A Field Guide to Writing

4845

A Field Guide to Writing

Chris M. Anson
University of Minnesota

Lance E. Wilcox
Elmhurst College

HarperCollinsPublishers

Executive Editor: Constance Rajala
Project Editor: David Nickol
Design Supervisor: Jan Kessner
Text Design: North 7 Atelier, Ltd.
Cover Design: Jan Kessner
Production Assistant: Linda Murray, Helen Driller
Compositor: TCSystems, Inc.
Printer and Binder: R.R. Donnelley & Sons Company
Cover Printer: Lehigh Press Lithographers

A Field Guide to Writing
Copyright © 1992 by HarperCollins Publishers Inc.

Library of Congress Cataloging-in-Publication Data
Anson, Christopher M., 1954-
    A field guide to writing / Chris M. Anson, Lance E. Wilcox.
        p.   cm.
    Includes index.
    ISBN 0-06-040292-X (student ed.)
    ISBN 0-06-500614-3 (teacher edition)
    1. English language—Rhetoric.   2. Interdisciplinary approach in
education.   I. Wilcox, Lance E.   II. Title.
PE1408.A6184   1992
808'.042—dc20   91-20468
                                                          CIP

91 92 93 94 9 8 7 6 5 4 3 2 1

Contents

Preface

This book is intended to foster what is probably the single most constructive movement in American college education in the last two decades, the movement known as *Writing Across the Curriculum* (or WAC). In every state and in every discipline, teachers are discovering that writing teaches the writer. History students can write in order to learn history, not just to become better writers or be measured for their knowledge. Chemistry students can grasp the logic and significance of an experiment by explaining it in prose. Mathematics students are being asked to discuss in writing the application of various formulas to different situations as a means of deepening their comprehension. Even students of dance are keeping journals tracking their progress, contemplating their control of various movements, and analyzing other people's performances. What was once the peculiar domain of departments of English and composition has become the responsibility of all college instructors. As English teachers, we wholeheartedly rejoice in this development and hope that, supported by *A Field Guide to Writing*, it will continue to expand.

Assigning written work in college classes is, of course, by no means new. Written assignments have been the staple of college classroom work for centuries. The major contribution of the WAC movement has been a shift of emphasis to the end for which writing is assigned. The traditional model sees writing as essentially and primarily a technique for evaluation. The student studies the content of a particular course, and then, either in a term paper or on a written exam, produces in correct English prose some sample of what he or she has learned. The instructor uses the paper as the tangible measure of the student's accumulated knowledge. Typically, the instructor collects the paper, weighs and assesses its content (and sometimes its style), and then returns it, annotated and graded, to the student. The grade goes permanently into the grade book, and the student decodes the instructor's marks and comments as well as he or she can, in hopes of doing better on the next assignment—by trial, error, and new trial.

The WAC instructor, though not denying written assignments an evaluative function, seeks to make a much more active and dialectic use of writing. The purpose of the WAC assignment is not primarily to assess a student's comprehension but to foster it. The effect of the writing activity on the student's understanding and knowledge is primary. The teachers of writing-intensive courses make heavy use of informal course journals, reading responses, short assignments, and brief in-class writings. Every time the student is asked to produce a text in response to something read, seen, or heard, the student's mind engages the material in a dynamic way. Not only does the student remember the material better, but his ability to think creatively and critically about it develops as well.

Instead of (or perhaps in addition to) a usual large term paper, the WAC instructor is likely to assign some sort of writing, however brief and informal, on a much more frequent, perhaps even daily, basis. Much of this may be merely checked and returned. Other assignments, however, may require as elaborate a development as any traditional term paper. Even with larger assignments, however, the WAC instructor seeks to make the writing as educationally fruitful as possible. A WAC instructor's "research paper" may require a written proposal, reading notes, a preliminary thesis or outline, a rough draft, peer group discussions about the rough draft, and only then a final draft. Each stage of the research and writing may be graded, with the final draft accounting for only a plurality of the grade, and any of the stages may offer an excellent opportunity for the teacher's intervention and guidance. Between the extremes of assigning one paper or thirty there is, obviously, a variety of individual styles and approaches by instructors.

In working with professors across many disciplines, we have found a number of recurring concerns and questions about writing across the curriculum. Professors are afraid of the increased time required to review and assess so much written student work. They are concerned with using writing in a pedagogical rather than primarily evaluative fashion and seek ideas and suggestions to accomplish the former. And they are uncertain of their own roles as writing teachers. Having never had any systematic training in composition instruction, they may feel uncomfortable teaching their students how to write, yet they hardly feel any more at ease simply assigning the writing and hoping their students swim rather than sink. We have tried to respond to the first two concerns in the Instructor's Manual that accompanies this book. Our response to the third concern *is* this book.

We have written *A Field Guide to Writing* as an adjunct textbook for writing-intensive courses across the various academic disciplines. Though the *Field Guide* could also be used in upper-division writing courses, its primary intended reader is the geography, history, psychology, or astronomy student in a course where writing is assigned. We imagine the student purchasing a stack of large, fancy, hardback textbooks for a semester's work, and then tossing on top of the stack our paperback on how to write. We have tried to provide the background on the writing process, approaches to different assignments, strategies for research, and methods of textual analysis which you, as a biology or theology professor, want your students to be exposed to but might not feel comfortable presenting. We can't, obviously, respond to or assess your students' writing—this crucially important task remains in your hands—but we can get them started and help guide their efforts with insights and techniques that have helped thousands of students.

Unlike many recent books aimed at writing in one specific discipline or another, *A Field Guide to Writing* works at a level of abstraction to make it uniformly useful to all disciplines. This, at least, has been our goal. The student who purchases the *Field Guide* for a writing-intensive history course will not have to return to the bookstore when he or she signs up for a course in population genetics which requires a hefty term paper. The strategies for developing ideas, refining and testing a thesis, organizing material, drafting, and revising remain largely constant regardless of content. We have tried in three of our chapters to address more specifically the most common writing assignments that occur in classrooms. And our final chapter, "The Comparative Anatomy of Texts," leads students to observe and analyze for themselves the distinctive characteristics of any specific text type—be it a movie review, a chemistry lab report, a mathematical proof, or a history article—in order to present their own discoveries in the language and forms of the intellectual community which the discipline represents. We don't teach any one given form. We teach how to observe, analyze, and reproduce the forms, and concomitant intellectual strategies, of whatever texts the student might be asked to read or write.

We hope that, with the guidance and support this book offers, you will feel more comfortable making a wider use of pedagogically useful and innovative writing assignments in your courses, and that your students, using the book, will benefit. In "To the Student" we explain further the pedagogical assumptions that underlie *A Field Guide to Writing* and present a brief overview of its individual chapters.

ACKNOWLEDGMENTS

Many people have helped us enormously in the writing of this guide. Our greatest thanks go to Lucy Rosendahl, whose excitement about this book got us started. For their encouragement and their gifts of time and thought, we would like to thank Quay Grigg, Donald Rice, Timothy Polk, Karyn Sproles, Jan Solberg, and Ted Lerud. We also thank the many scholars and teachers who reviewed the manuscript in its various incarnations: Gordon Schlesinger, University of California at San Diego; Ellen Strenski, UCLA; John P. Hewitt, University of Massachusetts; Peter Bardaglio, Goucher College; Beverly McLeod, University of California at Santa Cruz; Joan Mullin, University of Toledo; Joan Graham, University of Washington; Rolf Norgaard, University of Colorado; Stuart Brown, University of Arizona; David Jolliffe, University of

Illinois at Chicago; and Bruce Leland, Western Illinois University. Finally, we want to give a word of appreciation to Constance Rajala, who inherited this project. Her astute advice, helpful encouragement, great wit, and an unparalleled knowledge of our field helped the book to completion.

Three educational institutions also deserve our thanks: Elmhurst College, Elmhurst, Illinois; Hamline University, St. Paul, Minnesota; and the University of Minnesota, Twin Cities. Elmhurst College and Hamline University both presented models of what richly developed, highly integrated WAC programs could be. The success of the grass roots approach at Elmhurst, coordinated by Ted Lerud, reflects the enthusiasm of dozens of teachers working together to explore the value of writing for learning. Under Alice Moorehead, Hamline established in-depth writing curricula across an impressive array of courses and provided faculty with the guidance and support to make the writing as useful and interesting to their students as possible.

Faculty at the University of Minnesota also deserve credit for providing ideas, feedback, and materials helpful in the preparation of this book. In almost every department with which we consulted, teachers took the time to talk to us about academic writing, to provide us with samples of their assignments and papers, and to use or critique sections of the manuscript. We hope that in reflecting some of what they do with writing in their own courses, this book will reinforce and give strength to their voices. We also wish to express our appreciation to the Office of Educational Development Programs at the University of Minnesota for funding two grants on writing across the curriculum, from which we gleaned much information for this book.

We would like to thank our wives, Geanie Anson and Linda Roberts, for their belief not only in the *Field Guide* but in us. Without them, days would have passed without our having the courage or the energy (or even the time) to sit down and start typing. We dedicate this volume, finally, to our children: to Ian Geoffrey Anson (born while the book was gestating), and to Nathan and David Wilcox (veterans of an earlier father-with-book campaign). No one will ever teach us so much.

Chris M. Anson
Lance E. Wilcox

To the Student

WRITING TO LEARN, LEARNING TO WRITE

Suppose we ask you to describe, in as much detail as possible, the third house down the street from your own. Think about this a moment. Which house is it? What exactly does it look like? What could you tell us about it? Now, suppose we send you off with a sketch pad and a box of colored pencils, with instructions to draw it. We give you all the time you need and encourage you to make as many sketches from as many angles as you like. Then, setting your drawings out of sight, we ask you to describe the house a second time. No matter how good or bad your drawings may be, you can see that your *verbal* descriptions of the house will be fuller, more detailed, and more accurate the second time. What happened?

The first 537 times you walked past the house, the image fell on your retina, flickered briefly over your mind, and vanished. This time, however, you didn't just passively see the house, you actively examined it. You had to, in order to draw it. You had to count the windows, note the placement of the door and chimney, match the paint job against the pencils in your box, notice the colors of the windsock hanging from one corner. Recreating the house on paper forced you to observe it more carefully than ever before and drove it deeper into your memory as a result.

You can easily see how you might accomplish the same goal through writing. If you approached the house with a pen and notepad and wrote an on-the-spot description of it, the major characteristics of the house would again leave their traces in your mind, allowing you to remember the house in detail.

In your writing, furthermore, you could go far beyond simple physical description to consider the house in a wide network of relationships. When was this house built? Those elevated, metal-framed windows—those were the style in the early 1960s, weren't they? What was on this land before? Corn fields? When and why and how quickly did this rural community become a suburb? Where did the farmers go? Has this pattern been repeated across the nation? How do such developments affect the growth of transportation? Or did the building of roads and commuter trains, in effect, draw the suburbs out here? Who were the first residents of these houses? What kinds of people live here now? If interest on home mortgages weren't tax exempt, where would these people be living today? Why are Americans historically so partial to houses in the first place?

Writing about anything invites—almost compels—you to think more deeply about a subject than you have before. By putting your thoughts into permanent form, your written notes act as a sort of external memory, allowing you to preserve more questions, hunches, and intuitions than you could ever remember on your own. Furthermore, by pressing you to find the right words in which to capture your thoughts, writing demands a certain concretion, solidity, and definition in your thinking. The wispy, half-formulated ghost thought, rather than dissolving in a mist, gains body and firmness when you force yourself to find the words to record it. Your idea comes out of the shadows and into the daylight where you can then *do* something with it: affirm it, question it, share it, test it, research it, discredit it, prove it, modify it, develop it. Any of these will lead to more thought, and perhaps to still more writing. By now, of course, you have gone far beyond the simple memorization of detail to the development of genuinely new knowledge and new understanding.

WHY ANOTHER BOOK?

In *A Field Guide to Writing* we show you ways to use writing to explore your own thinking, to teach yourself, and to teach others. As you read and follow the suggestions here, you will write to learn, write to demonstrate learning, and write to inform others. As a result, you will be surprised by how much more fully you will be able to comprehend, recall, manipulate, and use the information that you confront. We can say this with confidence. We've seen this kind of development frequently in our students, in our colleagues, and in ourselves. A substantial body of research, furthermore, bears out our observations. Exercise builds muscle; writing builds intellect. It's a wonderfully reliable finding.

This simple discovery, in fact, is rapidly revamping American education. It lies at the heart of the movement known as *Writing Across the Curriculum,* or WAC for short. Professors from all disciplines have become aware of the fact that *writing teaches the writer.* Writing about history teaches the student history; writing about philosophy leads to deeper thinking about philosophical issues; writing about chemistry helps one to think like a chemist. In fact, even in mathematics departments, professors are asking students to write in plain English prose about complicated equations and proofs, with the result that the students become better mathematicians and, in the process, better writers as well.

Part of the excitement within this movement has to do with discoveries about the relationship of writing to reading. Students and teachers have long known that there's reading, and then there's *reading.* It's one thing to let your eyes drift listlessly over a column of prose and then walk away, letting the content of what you've read dribble out of both ears. It's quite another to read an article and then try to state on paper as accurately as possible just what the author's point was, and what you make of it. All of a sudden, a vague impression seems vaguer than ever: What *did* the author say exactly? And *why* is it important? Then you're back at the article, getting to the real heart of the matter. By comparing your attempted summary to the original source, you can refine your understanding of what the author actually said. A little further writing and thought can then lead you to an understanding of the significance of the author's ideas *for you.*

As a result, your reading sticks. You understand, you remember, and you've got a much clearer notion of what you
think of it all. By sketching or describing the house, you
learned to see it, and you were able to raise some questions
about its broader significance. By writing about a book, an
essay, or, for that matter, a lecture, you actually read it (or
listen to it) in a more searching and thoughtful way than ever
before.

For all these reasons, students in the 1990s can expect to
be writing more and more, regardless of their majors and
specialties. If you're a student, this probably doesn't strike
you as unalloyed good news. For one thing, writing is work.
Few tasks take as much time and energy—sheer intellectual
muscle—as thinking through a problem, organizing an answer, and stringing it across the page, word by word, paragraph by paragraph.

It can also be frightening. When you write, you're forced
to take a stand, to put your ideas on the line. You're exposed in
an essay in a way you never are in working out an equation. As
a result, most people tend to write slowly and painfully. Many
people sit down at their keyboards or their tablets, burdened
by the feeling, "I'm no good at this. I'm not a writer. Every
time I have to do this, it's a disaster." Writing is tough work
and it can be nerve-racking. We know this. As writers ourselves, we live with it all the time. Having studied, taught,
and practiced writing for many years, however, we have
learned helpful ways of going about it. Writing can be a useful, satisfying, intriguing business, and we'd like you to try a
few of the approaches that have worked for writers.

WHAT YOU CAN EXPECT FROM THIS BOOK

In *A Field Guide to Writing* we want to help you use writing
as effectively as possible as a means to communicate your
ideas, to learn the content, and to develop your thinking on
any subject you study. The *Field Guide* is not tailored to any
particular subject. Anything that can be talked about can be
written about, and anything that can be written about can be
thought about more deeply and learned more fully as a result.

We hope that this book will prove as useful to the biochemist as to the history major, to the seminarian as to the geographer.

Our book moves from the most informal and private writing to writing in the college classroom, and from there to work that requires you to know and follow all the conventions and formats associated with your field. We begin, in Chapter One, with the journal, a marvelous tool for sorting out and exploring new ideas, for getting a grasp on the material you're hearing and reading, and for developing longer, more formal classroom papers. Chapter Two considers what's required by a range of types of college writing. College writing assignments are meant to exercise your mind in a variety of ways, and in order to fulfill your assignments, it helps to understand what kind of thinking is called for by each. We examine these assignments and their related intellectual tasks in this chapter. In Chapter Three we look at that most common of all college writing tasks, the in-class essay exam. Chapter Four works through the process of writing more substantive academic papers, those for which you have greater amounts of time to think, plan, write, and rewrite. We provide strategies for understanding your audience, developing your ideas, and drafting and revising your paper. The most formal and complicated of these academic writing tasks is the research paper, which is covered in detail in Chapter Five. "The Comparative Anatomy of Texts," Chapter Six, leads you through the steps necessary to write the standard kinds of papers in any given field. Rather than telling you directly how to write a chemistry lab report, a psychological research study, a book review, or a biographical sketch, we point out what features of each kind of text you'll need to observe and understand in order to write one of your own.

We're admittedly trying to cover a lot here, and if you'll look at this book edgewise, you'll see how compact we've tried to make it. We know how busy you are. We'll try to move quickly, offer our advice as briefly as possible, and let you get on with your work. But this means you have to pitch in. Learning to write is like learning to play tennis. It takes only minutes to explain a forehand but years to master it. We can tell you what we know about writing, but to learn it, you have to try it out, experiment with it, and give it your best shot. We can't hand you knowledge. What we can do is suggest ways for you to use writing to derive greater knowledge and under-standing from any course of study you take. Write about what you hear, what you read, and what you think. Write *in order to* think. It really will make you smarter. And it can be very interesting.

Chris M. Anson
Lance E. Wilcox

A Field Guide to Writing

Chapter

1

The Academic Journal

TWO WRITERS LEARNING

Phil Braddock is a graduate student in marine biology working at a lobster research center and hatchery on the Massachusetts island of Martha's Vineyard. Phil has been gathering data on the survival rates of larval lobsters in the ocean and in captivity, and he's excited by what he's found. After four years of investigation, his studies have shown that baby lobsters raised at the hatchery have a much better chance of surviving past the first few weeks of life than those in the ocean. Phil hopes that if he can document the success of his pilot study, the federal government will provide funding to develop his research further. With a larger facility, he and his colleagues could raise more larval lobsters to survival size and perhaps even begin repopulating the New England coastline.

It's Tuesday afternoon on a hot day in July. Judy, Phil's colleague, is on duty in the outer visitor's room answering questions and keeping an eye on the tanks. This is a perfect time to begin his federal grant proposal for expanding the facility.

Phil opens the drawer of his desk and pulls out a battered spiral notebook. He locates a page in the journal titled "Ideas for Proposal" and begins reading his old notes—questions he asked himself about which studies he should cite, statistics on the survival of larval lobsters, attempts at an abstract for the proposal, miscellaneous jottings.

When he reaches a blank page in the journal, he scrawls "Grant Proposal—draft notes" at the top and begins thinking, jotting down ideas as they come to him. How extensively should he review the existing literature? Should he include the study by Pruett showing no significant improvement in survival of larval lobsters bred in captivity? If so, how should he handle it? He jots down "pilot study—Maine." Should he describe it in detail or only refer to the larger study he and his colleagues conducted later? How technical should he be in presenting all this? Who will his readers be exactly, and what knowledge will they bring with them? Phil writes for a few minutes on these questions and then lists the main features of his study: how the environments were controlled, how the percentages were derived, what procedures he used for collecting the data, and so on.

His writing flows freely, moving as his mind moves, raising and answering questions as he goes—sometimes in full sentences, sometimes in mere phrases and words connected by dashes. From time to time, he finds himself writing more formally, creating what looks like a full paragraph of usable prose, but soon he's rambling again. His pen glides across the page, rarely pausing, as he jots down ideas without worrying at all about style, structure, or correctness.

Half an hour later, Phil has written four pages. Tossing the notebook aside, he sits back and closes his eyes. He begins to see more clearly the outlines of his grant proposal. He knows that soon, after another session or two with his notebook, he'll be ready to begin drafting.

Sue Gonzales is a junior majoring in architecture. It's nearly mid-terms, and she's been worrying about an upcoming test in her History of Modern Architecture course. The test will cover a great deal of material on nineteenth- and twentieth-century architecture: major figures, famous structures, important theories and principles of design. She's nervous because her teacher, Professor Sims, has given the class few clues about what specific information will be covered on the exam. All she knows is that the test will include an objective section and a brief essay section.

July 16

Grant proposal — (Draft Notes)

First section: need to include comprehensive
review of the lit — but not so overwhelming
that it bogs down —
Esp. important:
   PRUETT, 1998 (because results = Method!!)
   Pilot Study — maine! — sets context
      for prop.: need resources
   One question has to do w/ collaboration — Woods
Hole — will gov't expect continued collab.
   ($-conscious, likes larger projects w/ more
      existing resources)
Background on Pilot Study —
   • Questions / hypotheses
   • Methods
      (controls, population size, location, variables?)
   • DATA gathering/analysis ⌐
   • Conclusions   ⌐ sep. sections?
   • Implications

➤ Sounds a bit too much like full-fledged report.
need to mention study but not provide so
much detail —
   Grant funders not interested in all
the minutiae —
(THEN): Rational for funding?

It's Sunday evening and the test is coming up the follow-ing Friday. Sue wants to get a head start on her studying, so she sits back on her bed, her lecture notes and textbooks scattered around her. Soon she's flipping back and forth be-tween her notes and her texts, comparing terms, and checking her textbook for ideas raised in class.

After a while, she finds her three-ring looseleaf notebook labeled "Learning Log—Arch." She flips through the pages. Then she begins jotting down questions and ideas, filling blank pages with terms, brief paragraphs, circled words, and lists. When did the Bauhaus movement really get started? She writes "Bauhaus" and lists four names, then circles Mies van der Rohe and adds "father of movement? 1910, 1920?" Then she draws a line down the middle of the page, writes the word "Bauhaus" on the left, and, without stopping, fills the right side with a running commentary about what she knows. Then she writes "Romanesque" and more commentary:

Good ex. is Trinity Church in Boston—1872—Henry Hobb Richardson, style of great prestige, used for churches, gov. buildings, business blocks. Richardsonian Romanesque—1885—1905? Characteristics: weight and mass, medieval qualities, minimal elements, rough masonry walls. Arches & towers? How related to Chateauesque Revival style of same period?

Each night, Sue returns to her notebook, reads what she's written, and continues to scribble more notes and ideas. She tests her understanding by trying to define major concepts in her own words, then turning back to her textbook to compare its definitions with her own. One evening she draws a time-line and places the various styles and developments along it as best she can. A day later, Sue studies photographs of build-ings in her text, writes down what features she sees, and then decides what these tell her about when the buildings were built, and by whom. In all of these sessions, she moves from her journal to her textbook and back again, and with every attempt to reproduce her knowledge on paper she develops a firmer grasp on the material.

As the exam nears, she poses possible questions to herself and writes out brief answers: "Describe the Beaux Arts Style of

10/5

Queen Anne -
1890's

Gothic - fullest form from 1860 → in church architec.

Also he pointed out that you see this in furniture - diff. types/colors of wood in a single piece

   most "literary" of styles. Dr. Simms pointed out that as you move westward in the U.S., you see buildings described as "Gothic" but that true Gothic was a rarety in so-called "frontier" cities/towns. These are basically (ITALINATE) with a Gothic overlay.

   One thing that seems to be coming through is (esp. in lecture) is the tendency for different arch. styles to appear in diff. types of buildings. So —

(Gothic) ⟨ Churches
         ⟨ Some Educational institutions
         ⟨ commercial blocks, occasionally (printers, newspapers)
esp. Ruskinian While ...
         County courthouses = (Italinate) (sense of "Etiquette" in styles)

Exam Q: "Architectural Etiquette"?

By 1880's → no longer mixed styles

Grecian - drum/dome 1870's
Then some buildings enlarged, remodelled to keep up times — so, you need to know something of the history of each structure - don't just identify cursorily!

Mixtures are important in the 1870's → 1880's
(French Second Empire Style (mansard roofs + pavillions on end) - lasted 10 → 15 yrs.

→ for some reason, this permitted more "Muddling" later - easier to adapt ???

the 1890s to 1930s and its main characteristics in City Beautiful Classicism. What did it borrow from late nineteenth-
century Parisian Neo-Baroque and Italian Renaissance?"
"Outline the main contributions of Frank Lloyd Wright to
modern architecture." "Explain why the Late Gothic Revival
style lasted for almost half a century in large U.S. cities." Five
days later, she's filled twelve pages of her notebook with
speculations and ideas.

When Sue walks into her History of Modern Architecture
course on the day of her exam, she notices the buzz of activity.
Other students are frantically comparing notes and flipping
through pages of their texts. Sue takes her seat, sits back, and
waits for Professor Sims to arrive with the exam. Her course
log, where she has written and learned for the past five days,
sits on her desk at home, no longer needed. The writing in it
has served its purpose. She has written her way into
knowledge.

Phil and Sue live in different parts of the country, are
different ages, study different subjects, and hold different
opinions and beliefs. They have almost nothing in
common—except that both, in their own ways, are successful
writers and learners. By successful writers, we don't mean
people for whom writing is easy, quick, or painless (much less
lucrative). We mean people who, instead of groaning with
dread each time they think about picking up a pen, use to their
advantage the uncertainty, intellectual struggles, and sheer
hard work that writing requires. By successful learners, furthermore, we don't mean people born with knowledge in
their blood, but people who have discovered ways to explore
and become expert in whatever course of study they've
chosen.

KEEPING AN ACADEMIC JOURNAL

In this chapter, we want to look at the writer's tool Phil and
Sue turned to again and again in their work: the academic
journal. Unlike the diary, in which you tell the continuing
story of your life, the journal contains discussions, ideas, issues, or information of a more academic, intellectual nature.
You carry on an internal dialogue, a personal conversation,
about some domain of knowledge.

If you don't currently use a journal, you may feel hesitant about starting one. Perhaps you kept one in a course you took and felt it was busy work. Or you decided one New Year's to try writing something every evening after dinner, only to discover that your entries fizzled out on January 8th. We've talked with a lot of skeptics and in almost every case of journal failure, the problem wasn't in the journal itself, it was in what the writer thought she was using it for to begin with. The problem stemmed from the way the writer was answering the question, "What's the goal?"

Many people wonder why anyone would ever choose to write more than they must. When they have a term paper to write, they want to punch in at the title and punch out by way of the bibliography—in as simple and quick a fashion as they can contrive. This "get it done" approach comes, in part, from the impression that writing is painful, hard, boring, and likely to yield frustration and possible failure—in other words, that the more time you spend with it, the more uncomfortable you'll feel. Ironically, this very approach has led countless writers straight to frustration and failure because it makes the wrong assumptions about the relationship between writing and learning.

First, it assumes that your thinking completely precedes your writing. It assumes that good writers, those people who publish articles in the *New England Journal of Medicine* or who write great novels, organize everything in their heads and then magically give birth to a perfect draft. But research on writing paints a much different picture. It shows that the best writers, when they begin a piece, are not at all sure of what they want to say and plan to use the writing to answer that very question. It also shows that writers spend a lot more time working on their prose than most people imagine, not creating perfect, stylish sentences, but rather exploring their topic in loose, often messy and very tentative ways. Good writers, in other words, tend to write first in order to learn, and then, only later, in order to create a polished draft.

Though few people sit down to write with absolutely no idea where they're going, experienced writers know that an immense amount of thinking, learning, and discovery occurs during the writing itself. A vague idea leads to some early, sketchy writing. In turn, these preliminary words produce richer and clearer ideas. These new ideas provoke more and better writing. And so on. Writing leads to thinking, and thinking leads to more and better writing. Ideas lead to words, words lead to ideas, and both expand and deepen and grow richer. It's a process that feeds on and fuels itself, and one that experienced writers learn to trust.

The "get it done" approach also assumes that whenever you write, you write for keeps. In other words, you write because you're trying to communicate—through a term paper, an abstract, a research proposal, a book report. It assumes that your writing should be well-structured and polished from the very beginning. But writing to "get it done" in this fashion puts you under a lot of pressure. Your words make you feel hopelessly inadequate precisely because you do have an audience in mind, weighing and criticizing (in your imagination) every word you write.

The difference between writing to get it done (for *them*) and writing to learn (for *you*) is important to remember as you start a journal. Sometimes you'll be writing purely for the sake of learning or intellectual exploration, and then your only audience is yourself. Sometimes, on the other hand, you write in order to grope your way toward a formal, public text. It may even happen, in fact, that you begin with purely casual, exploratory writing and wander by degrees into a fine piece of writing.

Ten Specific Uses for Journal Writing

If you haven't used journals much, try some of the following until you discover the strategies that best suit your needs. The list, obviously, is far from exhaustive, but all of these have proved helpful to students in the past. We have arranged the list, roughly, from the most purely private uses to those which may result in the production of a public text:

1. Make the most of lectures.
2. Explain the harder concepts to yourself.
3. Apply new knowledge; connect to other learning.
4. Pin down exactly what an author is saying.
5. Conduct an interview with a text.
6. Compare two or more contrasting positions.
7. Explore problems in your learning.

8. Prepare for an exam.
9. Extract information for later use or investigation.
10. Start moving toward the draft of a formal paper.

1. *Make the Most of Lectures.* 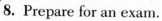 In many educational settings, it's all too easy to become a passive learner, sitting like an empty bucket waiting to be filled with knowledge. You listen to lectures, take notes, memorize facts and details, *et voila!*—you're trained. Well, maybe, maybe not. In any case, you're certainly not yet really *educated*, because you've hardly begun really to *think*. You should always go beyond whatever information you're given to ponder what it really means, what it adds up to, what difference it makes to anything.

You can start on this even while you're listening to the lecture itself. Take down your notes as usual, but try to raise questions and make connections in your mind as you listen. You might put these questions and ideas in square brackets to set them off a bit from the lecturer's own information.

Lincoln—early moves as President. After outbreak of war. Invited Robert E. Lee to be general of Union Army! [Why Lee of all people?!] Lee turns Lincoln down, stays with south. [Why did he choose that? what happens if Lee goes with North?] Lincoln, string of generals after that, none satisfactory. McClellan—"got the slows"—[McC's side of the story? Lincoln got "fasts"?]

Once you've taken your notes on a lecture, don't stop there. At the very least, back away from the trees and try once more to see the forest. You have three tightly-written pages of scribbled notes—excellent! Now, can you state in three or four pithy sentences the main points of the lecture? Try it—on paper. Don't worry about the details this time; try to extract only the major principles. This will help you grasp the significance of the lecture as a whole.

1858: Lincoln (R) loses Senatorial election to Stephen Douglas (D) but in the debates smokes Douglas out on slavery issue.

1860: The Democratic Party splits, with Douglas in the North and Breckenridge in the South. Result of 1858 debates, in part.

Though Democrats combined easily won popular vote, Lincoln won victory in electoral college.

The Southern secession prompted by wealthy landowners with poor whites following suit. South Carolina first, then ten others.

Many people feel rushed enough just taking notes without raising questions or jotting down reactions alongside them. In this case, their learning is significantly enhanced if they read over their notes sometime later, and then write something more about the material. If you're using a spiral-bound notebook, for example, you might try taking notes on only the right-hand pages, and then later go back and rework the material on the left-hand or facing pages. In reworking your notes, you might just summarize them, or you might raise further questions. Often, simply trying clearly to restate difficult material leads you to understand it better than you did the first time you heard it.

Here is an example from the notebook of a student taking a course in cell biology. Her right-hand page is covered with terms, phrases, and diagrams, but the exact meaning of the material still seems to elude her. A few hours after the lecture, she returns to her notebook, flops it open on a desk, studies the notes on the right-hand side, then begins thinking them through, pen in hand, on the facing (left-hand) page:

Experiment Dr. Cooper talked about in class—don't know what this is about—he said it proves the unitarian theory of Maximov—pluripotent cells in bone marrow that can produce all types of blood cells—part left out of the book, donor mouse given dose of x-rays (not lethal but chromosomally damaging) before bone marrow is drawn for transplant—shows that the cells in a single clone in the recipient mouse came from a SINGLE marrow cell because they all have the same karyotype. So this is supposed to prove that there is a single multipotent cell. So in other words 1: radiation halts blood cell production; 2: inj. cells from healthy donor; 3: mouse lives, healthy cells 2 wks. later; 4: spleen has nodules, producing cells. So what's happening here are CFU's, colony-forming units. How are the marrow cells affecting the spleen, though?

Notice in this excerpt how Jan not only restates some material that's confusing her, but raises further questions for study and analysis. She's assessing what she's learned by trying to cast it into her own terms, her own language, and coming to understand it more clearly as a result.

2. *Explain the Harder Concepts to Yourself.* Almost every intellectual discipline has its own terminology, its own special, and often highly useful, jargon. But it will only prove useful to you to the degree that you actually understand it. When you come across new terms, or specialized uses for old terms, try to define these in your journal in your own words. Try to pin down exactly what the terms mean in their current context.

Ralph here wrestles with the term "mass" in an Introduction to Physics course for non-science majors:

If one rock weighs one kilogram and the other ten kilograms, why does Dr. Lawrence keep insisting that "mass" isn't "weight"? It weighs one kilogram, what's the problem? Idea—does here—but on the Moon or Mars or the Sun would weigh something else. That is, its pounds would change—but it would still be "one kilogram"???? Or if floating in space—doesn't weigh anything. How could you tell a heavy rock from a light one (same size) in space? Could still push one or throw one faster than another. Push one big enough, it stays still and I fly away. Is this what "resistance to acceleration" is all about? It can weigh anything or nothing—question is, how far—fast?—can you throw it? Is that what "mass" means?

If Ralph now either double-checks his hunch against his textbook, or makes a point to ask Dr. Lawrence about the problem during the next class, he'll be very gratified to discover that he's pretty much figured it out.

3. **Apply New Knowledge; Connect to Other Learning.** Knowledge out of context is almost useless. If you can't apply new concepts to something real and concrete, the concepts won't stay with you, and you may be wasting your time. Your journal is an excellent place to try to connect your new academic learning with other events and situations in your life. What does the front page of the newspaper have to do with your Intro to Ethics course? How do the principles of aerodynamics—especially turbulence and drag—affect the movement of a hard slider or a big breaking curveball?

Here's an excerpt from the journal of Bob, a junior in a general course in social psychology:

> Just recognized (I think) a case of cognitive dissonance theory at work. Small collaborative group in Communications 310. We all knew we'd botched the oral project in various ways and this led to some misgivings. When we did our self-evaluations, though, we all agreed basically that the whole experience had been worth it anyway and that even though we'd gotten a C it had been meaningful. I know one thing, I wouldn't have felt that way if I'd been working alone. A C is a C, after all. But as the Aronson and Mills study showed, cooperative ventures have an effect on liking. So we liked each other in spite of our failure. "Dissonance reduction?"

All of a sudden, the classroom and the real world don't look so separate anymore. Not only that, Bob is a lot more likely to remember this term and its meaning longer and more vividly as a result of this bit of writing.

Part of finding wider contexts for your learning entails looking for connections between different classes as well. College courses are all too often presented as if they're totally detached intellectual domains, with nothing whatever connecting them. Your journal gives you a place to find the missing connections, to see what different aspects of your knowledge have to do with each other. Try juxtaposing your history and literature classes, or chemistry and biology, philosophy and fine arts, and see what you can say about them. Or stretch further and ask how biochemistry and theology, child psychology and international affairs, analytical geometry and Ancient Greece might stand to illuminate each other. If you have a paper to write for one of these classes, bracketing it like this with another and looking at what the combination suggests might lead you to an especially interesting topic for research.

4. Pin Down Exactly What an Author is Saying.   Writing not only helps you think; it also can help you read. It's one thing to let your eyes drift languidly over twenty pages of prose, close the book, and immediately either watch a soap opera or fall asleep. It's another to put real energy and effort into drawing out of that book everything it has to offer. When you're seriously trying to learn, reading with a pen in hand and your journal open can make a difference. Here are just a few ways to use writing to improve your reading:

- Glance over the chapter or article quickly just to get a sense of the shape of it. What subtitles or divisions do you see? Can you read a few sentences here, a few there, and get some idea of the general movement of the argument? Try sketching a rough, preliminary skeleton of the piece *before* diving in, or even just copy out the subheadings. Your outline will act as a sort of topographical survey, leading you into and back out of the forest.

   Owen, a student taking a course in ocean and land management at a small college in California, had to read through a packet of articles placed on reserve in the library. Here's his quick overview of "The Price is Wrong" by George Wuerthner, an article in the September, 1990, issue of *Sierra Magazine*. Though the article lacks actual subheads, it's visibly divided into major parts. Before deciding to read the article in its entirety, Owen was able to glance at the opening sentences of each part and create a brief topical outline:

Cattle raising as major cause of environmental damage in West.

Governmental support for cattle raising, despite problems.

Specific kinds, degrees of damage: birds, fish, plants.

Use, overuse, abuse of water sources in West.

Why we let it continue. Who's backing it.

For some purposes the outline may be all you need to know. Of course, it's no real substitute for a careful reading of the work; but if you're glancing through a stack of articles for a research paper, you may only want to note down this much for now, and then decide later if you need to read the article more thoroughly.

- Try to summarize the gist of the work in one pithy sentence.

    First ask: what is the work's dominant subject, or, what is it about? Find out and write it down.
    Now ask: what's the author primarily *trying to prove* about his topic? (In technical terms, what is he predicating of his subject?) Write that down.
    Finally, can you combine these into a precise subject-predicate thesis sentence?
    If Owen had done this on his *Sierra* article, he might have answered the questions as follows:

[Subject] The article is about: Cattle grazing on public lands in the Western states.

[Predicate] Regarding the subject, the author wants to convince us: It is environmentally destructive and expensive to taxpayers.

Thesis: Cattle grazing on public lands in the Western states is environmentally destructive and expensive to taxpayers.

Notice how much more exact such a summary statement is than something like "This article is about cattle out West." You should aim in your brief summary for a similar precision.

• Paraphrase the work in a page or a paragraph, trying to capture as much of the author's argument as possible. If you've sketched an outline of the work and formulated its precise thesis, you're already well on your way to a full, succinct, prose paraphrase of it. You can often use your brief summary as the topic sentence of your paraphrase, and expand the points in your sketchy outline to fill in the rest.

Cattle grazing on public lands in the Western states is environmentally destructive and expensive to taxpayers. Because cattle are not actually adapted to arid western conditions, expensive tax subsidies are required to allow ranching to survive as a business; this constitutes a form of welfare for ranchers. Cattle grazing has destroyed many entire species of birds, fish, and plants by their destruction of habitats, and have driven out many native mammal species. They also represent a huge drain on scarce Western supplies of fresh water. Despite all these costs to the environment and the taxpayer, ranching interests continue to compel Americans to support this industry on publicly owned lands through the Bureau of Land Management (BLM).

Once you're able to formulate such a paraphrase, you can feel pretty confident that you understand the work you've read. If at some point you're not sure quite how the author's argument ran, reread the work and revise your notes or paraphrase accordingly. Getting it right may take several turns from your notebook to the article and back again.

How thoroughly or carefully you should do this depends on your purpose in reading the work. Do you simply need a rough idea of its contents, or do you need to know it chapter and verse? If the latter, you probably want to work through all the suggestions given here. If you use the article in research, furthermore, your brief summary or one-page paraphrase may find their way straight into your own piece of writing. You'll be a step ahead of the game when you actually sit down to draft.

5. *Conduct an Interview with a Text.* The suggestions above are designed to help you arrive at as fair, even-handed and objective an understanding of an author's words as possible. But that's only half of the task. A good reader insists on having the last word. It's not enough simply to get clear on what an author wrote; you need to respond to it, to think about it, to reflect, brood, assess, raise questions. How does the book change or challenge your thinking? Suppose it's actually all true; then what? Suppose, on the other hand, that the author is seriously wrong in some or all of what she said—would it make any difference?

- Write notes and reactions as you read. You can make the same use here of square brackets as you did earlier in listening to lectures. That is, you can interpolate your own questions and insights into your notes, and set them off by [putting them in these]. Be especially alert for any questions, confusions, and reactions you may have. Whenever you're really confused by something you read, you should stop a moment and try to explain to yourself just where your confusion lies. This often proves useful even if you can't just then untangle the problem completely.

- Once you put the book down, and before you move to something else, turn it over in your mind a bit first and see what other questions, reactions, reflections occur to you. Jot those down. Think of questions you wish you could ask the author in person. If you had read the cattle-grazing article discussed above, you might find yourself asking the following:

How long has this been a problem?
What portion of American beef comes from these range lands?

What is the Bureau of Land Management exactly?

What do the ranchers themselves have to say about the problem?

Is there any way American tax-payers or voters can alter this state of affairs? Who decides these things?

Here's an excerpt from the journal of Shelley, a student in a course on American literature. Shelley is not so much summarizing a piece of writing or asking further questions about its subject matter as she is trying to puzzle out what it means in the first place. She has been reading a short story by Hemingway titled "Hills Like White Elephants" and now she's wrestling with exactly what the story was all about. Notice how she digs beyond her first thoughts about the story to try to discover its underlying significance:

> *I had no idea what was going on in this story. It seemed like these two people were really strange. I seriously thought they were retarded or on drugs. They conversed but not about anything. And then the landscape they're in was so weird. The hills were brown and dry. On one side there were no trees and no shade. It's like really dead. Then they began talking about this operation and how after it's done they'll be happy again. Why are they talking about that here? Some connection?*

Shelley has not yet found what she's looking for. But if you know the story, you also know that she's groping in the right direction. If she rereads the story with these questions in mind, she has a very good chance of unraveling the mystery of both the operation and the landscape.

6. Compare Two or More Contrasting Positions. When you read one author's work at a time, it's very easy to find yourself in agreement with her. The writer presents all the arguments in favor of one perspective, suppresses or confutes contrary arguments, and bears all away before her. Unless you're an extremely aggressive and questioning reader, it's hard to see where the author might be in error. But you don't want to rest there. Whenever you have the chance, you stand to learn more by reading two authors, and using your journal to work out the points of their agreement or divergence. Try to pinpoint (and write down) where the two are saying different things, presenting conflicting evidence, drawing contradictory conclusions. You can even write this as a sort of dialogue between the two if you like: for example, what Karl Marx and Thomas Jefferson would ask each other, or say to each other, if they could both be recalled from their graves. Your next step, of course, is to play judge at this trial and to weigh the evidence and arguments on both sides for yourself.

7. *Explore Problems in Your Learning.*   No one is immune to confusion or frustration in learning new and difficult material. But writing about those frustrations or problems can often help solve them by revealing the source of the confusion. Here's an example from Kelli, a student in a course in English linguistics, who is having trouble with phonetic transcription:

> This is my second reading of this chapter, yet there are some things that still seem contradictory. For instance, in the section on glides on p. 46, the following sentence is written about y's and w's: "When occurring in a word, they must always be either preceded or followed directly by a vowel." But in the word "merry" no vowel comes before or after the y. Or how about the name "Myra." The y is neither preceded nor followed by a vowel. . . . Maybe these examples are unfair since the y in "merry" is an "ee" sound, not a "y" sound. And the y in Myra is an "aii" sound, a diphthong, not a glide. Oh, get with it, Kelli! Y isn't a vowel. (Just checked on that, it's the English spelling problem again.)

Halfway through her journal writing, Kelli discovered where she was confused. And that may not have happened without her journal.

8. *Prepare for an Exam.*   Most of what we have to suggest on this topic has been illustrated by our description of Sue Gonzales' journal writing at the beginning of this chapter. You should start as early as you can, ideally a good week before the test itself. Several short sessions over the course of a week will benefit you far more than an eye-burning all-nighter on Sunday.

Use the time, first, to pull your notes into some sort of intelligible order. Make sure that you can extract the main points, that you can tell the major principles from the illustrative details. Make sure, too, that you have all the relevant terminology under control.

If you feel pretty confident about your general grasp of the material, use the time to practice for the test itself. Pose yourself possible exam questions and sketch out notes on how you would answer them. If possible, form a study group with other classmates and give each other problems to work on and discuss. Compare your answers with each other, or with your original lecture notes or texts.

9. *Extract Information for Later Use or Investigation.*   In school, if you know that you'll have a longer paper to write later in the term and that you can pick the topic, you probably want to be thinking about possibilities for it from early on. Whenever you're summarizing your lecture notes or reflecting on your reading, see if there's something that looks interesting to you, that you might want to pursue further. (The desire to know at least a little something more about practically everything that falls in your path is the sure sign of a lively, vigorous mind.)

Likewise, when you're in the middle of researching and developing a paper, keep an ear open for any stray pieces of information that might be useful and note them down. In any case, never throw anything away without first seeing if there's something in it that you might want to keep for future reference.

10. *Start Moving Toward the Draft of a Formal Paper.*   Whenever you face a specific writing task, your journal should be the first place to begin thinking about your topic. Such thinking can be in the form of sketchy notes, random questions, possible leads and information—or even the earliest rough drafts of passages that might find their way into your final text.

For example, one of the most effective methods for beginning a writing task is called *freewriting*. In freewriting, you write as fast as you can for some fixed period of time—usually 10 to 20 minutes. While the sand is running, you don't take your pen from the page for any reason short of fire. Keep writing whatever comes to mind about your topic. If you're making sense, great. If not, stay with it. You never know when you'll stumble upon a path. Then take a break, come back a bit later, and write for another short sprint. Does this produce a lot of waste, a lot of writing that just has to be scrapped? Well, yes, it does. But it may also lead you places you would never reach any other way. The long way around may be the shortest route home.

The two following brief freewrites come from Scott, a student in a child development course. Through his freewriting, Scott is feeling his way towards a term paper on research into the reflex responses of infants:

> The Morrow reflex is kind of interesting—seems to be an innate reflex related to monkeys clutching their mothers; but it's a startle reflex in humans. Lots of infantile reflexes in fact seem be very primitive and basic—makes it seem as if most basic characteristics of infants are the closest to our primitive ancestry, more they develop as humans the farther they go away from those.
>
> Possible thesis? Earliest reflexes most monkey-like? What would it take to prove? (How would I know if it's wrong?)
>
> Visual cliff—is that a reflex? Seems to involve some sort of vision/cognitive activity whereas others don't. The Babinski reflex, now theres a weird one, set off by stroking the soles of the feet (also the hand-to-mouth and that other one). Gagging and rooting.
>
> Is there a continuum from "most involuntary" to "most voluntary" or are all reflexes by def. involuntary? Invol. ones closer to primitive roots? Vol. reflex—what do I mean?

Contradiction in terms? Also why babies don't blink when something rushes toward their eyes. When learned or developed?

Notice how, simply by freewriting about his topic, Scott begins to review the current issues and research, define key terms, consider a possible thesis, mull over methodological problems. If he puts in a number of such short, high-speed writing sessions, he'll be in excellent shape when he actually starts poring through *Psychology Abstracts* in search of the most relevant theory and research.

Some Tips for Keeping a Journal

Use a Comfortable Style.   You'll notice that many of the journal entries here are messy, associative, sometimes almost incoherent. This is all as it should be. Keeping a journal means learning to take a lot less seriously much of what you know about "proper" or "correct" writing.

In well-used journals, you'll find abbreviated words, sentence fragments, grammar and spelling errors, haphazard punctuation. Paragraphs may be unstructured. There may be cryptic remarks, meaningless except to the writer. Sometimes an entry will ramble on for pages—far more than the topic would deserve in a formal paper. At other times the writer may skip through an issue far more briefly than you would expect in a good piece of prose. But who cares?

Which leads us to this profoundly important point, the Cardinal Rule for all good journal writing: **If writing in the journal is helping you to clarify your thinking—YOUR thinking, not a reader's—you're doing it correctly. There is no other criterion.**

Choose a Medium Appropriate to Your Purposes.   If you plan to use a journal in more than one context, get yourself a three-ring notebook that will let you remove or add pages. The reason for this is versatility. You can insert pages in this more permanent journal from other, temporary ones (such as the three-hole spiral-bound variety). You can also remove pages when you're working on specific projects and share these with colleagues, or turn them in to your teacher for comments. And, of course, sometimes a little simple house-keeping is in order. If you're quite sure you're done with a few pages, toss them. Cut away at the underbrush. Or transfer the most important material onto a fresh page, and then throw out all the earliest, roughest sketching.

If you're keeping a journal for one specific purpose (such as a single college course, a special project at work, or a paper or article you plan to write), you might want something less bulky. In this case, try spiral notebooks of various sizes, or even small, briefcase-size pads. Since this is for you, indulge yourself. Buy whatever you think you'd like to write in. Here's your opportunity to write with a peacock blue soft-tip pen in a 5″ × 8″ spiral-bound notebook with eighty wide-lined, pale gold pages.

Write at Least Something in Your Journal on a Regular Basis.   Academic journals thrive on regular attention. If they don't get it, they begin turning pale, dropping leaves, eventually dying of starvation. To keep your journal healthy, green, and glossy, feed it often—daily if possible, three times a week at the least.

No matter how well you're using your journal, however, there will be occasions when your mind simply refuses to engage. You feel blocked. If and when this happens, try doing a ten-minute freewrite. And let this be the slackest kind of writing—a real undisciplined meander, or even simply a list. See if you can stand this for ten minutes; if you succeed, congratulate yourself for having gotten something solid accomplished. Over time, a fine house can be built of just such bricks.

If that doesn't work, write about your problem getting started as a puzzle in itself. This, surprisingly enough, may get you started even when nothing else seems to help.

Start With the Obvious; Wait for the Brilliant.   Some students have trouble with journals because they're trying to be too brilliant, too insightful too soon. Don't sit there with your pen poised like a hawk over your pad, waiting to let rip with a series of lightning-flash Nietzschean aphorisms. Instead, put down the obvious, ordinary, garden variety observations as they occur to you, and wait to see what patterns form. The journal isn't a place simply to capture and cage your more dazzling insights (though that does happen sometimes, and it's hugely gratifying when it does). Instead, think of yourself as growing crystals. Write down simple, unflashy, ordinary sorts of facts and ideas about your subject, and see what they combine to form. Don't hesitate to write something down because it's too simple, too obvious, too dull. Write it and keep going. What we call insight, after all, isn't usually sight *into* anything; it's a perception of pattern, of order, of form.

Notice the journal excerpts above. One student, thinking about rocks bobbing about in space, was able to arrive at a scientifically sophisticated understanding of mass. Another, by jotting notes about dry hills and weird talk of operations, was just about to stumble over Hemingway's powerful matrix of symbols. So go easy. Write down one thing at a time. Don't flog yourself for your lack of astounding perceptions. Let your mind have the time it needs to do its magic. Let the developer work, and the image will appear in its own sweet time.

VARIETIES OF ASSIGNED ACADEMIC JOURNALS

Throughout this chapter, we've described academic journals in a fairly consistent way, as a mainly private tool for intellectual exploration and the learning of subject matter. As assignments, however, academic journals can be as varied as the college curriculum. They come in many forms and are accompanied by varying requirements, standards, and rules of appropriateness. In some courses, for example, an academic journal might be collected weekly and assessed in some way. In other courses, the journal isn't collected until the very end of the course. Some teachers apply more rigorous standards to their assigned journals than others. We want to conclude, then, with some advice for understanding certain varieties of academic journals that might require some more specific strategies than those we've outlined in this chapter. Three common types, all different in their forms and structures, show up frequently in many colleges and universities around the country.

The Repository of Short Assignments

Many teachers think of an academic journal as a kind of portfolio, where students collect short, sometimes informal, writing assignments or focus papers which the teachers describe in class or on a syllabus. In Chapter Two, we discuss the nature of typical college assignments, how they work, what they're for, and how to go about doing them; if your assigned journal is a place where such papers will be housed, you might turn to that chapter next. As a compilation of more formal papers, such a journal doesn't much resemble the loose, exploratory kind of writing we've spent much of this chapter describing. Nevertheless, it may well share some features, especially if it reflects a kind of journey through the subject of your course.

Most journals as repositories mix assigned and self-sponsored entries. One of us requires this kind of journal in almost every course, finding it especially useful as a way to encourage free exploration while also providing occasional common focuses for class discussions. In this arrangement, the standards applied to the two kinds of entries are different; the casual, freely written, self-sponsored entries are not assessed for style, structure, etc., but mainly for their frequency and length. The regularly assigned journal entries, on the other hand, are collected when they're due and then informally graded. When these are inserted into the journal, they become part of the grade for the entire compilation, which is judged at the end of the course.

If you're assigned a journal of this type, you might find the following tips useful:

- Learn to vary your entries according to your teacher's expectations. If assigned entries should be more structured and formal than unassigned ones, learn to differentiate the two. Try not to slip into the more casual and personal language of your own entries when responding to a journal assignment, even though both may be written in the same context of the larger journal.
- Be sensitive to length requirements. Your self-sponsored entries might ramble on for several pages, but an assigned entry might need to be tighter, more controlled, and shorter. Find out.
- Consider your audience. While no journal writing will,

by definition, require elaborate adaptation to a reader, your teacher may read and informally grade or check your assigned entries, or may even *assign* a specific imaginary audience to address. These sorts of entries will differ from ones you write primarily to and for yourself. Abbreviated language, notes, and other time-saving devices useful in personal journals may mean next to nothing to a reader (such as your instructor) who wants, in an assigned entry, to understand the ideas you're exploring or the points you're making. As a result, you'll need to be a bit more conventional in your writing, even though (depending, again, on your teacher) this might not mean writing highly styled, well-crafted sentences and paragraphs.

- Finally, try to figure out what, specifically, the teacher is up to: why would he or she ask you to respond to a topic in your journal instead of simply asking you to write anything that comes to mind? If it's to provide some common experiences for class discussion, then you might anticipate that discussion as you write. If it's to make sure that you and your classmates have understood a difficult idea or concept, then you might review your notes and readings first, pushing your understanding as far as you can, perhaps in preparation for a test.

The Dialogue Journal

The most popular form of academic journal asks you to carry on a conversation with *yourself*. Although it's a kind of internal dialogue, you essentially have no regular reader unless your teacher frequently collects and responds to your entries or organizes your class into groups to react to each other's entries.

A second, increasingly popular kind of journal takes all the principles of the typical self-directed journal but turns it into an academic dialogue between you and (usually) another student in your class. It works like this: you and a partner both begin keeping an academic journal, writing about an assigned reading or some other aspect of your course. On a given day, you swap your entries. After reading your partner's reflections, questions, musings, and uncertainties, you respond in

Victor: I had a tough time on this scenario! I realize that getting a media job would be great for the guy in the scenario, but then I got puzzled about whether he should get rid of his Brooklyn accent to get the job or else assert his rights. Most people don't have an accent in the media that is recognizable to me, anyway, except when I was in Atlanta last year the local networks did seem to have a different accent. But I can't seem to figure out why there should be this norm in accent for those in the media field. People from the south and southwest like Dan Rather, and people from different ethnic backgrounds like Bryant Gumbel, they all have not much accent, but then look at Jimmy Carter and the Kennedys and Lyndon Johnson all had pretty heavy regional accents. I just don't know where the source of the problem is. It should be the audience, because they should be able to understand all the various accents of the states-- but then why would we even have all the accents that we do? This does get complicated, doesn't it? So I'm sort of baffled by this one. I guess my advice to the guy in the scenario would be to go ahead and enroll in the accent eradication course. I mean, it can't hurt him, and he can always use his old Brooklyn accent at home and at the ball game. What do you think?

--Carmen

Carmen: I agree totally (not with your confusion!). I think there are two problems here. One is whether the guy should do certain things (like changing his accent) to get a job. The other is whether the media should have accent as a requirement for the job. The first seems like a short-term problem for the guy in the scenario, and I think, why not, go ahead and take the course. If I was applying for a job as a golf pro at a country club and one thing I had to know about was the use of videotape to help people with their swings, and if I didn't know diddly about video, I'd take a night course or something so I could market myself better. That's all this guy would do, just speak the way the media wants him to. It's no different than him taking a grammar course or a course in how to use his voice over live TV. Now the other issue is tougher because it's long term. I think this is where I feel your confusion, because *should* the media exclude people on the basis of their accents. And it's even tougher when you think that maybe there are subtle dialect things like what we've been studying about Black English Vernacular that could exclude whole groups from consideration, and that's just plain discrimination. But here's one other thought. If the guy were to go somewhere like Wisconsin or Utah or something, wouldn't a Brooklyn accent be sort of neat? Think about the Australian reporter on channel 4 news! Everyone thinks his accent is great. So maybe he *shouldn't* take the course!

--Victor

your next entry *to some or all of what your partner said*. He or she has, in the meantime, done the same. You swap again, and again respond, and so on, throughout the course.

To get some idea of what a typical dialogue journal might look like, consider the sample on p. 26 from a course in the English language. (The original, handwritten material has been set in type for clarity.)

The principle behind dialogue journals strikes most people as startlingly simple, once they clear away some of the logistical questions that usually surround them: *learning together provides a more fulfilling, enjoyable, and intellectually stimulating experience than learning alone*. But the logistical questions still must be answered. Here are a few of the more frequent ones we hear.

- *Should every entry respond to the partner's entries?*
  No, especially because at some point you would be responding to a response to a response to a response . . . clearly, not a very fulfilling way to write. Some dialogue journals do turn into a series of directly addressed letters, each entry carrying the discussion a step further, as if the two partners were having a phone conversation. Most of the time, however, your dialogue journal will represent a mixture of writing to yourself and responses to your partner's writing. This happens because you *select* entries either to share or to respond to, and these may be only a small percentage of an entire journal. It also happens because, at least in most classroom situations, you'll want to write more entries than the number of times you're able to swap them when you meet.

- *Should the writing always keep the partner in mind?*
  No. You'll keep writing at least some entries for yourself, focusing on your own learning. Your partner, looking through a kind of window into your relationship to the subject matter, may be struck by a similar experience and write about that; or she may address you directly. Sometimes one partner will voice a confusion only to have it cleared up or answered by the other. In many dialogue entries we've seen, both partners may struggle toward some understanding—together. Usu-

ally, there will be a mix of entries addressed to the partner and addressed to oneself.

- *Must all entries be shared?*
  No. You might choose to keep some entries private. Others may be too boring to share (for example, fairly rote rehearsals of class lectures or readings). If you're not sure initially what sorts of entries will spark the most response from your partner, after a week or so of sharing you will.

- *Is it acceptable to write* on *your partner's entries?*
  Many dialogue partners do (as illustrated in the second sample above). Instead of responding with new entries, they simply annotate their partner's entries by writing in the margins or on the back of the page. But be sure to ask before you cover your partner's entries with ink.

- *What happens if your partner loses your entries?*
  This is a common problem, even to the extent that a partner can unexpectedly quit a course (accompanied by all your entries) and be unreachable for the rest of the term. You can avoid this problem by photocopying your entries before swapping them.

- *If your teacher is collecting all the entries, how will he or she know who wrote what?*
  Simple: put your name on all your own entries.

- *What happens if your partner is unbearable?*
  The notion of dialogue must be preserved in dialogue journals. Ninety-nine percent of the time, you'll find yourself becoming well acquainted with (and liking) your partner. On rare occasions, however, the partnership breaks down. When this happens, the journal writing itself can often repair the damage, especially if you address the problem directly. When this fails, you might need to make arrangements for a different partner, or simply drop the dialogue.
  If a partner seems reticent and isn't keeping up his or her end of the conversation, try addressing the partner directly. Ask a specific question: "What did you make of Prof. Stainton's comment about the history of

Black activism in the 1900s? I wasn't sure what he was getting at; did it make any sense to you?" If you still don't get an answer, talk to your partner during a class session and ask why she's not responding (it may be something simple, e.g., she didn't read your entry). Remember that the dialogue journal must be a *dialogue* to work well. Simply looking over the shoulder of another class member while he writes may be more useful than being totally cut off from other people's ideas but it's no match for direct communication.

- *Do dialogue journals ever get carried on by computer?*
  Most certainly. In fact, it's the principle behind the concept of electronic mail, which is used in many business and professional settings. Dialogue journals can be computerized in two ways: if both partners have access to an electronic mail system or can link their computers by modem, then they can carry on a dialogue quite easily and even, in fact, more naturally than by paper since they can respond to each other instantly. Alternatively, if both partners are using compatible computer and word-processing systems, they can swap disks (instead of paper) or even use a single disk and keep shipping it back and forth, adding to the ongoing conversation each time they open up the file.

- *Must there always be just two partners?*
  A dialogue journal can be carried on with as many participants as can be reasonably coordinated. In most classrooms, however, more than three becomes unwieldy and complicated. Computer networking solves many of the logistical problems when several people dialogue together.

The Double-Entry Notebook

Several times in this chapter, we've alluded to a third, also increasingly popular form of journal writing usually called the double-entry notebook. In the classes of some teachers we've consulted, every entry in a student's journal must take the form of a double entry. On one side of the page, usually the left, the writer jots down an idea, an excerpt from a reading, a quotation, a bit of a lecture, or a factual description. Then, on the right side of the page, the writer comments on or explores in some way the material on the left. In most double-entry notebooks, the amount of commentary exceeds the amount of original text, as illustrated in an example from a course in cultural anthropology (see p. 31).

However, there's nothing about double-entry notebooks that says you have to write more commentary than original text. It may be valuable, for example, to keep track of useful or interesting information and then simply write a line or two alongside of it, commenting on what it means or what you might do with it later on (in a class discussion, research paper, or the like).

The difference between conventional journals and double-entry notebooks concerns the *focus* of your writing. In a typical academic journal, you're usually free to explore whatever new ideas and knowledge occur to you, in whatever way you wish. In double-entry notebooks, you're more likely to focus on something concrete and tangible, such as a piece of text. Your entry in a typical academic journal might jump from topic to topic or take a loose, associational form. A right-side commentary in a double-entry notebook, while not absolutely requiring that you stick to the left-side material, tends to rein you in a bit more. Your entry fizzles out when you have nothing more to say about the left-side entry.

Double-entry notebooks can be used in any field. Their value lies in their critical edge: they force you to study and contemplate specific ideas, words, or data. They can also be easier to start and keep up, especially in the context of coursework. It's virtually impossible not to think *something* about a bit of writing, no matter how mundane the thought might be. If you were keeping a double-entry notebook at this moment, that last sentence might give you pause: is it possible, in fact, to think *nothing* about some piece of language? On the left side of your notebook, you would write down the line, "It's virtually impossible not to think *something* about a bit of writing, no matter how mundane the thought might be." Then, on the right, you might spend five minutes contemplat-

10 - 12

"patriarchies are prevalent, and they appear to be strongest in societies that in which men control significant goods that are exchanged with people outside the family." - p. 159, Spradley and Mc Curdy

I'm really interested in this material on matriarchies/patriarchies because I keep hearing the terms (esp. patriarchy) used in connection with our American culture. This quote focuses on the economic aspects of patriarchies, and I can't help seeing the connection to the argument that our society is (business wise) controlled by men, mostly. I wonder if, in 100 years, that situation has changed, if we won't be matriarchal, or if there's some gender-neutral alternative, a kind of balanced economic/control system. I also am finding it interesting to note how few human societies have ever been controlled by women. The Iroquois and the Lovidu (Africa) came close - that might make a good term paper, to look into how those gender roles were set up and esp. what role the men played in them. Because

ing the implications of such a statement:

Right. All language seems to create thought because language is thought. Unless it's not comprehensible language, like cat muffin I the field in something off to sky entertain by me I. Even then, it's impossible not to "think," because the words carry meanings and associations. But it depends on what we mean by "thinking." Subliminal? Advertising as a case in point. We see the words, try to ignore them (and sometimes do), but they're said to get into our consciousness somehow. And then what? Is that "thinking about" them? And what about words we see when we're simultaneously processing other language—we pass a highway sign and someone's in the car talking to us and the radio's on. Are we "thinking about" the highway sign? What does it mean when something goes "in one ear and out the other?"

As this entry illustrates, when you're at a loss for something to write about, trying out a double entry will certainly get you at least started thinking and writing. This strategy also works well when you need to begin a more formal project such as a term paper.

Double-entry notebooks come in various styles and are used for different purposes. Sometimes a teacher will assign a double-entry notebook with no restrictions on what gets entered on the left-hand pages—only, for example, that it should come from the material of the course. Other teachers may require that you pull out five interesting passages or ideas from each of ten assigned articles, and comment on all five. Still others may actually assign the passages themselves, or provide you with specific bits of information or data, which you copy into your notebook and then analyze in your right-hand entry.

In the least restrictive kind of double-entry notebook, try to be diverse in what you choose to comment on. Don't feel compelled to write only about other people's words. Consider clipping and pasting into your left-hand pages cartoons, newspaper pictures, or snapshots. Or describe objectively in your own words a particular scene or event; then comment on it in your right-hand entry. If you're involved in any clinical or visual field, such as botany, dance, art, anatomy, mechanical engineering, or chemistry, such factual observations can be excellent left-hand entries which you can then evaluate, analyze, or discuss in a way that looks beneath the surface of your observation.

If You're Still Uncertain

Of all the assignments we give in our courses, the one we find ourselves having to describe in greatest detail to students is the academic journal. This is because, as we've pointed out, the academic journal is neither a well-defined nor a consistently used genre of academic writing. The three variations we described above come up fairly frequently as alternatives to the typical reflective, self-directed journal. But they're just three. One professor we know who teaches a course in women's studies requires that her students write only autobiography, exploring their lives growing up and living as women in a changing culture. In her course, an entry focusing entirely on a course reading, without reference to one's own life, beliefs and experiences, would be inappropriate. In contrast, in a dental course at one of our universities, students must record clinical observations in their left-hand entries and then comment on these observations in their right-hand entries. Here, reflections about one's own life and experiences (the required focus of the women's studies journal) would be inappropriate and might even lead to a low assessment of the journal when it's turned in.

    With such a wide spectrum of uses for academic journals, we hesitate to conclude by suggesting habits or conventions that *all* journals should promote, besides our Cardinal Rule that journals should always encourage learning. In cases when you're assigned a journal, however, be sure you know what's appropriate to include in it, how often you should write, and so on. When in doubt, *ask.* Is it appropriate to include entries not related to the course? Can you rehearse lecture notes in your journal? How long should your entries be? Will your style matter, or does anything go? Should you date or number your entries? Is it at least *possible* (if it's not required) to keep a dialogue journal with a partner in the course? Are there any specific requirements as to the format or kind of notebook you turn in? Should other assignments go into the journal? If you're working on a term paper, is the journal a place where you should do all your preliminary brainstorming, drafting, and note-keeping? Can you keep your journal on a computer?

If after a day or two of journal keeping, you're still unsure about some of the expectations for your writing, you may find that what was supposed to become a freewheeling, exploratory kind of experience is feeling more like writing a term paper, harassing you with all sorts of tough questions about your reader's reactions. An excellent strategy is to *turn in a page or two of your journal* and ask your instructor if he or she has any suggestions. At the very least, you can feel assured that the sorts of goals your instructor has in mind for your journal are reflected in what you're doing. And that assurance may be enough to loosen up your writing and make the journal experience richer and more fulfilling.

Finally, if you're not assigned a journal at all, keep one anyway. Use the most comfortable or appropriate of the suggestions we've made in this chapter. Find a partner, if you can, and keep a dialogue journal. Once you get used to writing regularly, you'll find that much of your learning will become more interesting. Your final goal should be to feel good about writing in the journal, to want to return to it as a place of your own, a kind of haven for thinking, learning, musing, talking with yourself or, occasionally, someone else, about knowledge new and old.

Chapter
2

Tracking the Short Writing Assignment

THE NATURE AND HABITAT OF THE SHORT ASSIGNMENT

You probably weren't in college more than three or four days—just long enough to receive the syllabi for your first term courses—before you realized what a tremendous amount of written work you could expect to face between then and graduation. All your humanities courses, your history courses, many of the social sciences, even some of the hard sciences would require you to spend hours at your keyboard, hammering out answers to questions of varying degrees of complexity and detail. If you were to add up the number of pages of all kinds that you will write in college, it could well come out to a standard book-length manuscript or more. This also means, of course, that your professors can expect to read, assess, and annotate all those hundreds of pages, every class, every term, from their graduate T.A. days to their retirement forty years later.

Whenever you see human effort on this scale, it's perfectly fair to ask the question, Why? Why do professors assign all this written work? What is all this writing intended to achieve? Such questions are not only fair, they're useful. The better you understand the purpose of any activity, the more likely you are to fulfill it. The more clearly you perceive the role of written assignments in college, the more you will get out of doing them, and the better performances you'll turn in. Your work will be both more rewarding and more successful. In this chapter we examine in detail the role that short writing assignments play in college and offer suggestions on how to understand and approach them.

Although all writing, short or long, demands similar thinking and composing processes, we have given the essay exam special treatment in Chapter Three. If your assignment exceeds four or five pages and requires multiple drafts, Chapter Four will help with some useful strategies for coming up with ideas, structuring and drafting your paper, and revising for clarity and polish. Full-fledged, sustained, documented research papers, because of their size and complexity, we save until Chapter Five.

Writing Assignments as a Means of Assessment

One of us remembers entering a classroom once for an exam and overhearing a student mutter, "I hate this part. I wish they could just x-ray our brains and let us go home." It might be nice. But since it's also impossible, the fact remains that a major function of writing in college is assessment. By asking you to reproduce on paper some portion of what you've learned, your professor hopes to gauge the extent and depth of your acquired knowledge.

What precisely your professor is assessing varies not only among your courses but sometimes even within the same class. Your teacher will almost certainly be looking for somewhat different qualities in your work on an in-class essay exam than on a full-dress research-based term paper. Roughly speaking, your professors are probably looking at one or more of four possible characteristics in the evaluation of any piece of writing:

1. *Grasp of content,* or how well you know your material. A teacher grading a midterm or final exam essay may be especially interested in the sheer amount of knowledge you've acquired in the course.

2. *Sophistication of thinking.* Are you able to go beyond blunt facts to more complex inferences? Can you resolve contradictions between seemingly incompatible positions? Can you understand and express complex relationships between ideas?
3. *Ability to handle English prose.* Don't expect only your literature professors to care about the clarity and correctness of your writing. We often find astronomers and engineering professors as demanding of proper English style as anyone on the English faculty.
4. *Mastery of particular text forms.* You may need to demonstrate, especially in advanced classes, that you understand the format and logic of particular kinds of texts: psychological research reports, business proposals, abstracts, news articles, or whatever.

Any or all of these might be the focus of your professor's attention in grading a piece of writing. It behooves you to know exactly what's being assessed in anything you write.

Writing Assignments as a Means of Intellectual Development

The main argument of this book (and indeed, of the writing-across-the-curriculum movement as a whole) reflects many teachers' purpose for giving you assignments: *writing develops thinking and helps you learn whatever you're writing about.* Teachers who use writing in this fashion often give a number of shorter, informal assignments, either instead of, or in addition to, their more formal ones. Under such an instructor, you may find yourself writing almost every day, if only a quick, hand-written paragraph or two. Your journal itself may become part of the graded homework.

Such assignments can be used to open up your thinking, by asking you to brainstorm or speculate freely about some question or issue or piece of information. They might also be used to direct your attention to matters of particular importance. Your English professor, for example, might ask you to write something about a particular symbol or setting in a novel, in part to make sure you become aware of its importance. Such assignments can even be used to prepare for in-class discussions. Your religion professor might ask you to write a brief explanation of a chapter in *Romans* in preparation for a detailed discussion of the passage in the next class. Not only can writing open up your thinking, making you aware of more possibilities and options, but it can force you to refine and clarify your thoughts as well. A short, focused analytical paper can force you to mold and shape and distill your original hazy impressions into sharp, precise conceptions expressed in clean, smooth English.

Writing Assignments as Practice in Professional Communication

Almost any career for which college is required demands a certain amount of writing on the job. Every profession or field, furthermore, has developed a variety of more or less fixed kinds of texts to carry on its business. Some of your college writing is assigned specifically to help you develop an understanding of these text types, the forms they take, the purposes they serve, and the logic they embody. At a simple level, this means at least learning how different kinds of texts are laid out, how they're structured, what style they're written in. But more profoundly, each kind of text represents an entire system of assumptions and beliefs, a way of organizing and using information, of making sense of some area of experience. Learning how to write in these forms entails understanding the assumptions and logic each one reflects.

APPROACHING AN ASSIGNMENT: WHAT YOU NEED TO KNOW

By the time you arrive at college, you've obviously undertaken, with more or less success, hundreds of assignments from elementary, junior high and high school. It may seem, thus, a little gratuitous to start *now* into a discussion of how to approach them. But we want to look at this as a tennis coach might, if you were suddenly to make the varsity squad. Even realizing that you had been in tennis for several years, the coach would want to train you for a higher level of play by studying each part of your game—serve, forehand, backhand, lob, volley—separately, and seeing where there might be room for improvement, some change in style that might make your play more effective.

Understanding the Assignment

It almost goes without saying that the first thing you should do after getting any writing assignment is to think about what's being asked of you. Launching right into the writing, unless you're thoroughly familiar with the type of assignment you've been given, would be like trying to create a good *paella* without knowing to check your spice rack for saffron. In short, it helps to read the recipe *carefully* before you begin.

Form of the Assignment   Assignments will come to you in at least three forms, each presenting different opportunities to clarify what's expected of you. No end of students have missed the mark on an assignment simply because they missed something in the assignment itself, perhaps because they were hurried in taking down some notes, didn't bother to think carefully about the precise wording of the assignment, or didn't bother to ask for clarification if something didn't make sense.

   The Handout   The majority of assignments in college courses come to you in the form of a handout. The instructor has usually designed and written the assignment him- or herself and then typed it up on a syllabus or separate sheet. This is done for a simple reason: to ensure that the entire class understands exactly what is expected and will follow through in a systematic way. Written assignments also allow the teacher to make certain specifications that might take up valuable class time rehearsing.

   Whenever you have a written assignment given to you directly from an instructor, *write additional notes on the same page.* In other words, annotate your assignment, *especially* if your teacher makes any comments in class about it. When it comes time to think about your writing, you'll have additional ideas and details in the same place. It also helps to do some preliminary brainstorming, perhaps in the form of bulleted possibilities for completing the assignment.

Oral Assignments Sometimes, a teacher will give you a writing assignment in class only orally, or at most accompanied by some notes on a blackboard or overhead projector. In our own experience, students often miss something in the *oral* part of the assignment because they're so preoccupied writing down what's on the board. Tip: write down what your teacher is saying *first*, being sure to understand as much of his or her suggestions or requirements as possible. Once you're sure you've understood the orally delivered parts of the assignment, then write down whatever may be on the board. Sometimes this will just be a sort of précis of the orally explained assignment: "For Mon.: 1-2 page analysis of how Cardinal Newman defines 'Liberalism.'" Your teacher, meanwhile, may be explicating this assignment orally: "So what I'd like you to do for Monday, then, is to reread the sections of *Apologia Pro Vita Sua* in which Newman talks about this notion of Liberalism and then write a, um, *analyze* what he says here, OK? Try comparing this notion with Ward's philosophy in the *Ideal of a Christian Church.* You might want to go back to that and, um, review the relevant sections as well. Then we'll use your analyses for a discussion on Monday. See you next time." Notice that the written assignment says nothing about the comparison with Ward. In this case, it would help you enormously to have, alongside the exact wording of the précis, a transcription of what your teacher said to flesh it out.

The Textbook Assignment Finally, if your textbook includes writing assignments, your teacher may simply ask you to complete "Exercise 2.6 on page 159." In this case, everything you need should be contained in the pages of the text, since the exercise will almost always be tied to the exposition that precedes it. It would be odd, in other words, for a teacher to assign a textbook exercise and then expect you to respond to it only by referring to material given to you in lecture or in another reading—unless she *said* so.

The same principles for analyzing the assignment apply here, except that you already know which material to review (or read for the first time!): it's contained in the sections or chapters immediately preceding the assignment. Before launching into the assignment, go back through the preceding material, looking for key ideas or concepts to use when responding to the assignment. In class, be absolutely sure to listen to your instructor if he or she makes the assignment orally, and follow the guidelines above for oral assignments. Sometimes teachers will add to or change a textbook assignment in some way in class, and the last thing you want to do is compare the views of Descartes and Locke on the existence of matter (the textbook assignment) if your teacher has substituted "Hume" for "Locke."

When You Miss an Assignment   It happens: you're not in class, for whatever reason, when an assignment is given. Students almost unanimously would rather ask another student in the class for the assignment than seek out the professor, who, as the general lore goes, is likely to say, peering over his glasses, "Why weren't you in class, Mr. Jones? We went over the assignment there." In reality, most teachers are glad to give the assignment again over the phone or in their office, and as a general rule *it is always better to go to the source than rely on hearsay.* (You may even get some valuable clarification or elaboration as well.)

If, however, you choose to ask your classmates for the assignment, be sure either to get it from someone very conscientious or get more than one rendition. Above all, ask for elaboration. If your friend says, "Oh, it was just something to do with Kennedy's actions during the Cuban Missile Crisis, um, yeah, just, um, write a page or two about the Cuban Missile Crisis, that's it," you may be in for trouble. Were any readings assigned? Was there a written version? What *about* the Cuban Missile Crisis were you supposed to focus on? Keep probing, and you're likely to mine a richer vein in your friend's memory. And if it turns out you've stumbled on a dead mine, find someone else.

Phrasing of the Assignment   All assignments, whether they come to you in a quick oral remark or are spelled out in great detail on a hand-out, can be analyzed in terms of what they expect you to *do*, and those expectations are usually retrievable, even in not very explicit assignments, from the exact phrasing of the question itself.

In Chapter Three, we spend considerable time describing the various commands that appear in typical essay exams. To some extent, essay exam questions may resemble short writing assignments in that they ask you to engage in similar sorts of intellectual activities as you write: Compare, analyze, trace, describe, enumerate, discuss, extend, and so on. For detailed treatment of these command verbs, we urge you to read pp. 88–98 there.

In addition to reading the assignment, word for word, with the care we recommend in Chapter Three, a few additional brainstorming strategies can help you before you begin responding to the task.

Levels of Formality   Longer writing assignments, other than journals, almost always require a fairly high level of stylistic, intellectual, and structural formality. Shorter, more routine papers, on the other hand, can be dressed in many ways depending on your teacher's expectations and the kind of assignment you're writing. Your teacher in your cultural anthropology course may be expecting nothing more polished than a quick freewrite in response to her question, "Compare the status of women in nineteenth-century Japan and nineteenth-century America," while your teacher in sociolinguistics may want a structured, carefully edited text of the same length in response to her question, "Compare Labov's and Wolfram's definitions of *dialect*." As we explain in more detail below, knowing what level of formality to use in your writing will depend in large part on knowing your context and the *purpose* of your assignment. When in doubt, especially at first, *ask*. If you still don't know, always, always err in the direction of formality. It's much easier for a teacher to give you permission to relax and loosen up than to have to ask you to exercise some academic decorum in your prose.

In the absence of any contextual information that might clue you into the proper dress of your writing, try thinking about the wording of your assignment itself—its own garb. Compare these two:

Take a look at the stats on how many folks were living in big and small Italian cities in the years before and after the plague; notice any patterns? Jot down some ideas and bring them to class.

Examine the statistics for density of population and urban index for large and small Italian cities in the years preceding and following the plague. Then analyze any patterns discernible from the statistics, paying special attention to the relationship between urban centers and the low country regions.

Clearly these two assignments suggest different styles, and you might write the first in a more casual form than the second. Some teachers, however, like to *sound* casual, perhaps to ease tension in the classroom, even when they expect nothing less than black tie and evening gown when it comes to your writing. Again, when in doubt, don't take a chance: dress up.

Range of Territory   By nature, assignments define an intellectual territory and assume that you won't stray much beyond it. Just how far you might wander, however, can vary considerably from teacher to teacher, assignment to assignment. Imagine you get this assignment in your history course:

Analyze what might have happened to the military events of World War II if Hitler hadn't inexplicably stopped his army's advance at Dunkirk when it was on the verge of completely annihilating the British, French and Belgian armies there. How might this have changed, in particular, Churchill's next move?

Here you might speculate freely on at least some events following the battle of Dunkirk, paying, of course, special attention to Churchill. You might even speculate a bit more and discuss the implications of such a large loss of manpower for the Allied forces, especially the British. Stretching further, you could even discuss how such a defeat might have affected the morale of the French and the strength of the underground resistance movement. But be careful not to roam so far that you lose sight of the intellectual path of the assignment (to stick to military strategy, especially Churchill's, perhaps to demonstrate that you have a good handle on the major military and political events of the Second World War). If you start considering whether Hitler would have committed suicide with Eva Braun and (so one theory goes) had his chauffeur cremate their two bodies with gasoline, you may not find your way back by nightfall. Worse still, your *teacher* may think you're lost.

Some assignments may deliberately encourage imagination and free exploration, perhaps as a way to interest you in the topic. Would you have been born if so many British troops hadn't escaped from Dunkirk? Would the U.S. have continued to develop the atom bomb? Would there have been a cold war? Would Hitler's master race have succeeded? Would there have been global genocide? As it stands, the assignment above doesn't seem to suggest such a wide speculation, but the change of only a few words in the assignment might open a wider territory to explore, or, for that matter, run off the maps altogether.

Once again, we can't stress how important it is, when trying to understand the nature of any assignment, to ask your instructor what may or may not be appropriate. Teachers are used to defining and sometimes refining their assignments: it comes with the territory. Make use of their interest in their own assignments to help you to understand their nature and parameters.

Purposes of the Assignment

Many students run into trouble in their writing because they have little or no sense that their papers should *do* anything. They think of writing as vaguely "informative," with "to inform" meaning simply to "write stuff down." Since they have no goal or aim in their work, they get stuff down all right, but their papers turn out formless, haphazard, and dull. They select their material according to no particular criterion, write it down in no particular order, and lead their readers in a meandering track through an unsorted verbal museum—a fossil here, a suit of armor there, a Gutenberg Bible in the corner. Because they have no real purpose for their work, they find the writing itself laborious and dreary, and they produce papers of a confused gray quality. Life is too short for this.

In approaching an assignment, you need to give some thought to what you want your paper *to do*—and that means, *to your reader*. What effect on your reader do you want your paper to have? How should your reader be changed as a result of reading your paper?

Occasionally your purpose will be dictated by the assignment itself:

> Write a one-page letter to the CEO of your chemical prod-
> ucts company trying to convince her to adopt the proce-
> dure for assessing the purity of liquid nitrogen explained
> on pages 327–334.

> Write a speech to be delivered to a gathering of voters of
> the political party of your choice. Try to get them involved
> in campaigning for the upcoming senatorial election.

In these cases, obviously, your writing should take its
direction from the purpose given in the assignment itself:
secure adoption of the chemical procedure, get out the vote.
Your task is simply to hold the purpose firmly in mind at every
moment as you write, thereby giving your paper real direction
and energy. You only run into danger by letting the purpose
slip away from you and lapsing back into the old, purposeless,
dull informative paper that your professor has gone to some
trouble to avoid.

Assignments in which the purposes are this sharply defined for you, however, are rare. Far more often, you'll be
asked to write without anything being said of your paper's
effect on its reader. Nonetheless, you can still often infer the
appropriate purpose even if it's not explicitly stated. Suppose
you're given this assignment in a course on medical ethics:

> Do you think, on the basis of the facts in your casebook,
> that the Cayhills should or should not be allowed to re-
> move their infant son from life support? Write a report to
> the West Prairie Hospital Ethics Board presenting them
> with your recommendation and your reasons for it.

The formal command of the assignment is to write a report—a
sufficiently neutral request—but this is hardly a neutral topic;
it's literally a matter of life and death. You're not writing to the
Ethics Board simply to entertain them or to make idle conversation; you're determining whether a child lives or dies. Do
you simply want to inform the Board of your opinion? No. You
want to *convince* them to do what you suggest. You might
inform them of the physician's opinion, the parents' wishes,
the child's medical problems, the state's laws, and so forth—
but you want to *persuade* them to follow your recommendation. Depending on your opinion, you want your report to so

affect the Board that they will either discontinue treatment or keep the child on life support for the future. Just as in writing to your CEO or the party faithful, you're seeking to provoke a very specific action.

But even an assignment such as the Ethics Board Report offers you at least an implicit purpose for your work. Most assignments offer nothing of the kind. What are you to make, then, of assignments like the following?

> Discuss the significance of Harry Harlowe's primate research on current theories of early family relationships and their effects on later psychopathology.

> Compare and contrast the ways in which Aristophanes and Euripides respond in their plays to the Peloponnesian War.

Nothing in the way these assignments are phrased suggests a real, dynamic purpose. "Discuss . . ." Well, why? "Compare and contrast . . ." In order to do what? What possible purpose can you adopt in responding to assignments of this nature? Are you left once more simply with the goal, "to inform"?

No. Though it may not be much less vague than informing, you can still adopt a goal with more life to it than that. If the assignment offers no other particular purpose, make it your goal to *convince* your reader of the truth of your assertions. *Prove* that you're right. In effect, you approach such an assignment as you do the report to the Ethics Board. You seek *to compel your reader* to see matters your way. You present your thesis, pull your reader step-by-relentless-step through your reasoning, marshal your evidence clearly and forcibly, and draw your threads together in a way that leaves your reader no room for quibbling or doubting. You don't leave your reader the option of remaining neutral or undecided regarding your belief. You seek to make the reader your disciple. Even if you never again plan to read about Harry Harlowe or the Peloponnesian War, you write your paper as if nothing could be more important than the truths you have to tell concerning them.

The difference between *informing* and *convincing* may not seem at first all that important to you, but if you make the shift you'll see the improvement in your writing. You'll find it easier to formulate a clear, definite, arguable thesis. You'll be more sure-handed and confident in selecting and arranging your material. The language you use will almost automatically become more clean, direct, and energetic. And, finally, you'll have a better sense of what to do with the two most crucial and difficult parts of any paper, the introduction and conclusion. You will no longer simply drift in and drift out of your paper; you'll start and end it more vigorously, more decisively.

Have we convinced you?

Purposes of the Instructor

We have spoken so far as if your own purpose for the paper were the only one that mattered. But in order to write most effectively, you also need to consider your instructor's purpose in giving the assignment. As we noted earlier, your teacher might be assessing your grasp of the course material, the complexity of your thinking, or your ability to write standard English prose. Or he might be using the writing to expand, deepen, and refine your thinking, or even to fuel a class discussion. Which of these he intends to accomplish by the assignment should in turn affect how he grades your work.

If your instructor intends the writing to open up your thinking, to help you study some phenomenon from a range of different perspectives or to see different angles to it, you can assume that a rich welter of ideas, however loose, will earn more credit than a tightly polished single thought. You want to stay with the question and thrash it out on paper—thinking out loud, as it were—rather than giving up too soon or spending much time in revision. Essay exams, on the other hand, are given to assess the depth of your learning. You're asked to display what you have learned, and within the confines of the question you're answering you should do just that—show off, lay it out there, demonstrate your wares. If your professor intends the writing to discipline or sharpen your analytical skills, he will probably look for writing that reflects precision, acuity, even elegance rather than the casual heap of ideas more typical of journal work. In a brief, focused analytical essay, you may only write two pages, but those two pages may require several drafts before you've honed your analysis to a sufficiently fine edge.

Try to assess, then, what your professor is using the assignment to accomplish, what his educational goals are, and write with those in mind. If you're not sure of the educational goal, you should ask. The conversation that ensues may help both you and your instructor do your respective jobs more effectively.

Audiences for Assignments

When responding to a writing assignment in college, the audience or readership of your paper both is and is not your professor. You need to write *for* your professor without, as a rule, writing *to* her. You can hear for yourself how silly it sounds to begin a formal paper something like this: "As you were saying in class last week, Dr. Harris, Jim doesn't seem much like either a man or a woman in the book." Dr. Harris, of course, knows that the book is Willa Cather's novel *My Antonia;* that Jim is the novel's narrator, Jim Burden; and that, in fact, Jim Burden's gender identity really is a bit ambiguous. But the student, by relying so heavily on Dr. Harris to make sense of his paper, is shirking part of his responsibility. Dr. Harris, in fact, will be more impressed if the opening is something like this: "Willa Cather, in her novel *My Antonia,* tells her story through a first-person narrator, Jim Burden, whose interests and attitudes seem to mix traditionally male and female characteristics." The opening in effect ignores Dr. Harris completely, and will impress her more as a result.

In the great majority of cases, then, you will be writing *for* a professor but *to* an audience which is more or less fictional, invented, imagined. In some cases, the audience may be designated, as in the assignments above where the students were to write to the CEO of their chemical companies or to their party regulars. But an explicitly designated audience is as rare as a specifically designated purpose. More often, you'll be writing to one of two other, more general audiences: scholars in the field, or readers of about your own background and training.

In specialized upper-division courses, you may need to address a readership of fully-trained experts in your area. You can assume they know all that you do and more about the general field, although you certainly may, by virtue of your research, have something new to tell them about some aspect of your subject. You can use all the technical language of your field without defining it, and you won't need to document many facts that will constitute common knowledge among this community of scholars. On the other hand, you will need to be doubly scrupulous about using technical language correctly, and you'll need to follow the standard text forms of the discipline with absolute fidelity. You will have less background material to explain, but you will also be held to higher standards in your logic and evidence. Again, only one person may ever read your work—that is, your professor—but your professor will be reading your work *as if* it were written for an academic conference or journal, and will assess it accordingly.

For the great majority of college assignments, however, you'll be writing for what is loosely called a general audience. *If no particular readership is specified for an assignment, you should address an audience comparable to yourself, as you were before starting work on this particular paper.* Assume readers with your own level of education and interests, and tailor your work for them. You could also get roughly the same effect if you model your imaginary audience on the other students in your class. One professor we talked with tells his students, "Write for the student who missed class the day we discussed this material." Another suggests that his students imagine themselves writing chapters for a study guide for the course to be placed at the reserve desk in the library for students in the future. Both professors are helping their students picture a general audience in similar ways.

The important thing in either case is to keep the needs of some reader or another before your mind whenever you write. You need to provide your reader quickly with the necessary context to follow your paper, and you need to make sure at every point that he or she can follow what you're saying. If you analyze your assignment in terms of its purpose and audience from the very beginning, and keep these before your mind the whole time you're working, your draft will prove stronger, more coherent, and more alive when you finally submit it to your real reader—your professor.

INTELLECTUAL DEMANDS OF COLLEGE WRITING ASSIGNMENTS

In our discussion with teachers in all disciplines, we hear a common concern—one which reveals the good will of the teachers themselves (their desire for students to learn) and a little anxiety as well (the creeping sense that students don't learn quite as well as they might). The concern is often expressed in the phrase, "I want my students to think critically." What this suggests is that teachers are not looking for students merely to absorb information and parrot it back. They want students to analyze and evaluate what they study, to take it apart, to examine it piece by piece, to weigh it, judge it, perhaps (who knows?) to doubt or reject it—perhaps even to improve on it, add to it, develop it further. Teachers want students to be active in their pursuit of knowledge while at the same time exercising a little healthy skepticism. They want students going after knowledge with a pick and shovel and then putting everything they unearth to the acid test—not to be captious and negative but in the restless search for True Gold.

But this is a lot of work. Memorizing and replaying information is easy. Critical thinking demands effort, active questioning, a sharp eye, a deeply ingrained restlessness, a refusal to be easily satisfied. It also demands some sort of method, a place to start. If you haven't often been asked to think critically and analytically about what you study, you may feel at loose ends. Where do you begin? How do you gain entrance? Which nuts and screws do you have to remove first?

It helps to have some general idea of the intellectual operations you may need to perform in responding to written assignments, especially for those that call for sophisticated critical thinking. The major intellectual operations are like the basic moves in ballet; whatever dance you perform will be largely built on some combination of them. The operations are not to be simply confused with the commands of the assignment (describe, evaluate, trace, etc.), even though they often carry the same labels. The operations, as opposed to the explicit commands, represent a deeper structure, a more basic activity of the mind. They have less to do with the actual final form of your written work than with the thinking necessary to develop your material. All five of the operations discussed here—description, analysis, synthesis, evaluation, and interpretation—may be involved, for instance, in an assignment that reads: "Trace the development in effectiveness of computer programming languages from BASIC to Pascal and speculate about what this development suggests for the future."

Description

Probably the simplest of these mental operations' to "describe" means simply to record the specific details of some phenomenon, to produce an accurate picture or account of it. You don't need to explain anything yet; that comes later. For now you're simply logging facts, collecting raw data. It takes time, patience, and meticulous observation. An excellent introduction to the art of observation, by the way, is A. Conan Doyle's first Sherlock Holmes novel, *A Study in Scarlet*. It is there that Holmes keeps chiding his companion, "You *see*, Watson, but you do not *observe*," and then demonstrating what real observation entails.

Teachers often assign problems requiring description in some form to help students develop their powers of observation. In the health sciences, for example, one of the most important processes for clinical practice is looking carefully, noticing unusual characteristics or symptoms. A doctor, nurse, dentist, or other clinician will generally postpone her formal diagnosis of a patient's problem until she's made a full description, which may come from notes she keeps during the examination. A historian or biographer dare not start expounding an interpretation of a life or event until he's ferreted out and sorted all the available facts. A newspaper reporter can't park near a political rally and take notes from her car; she has to get in close, ask questions, read signs, listen to chants and slogans—observe the events. Even writing down readings from a barometer qualifies as a sort of description.

Many assignments may involve other thinking processes, such as analysis, assuming that you've observed and described something carefully first. Because such assignments don't always remind you to begin by describing what you see, it can be tempting to give short shrift to the observational process. But don't. An excellent way to begin many writing assignments is simply to describe, as fully as possible, exactly what you see or what's happening in the painting, cadaver, tribal community, microscope lens, film, or Shakespearean sonnet you'll be analyzing. As we suggested in the last chapter, start with the obvious and wait for the brilliant. If description teaches you nothing else, it teaches you that the obvious is often not so obvious after all.

Analysis

From the Greek word for loosening up, *analysis* means, strictly speaking, taking something apart for the purpose of looking at its constituent elements. In quantitative analytical chemistry, this something is a substance whose constituents are measured in amounts and proportions: what elements make up this compound? In cultural anthropology, the "something" might be a community of people, and your analysis might entail sorting out and examining separately their familial, political, commercial, and religious institutions and structures.

Freud, for instance, strove for decades to arrive at the most useful division of the mind into its major components. "Psychoanalysis" means literally "analysis of the soul." In his early model, he divided the mind into unconscious, preconscious, and conscious. Not entirely satisfied by that, he later reanalyzed the psyche into ego, id, and superego. Modern chemistry only developed after scientists abandoned their early attempts to analyze all substances into earth, air, fire, and water, and learned to analyze them instead into homogeneous elements comprised of structurally identical atoms.

Once you understand what kind of mental operation analysis represents, you can deliberately carry it further. Given any topic, you can search for several ways to subdivide it or break it out into its components, and assess what results you get from each division. Suppose a professor (we won't specify in what discipline) hands you a letter written by Benjamin Disraeli, a Prime Minister of England under Queen Victoria. How many different options can you find for ways to analyze this phenomenon?

1. You could analyze the letter by author, audience, and topic. Who was Disraeli? Whom was he addressing? What was he discussing?
2. You could analyze the letter as a political act. What was the situation? What did Disraeli seek to achieve? How was he using the letter to achieve this?
3. Knowing that Disraeli was a novelist as well as a politician, you could analyze the letter on literary dimensions. How would you characterize Disraeli's style?

What images or metaphors does he employ? Are there
examples of allusion or parody in his letter?
4. You could even, if you had the original document, subject it to physical analysis. What kind of paper and ink
are these? Where must he have procured them? Is it
possible that the letter is actually a forgery, and could
this be established (as it was with Hitler's bogus diary a
few years back) by an analysis of the paper itself?

Analysis, like description, is more often assumed or implied in the way an assignment is presented than stated outright. (When the term *is* actually used, curiously enough, it
usually means to *interpret*—strictly speaking, a rather different intellectual operation which we'll describe shortly.) It's
also the case that analysis as a mental operation is rarely an
end in itself. Far more often, analysis represents the necessary
prelude to synthesis, interpretation, or evaluation. You analyze a play—as in break it down into its constituent aspects—
in order to assess the artistic contributions of each: its script,
direction, acting, lighting, score, etc. You anatomize a fish in
order, ultimately, to understand how the organs work together, not just separately.

Synthesis

If analysis involves taking something apart, *synthesis* means
putting things together—combining elements or entities to
form a conceptual whole. At some level, for example, all fields
are involved in building theories about their objects of study.
A theory is, in fact, a set of more or less elaborate generalizations based on a large-scale synthesis of what a field has observed about its subject.

Darwin, in a sense, constructed his theory of evolution
from a lifetime of careful observations and analyses. As Darwin drew on more observations about various animal species
and their behaviors, habitats, and biological characteristics,
he was led, finally, to *synthesize* his findings into a model of
genetic variation, differential reproduction, and speciation
that has had an enormous impact on how we think. By contrast, Tycho Brahe put years into making meticulous observations of the movements of the stars and planets, but got no

further. It was left to Johannes Kepler to synthesize Brahe's data into the Three Laws of Planetary Motion, which in turn paved the way for Newton's still broader synthesis, resulting in his formulation of the Law of Universal Gravitation.

The moral here is that *collection* is not in itself *synthesis*. Description does not automatically yield more than a heap of givens ("data" in Latin). Synthesis entails finding the *connections*, the *linkages* between the various facts before you. To synthesize means not just to add one thing to another to another, but to see what new entity they form among them, to see what pattern or patterns hold the givens together. It's also important to note that *synthesis* generally requires or presupposes a preliminary *analysis* of the data—a sorting of the data into its major categories.

Suppose you're required, in a course on child psychology, to read and report on ten different studies on the attention span of children between ages six and eight. A mere summary of each of the studies won't tell you much. You need first to *analyze* each study by examining separately its hypothesis, subjects, assessment instrument, methodology, statistical analyses, and the results of each. This guarantees at least that you won't later end up comparing apples and oranges. Thereafter you need to ponder the evidence you have analyzed and try to *formulate a model of the underlying reality which could account for all these findings.* Are there studies which need to be rejected on methodological grounds? Of the better studies, what are the consistent findings, and where are there discrepancies? What might account for the discrepancies? What else would we need to know to fully understand the child's attention span?

Synthesis, then, doesn't mean simply glomming information together or listing stray facts or just counting things up. To synthesize means, after careful observation and analysis, to formulate a model of reality that binds all your information logically together into a coherent whole. You will find that many college assignments call for synthesis under one name or another, though the word itself almost never appears as an explicit command. If you examine the most famous figures in any discipline, furthermore, you will find that it is often this particular mental operation that they excel at.

Evaluation

If you analyze the word *evaluation* according to its roots, you get e-valu-ation: that is, the act of drawing out the value of some thing—or, to put it another way, of determining its worth. If a writing assignment calls for evaluation, then it's no longer enough to describe or explain whatever it is you're discussing; you are now called upon to say *how good it is*, according to relevant criteria. The term "evaluate" is often used as the explicit command in college assignments and, unlike the all-purpose "analyze," usually does mean precisely the operation we're describing here.

The range of things you can evaluate in an academic setting is extensive. You can, perhaps most obviously, write a movie or drama review, evaluating the quality of some cinematic or theatrical production. Or, you might evaluate the success of Washington's military tactics in the Revolutionary War. Or, you might evaluate the cogency of Socrates' arguments for remaining in Athens and drinking the hemlock after his conviction. Or, you might evaluate a particular research design in biology: will this experiment indeed answer the question it was designed to address? Evaluations themselves, in fact, can be evaluated in turn. How often have you watched a movie, read the review in the paper, and wondered how on earth the critic could come to such silly conclusions?

In every case you have several different steps you must work through. To evaluate anything, you must understand what the entity is; you need to formulate appropriate criteria for evaluation, measure the object against those criteria, and draw your various measurements together into one overarching assessment. That is, you will need to *analyze* the entity into its component aspects and decide on standards for the assessment of each; *observe* and *describe* the object itself, to see how it measures up on each criterion; and *synthesize* your assessments into one coherent, evaluative conclusion.

The establishment of the evaluative criteria themselves can often be a major part of the intellectual challenge. How do you assess, for instance, the action of a particular political leader in the past? By how it served the interests of her own nation? By how fairly it dealt with all concerned parties? By how it strengthened or weakened the leader's political power? By whether it resulted in the greatest good for the greatest number—even if it destroyed a few lives on the side? By how consistent or inconsistent it was with the leader's campaign promises? You can't judge anything except by some particular criterion—every measurement implies some sort of ruler—and sometimes you will need to evaluate the criteria in their turn!

Finally, to evaluate something implies more than simply registering whether you happen personally to like the thing or not. You're trying to assess some quality believed to inhere in the thing itself, not simply in your own eye as the beholder. Observing and recording your initial rough impressions of the object often provides a fine starting point—but that's all. A raw opinion is not yet an evaluation. For that you need to ask yourself what it is about the book, movie, theory, policy, experiment, etc., that strikes you as good, bad, or indifferent. Furthermore, once you've isolated why the object affects you as it does, you need to consider whether your original impression is actually well-founded.

Suppose you're taking British History from Elizabeth to Victoria and you begin reading about the British treatment of the American colonies in the early 1700s. As an American with years of July 4th pageants in your past, you may feel that the British policies were brutal and stupid—but were they really? Once you examine the situation more closely, and once you've developed your criteria for assessing foreign policy, the British policies may appear more restrained and fair than you had supposed—or they may look worse. In any case, you'll no longer simply be registering a gut feeling but a careful, responsible assessment.

There is nothing easier than offering a snap judgment on something on the basis of your immediate gut level response to it. Developing a careful, precise, even-handed, conscientious evaluation, however, requires every bit of intellectual energy, care, and maturity you can muster.

Interpretation

The term "interpretation," like "evaluation," does occasionally turn up as the command in an assignment, and, again like "evaluation," it tends to mean there pretty much what it means as an intellectual operation. To *intepret* anything means to *say what the entity means or points to beyond itself.*

What does a particular sonnet *mean?* That is, what does it say about life, truth, beauty, or whatever?

What do the results of this physics experiment *mean?* What do they tell us about the hypothesis being tested, or about the broader theory from which it was derived?

What do the recent fluctuations in the Dow-Jones *mean*— or tell us—about the future odds of an economic recession?

What does a particular bit of body language *mean?* Does an interviewer's crossed arms on his chest actually suggest displeasure with the performance of the job candidate? Does that crossed leg spell trouble?

All of these are questions of interpretation, of reading, in a sense, the meaning of some phenomenon. To interpret anything is to view it not just as itself, but as a symbol for something else, as a sign indicating a reality in some other context. To take a classic example, consider the problem of interpreting the Bible. Are you to read it as a literal account of the history of the earth? Or as a purely secular anthology of historical and literary writings of various ancient Middle Eastern peoples? Or as the major source of Western ethics? Or as poetry still possessed of all its artistic value? Or as a historically conditioned human document which is yet still revelatory of Divine Truth?

Or, to take another example, what does the Constitution actually have to *say* about the right to privacy? The actual phrase occurs nowhere in the Constitution, but does the document as a whole nonetheless actually mean or intend to guarantee some such right to American citizens? And if it does, what in turn would such a right to privacy *mean* for women seeking abortions, for the terminally ill seeking to be released from life support, for confidentiality of credit records? Some questions of interpretation have literally had wars fought over them—and may well have again.

Any object, furthermore, can be read in the light of multiple contexts or languages. Konrad Lorenz, for example, began his famous studies of animal aggression when he noticed how intense and varied were the colors of the tropical fish in his aquarium. They were beautiful, to be sure, but Lorenz went beyond their obvious aesthetic appeal to wonder if their colors, in fact, *meant anything.* Did the colors serve some purpose, or point to some reality or system beyond themselves? Years of observation and thought in time convinced Lorenz (and others) that the colors of the fish were essential in determining social behavior and thus survival in their natural environment. That is, at least, what the colors mean to a biologist; that is how he reads them in a biological context. You could also imagine, however, variously colored fish showing up as symbols in a literary work, like the crystal unicorn in Williams' *Glass Menagerie.* Or they might appear as symbols in dreams. Or a South Pacific island nation might even use fish of different colors as symbols on different kinds of postal stamps. What the colors of the fish mean in each case would depend on the context or language through which they were being read.

Interpretation, like the other mental operations discussed here, can be conscientiously practiced, once you understand what it entails. In large part it's a matter of developing a consistent habit of asking, over and over again, about almost anything that floats past, "That's curious. I wonder *what that means.*" And then you're off.

TWO WRITING ASSIGNMENTS

So far in this chapter, we've been providing some general tips and strategies for analyzing and responding to shorter writing assignments. To show you more specifically how that kind of analysis can help you to think about your writing, we want to examine two short, college-level writing assignments from quite different courses. In particular, we want to focus on the role that the basic mental operations described in the previous section play in college writing, and how they might help you think through and plan your strategy.

Assignment 1

Let's return for a moment to the sample assignment given a few pages back:

> Trace the development in effectiveness of computer programming languages from BASIC to Pascal and speculate about what this development suggests for the future.

Source, Level of Formality, Range of Territory   This assignment comes from an introduction to computer programming in which, in addition to writing short computer programs, students read about the history of computer technology in a series of articles and reports. The assignment appeared in the syllabus about midway through the course and was not elaborated on in class by the instructor. The language of the assignment seems to suggest a formal, structured response. No goofing around here: get to the point, marshal the appropriate information, and write the response cleanly and effectively. Notice, however, that there may be at least some room for ranging beyond pure history. The last section asks you to speculate. How have the most recent kinds of programming languages progressed beyond the dreams of the first computer technologists? What might the union of programming and more theoretical notions of artificial intelligence yield in the next decade or two? Can you even toss in a paragraph about that article you found in *Time* magazine on virtual reality? Maybe—but see how far you get first with the more straightforward material from the readings.

Audience   Since nothing about the assignment suggests any specific readership, you're probably safest writing for the default or general academic audience. Remember, this does *not* mean writing directly *to* your professor. You probably do best, as you write, to address a readership made up of other students with approximately your own general level of computer literacy but without the special expertise you've developed in this course. And you'll want to address them on the assumption that they've never seen you or your professor or your class before in their lives. Provide them with the background they need from the beginning. They know something about computers and programming, but otherwise they're starting from scratch.

Purposes   Think through first what your professor is attempting to exercise or assess in your understanding. She'll want to see evidence that you understand the major aspects of programming languages; that you know the exact characteristics of a number of specific languages, including at least BASIC and Pascal; and that you can compare these appropriately. She also clearly intends to develop and assess your more abstract understanding of programming language development. Can you assess the direction and speed of this development, and accurately forecast where it will go somewhere down the line? Since the assignment seems fairly formal, you can expect the clarity and economy of your prose to make some difference, but you're not being asked to use the conventions and structures of a particular scholarly or technical kind of document.

Since the assignment is every inch the classroom exercise, it does not suggest a specific practical purpose. You're not being asked, for example, to make a company-wide decision on whether to adopt a particular currently-existing programming language, given the possibility of better ones coming along soon. Then what should you be *doing* with your paper? When in doubt, again, adopt the goal of *convincing your readers of the logic or correctness of your claims. Prove* to your readers that the major trends in development are such-and-such, and leave them in no doubt that ten years from now state-of-the-art programming languages will do thus-and-so.

In short, no matter how abstract or technical the assignment seems, you're still not writing in a social void. You're *doing something to or for someone* every time you write.

Mental Operations   Given that none of the five basic operations is mentioned here, what does such an assignment require of you intellectually? You will need to *analyze* the grounds for comparison of computer languages generally (user-friendliness, speed, power, flexibility, etc.). You will need to *describe* each language along these and probably other relevant lines as well. Your analyses and descriptions should then allow you to *evaluate* each language on each major criterion. You must then *synthesize* your separate evaluations into one overarching judgment on each language. And, finally, you will have to *interpret* your findings as signs of what lies in the future for computer programming languages; you will need to read the sign of the times as it appears in your collection of completed evaluations.

You can imagine how, once you've diagnosed the assignment along such lines, you can begin work on it with greater efficiency and confidence. There's nothing like knowing where you're going.

Assignment 2

Assigned Journal Entry (to be collected):

> Imagine that you've been sent to India on a peace and negotiation mission to try to bring some compromise in the religious wars between Muslims and Hindus. Your focus is the mosque in Ayodhya which we have been discussing in class. You decide that the best way to end the conflict would be for the Muslims to sell the mosque to the Hindus for a very profitable sum. Since for the Muslims the mosque is not an extraordinarily sacred site as it is for the Hindus, you reason that they stand only to gain (by, for example, building a spectacular new mosque nearby), while the Hindus get back their temple, the purported birthplace of Rama. What will be the reaction to your plan on both sides? Will it work? Why or why not? Write a diary of the events of your visit. Be sure to make use of our readings on the relationship between Muslim and Hindu beliefs and recent events in India.

Source, Level of Formality, Range of Territory   The assignment, given in a course in modern world religions, appeared on a dittoed handout. When the teacher passed it out, she added little to the actual specifications of the assignment, but told the class that she thought they would enjoy doing it and that she would be forming them into small groups during the next class to compare their responses. These comments, together with the form of the assignment (a kind of miniature case problem or scenario), suggest that it is appropriate to be imaginative while also being sure to integrate into your response the material from the course readings. This is also clearly an *assignment* (and will be collected and assessed). For that reason, it's important to take it more seriously than a casually written journal entry, and to move back and forth between the readings and the paper as you write it.

The intellectual territory of the assignment seems, in this case, to restrict you to the beliefs and actions of the two groups (Hindus and Muslims living in India) and their religious convictions as these relate to recent events there—all through a sharp focus on the ownership or control of the mosque at Ayodhya. All this information, furthermore, comes from several course readings and class discussions—material it would benefit you to review carefully before writing.

Audience   The audience for this assignment is curious. Notice first that the assignment calls on you to write a diary concerning your imagined peace-keeping mission. Normally, a diary is the most personal of documents; you write a diary entirely for yourself—you are your only reader. But your instructor also intends for you to share this diary with classmates and, finally, to turn it in for a grade. This probably means, when you add it all up, that you should write something more like a journalist's log of your trip, telling the imaginary story as it unfolds over time. You obviously write in the first person—I did this, I saw that—and your style can afford to be fairly casual, even to the extent of writing in occasional fragments. But still, the entries have to be self-standing. That is, a newcomer has to be able to read your entries and follow what's going on. You can't leave as large gaps in your account as you might in a real diary, and you can't use any private shorthand. In other words, you *do* have an audience, even though you're pretending you don't. The following excerpt from one student's response seems to have gauged this about right:

> Saturday. Talked to Hindu group who say the temple is just the tip of the iceberg (my metaphor—it was already broiling by noon!). Another big issue is the Muslim defiance of voluntary birth control program. Seems to be a threat to Hindus in terms of future population. Just one of many intertwined complaints against Muslims.

The implied audience, in this response, is the self (a nice parallel to the location of the assignment in the course journal). But far from being an entirely self-directed piece of writing, this response anticipates both the teacher as reader/evaluator (hence the overt display of references to other Muslim/Hindu conflicts from the course readings) and other students as discussants in the small groups (who might like the humor of the iceberg metaphor).

Purpose   In addition to the obvious purpose of sharpening your focus on the relationship between religious belief and political action among Hindus and Muslims, this assignment seems designed to encourage several other kinds of thinking and learning: 1. making the study of world religions immediately relevant to your knowledge of world politics; 2. helping you to make concrete and real certain events taking place halfway around the world; and 3. encouraging you to take an informed, pluralistic position on an important source of human emotion, conflict, and action: world religions. Once you realize some of these goals, then it follows that you can benefit from aligning your own purposes with those implied in the assignment: *make* your review of the material relevant; *put* yourself in the shoes of a mediator, balancing both sides of the issue; *integrate* your other knowledge of Islamic and Hindu religion into your response. And enjoy learning in the process.

Mental Operations   Once again, the mental operations required of this task don't appear explicitly in the command of the assignment. In fact, the actual task emerges from a series of questions ("What will be the reaction to your plan . . . ? Will it work? Why or why not?") followed by the imperative to write a diary of the events of your visit. Writing a diary does not, in itself, lead to a specific sort of thinking, since most diaries simply record the daily narrative of the writer's life. The key to the assignment's intellectual demands must be found elsewhere.

In short scenarios like this one, the context or domain of your thinking is established initially, in the opening description. Here, it calls for the *analysis* of a controversy over a mosque/temple in northern India, including a *synthesis* of the positions surrounding the controversy and, finally, an *interpretation* of what might happen, relative to that synthesis, if one course of action were proposed (selling the mosque). An excellent way to follow through from these mental activities, in completing the assignment, would be to: 1. review the readings on Hindu and Islamic faith, asking what stake each group has in control of the mosque; 2. extend the belief systems of each group to the causes of the factionalizing and tension in India; 3. ask yourself how each group would react to ownership of the mosque shifting from Muslims to Hindus. Can there be, in fact, a purely economic solution? How tied up in the controversy are the issues of pride or hatred? What is the historical relevance that the mosque was once a Hindu temple before it was demolished several hundred years ago by Muslim invaders who then built the mosque on the same site? How might the events of October 30, 1990, when thousands of Hindu protesters swarmed into the mosque and were fired upon by police, figure into the reaction to your plan? And so on.

It should be clear that each of these three processes in completing the assignment actually *creates* fuller and better learning. It's clear, too, that the instructor has done her part to encourage that learning. The rest is up to you.

A CATALOGUE OF COMMON WRITING ASSIGNMENTS

College writing assignments come in every shape, color, and flavor. Baskin-Robbins has nothing on the standard college curriculum. There are, however, some kinds of assignments that you'll probably run into again and again. On the basis of our discussions with teachers across a range of disciplines, we have developed the following catalogue of assignments. For each, we have tried to apply the thinking outlined throughout this chapter to diagnose the intellectual tasks they entail, how you might approach them, and the grounds on which they are likely to be assessed.

The Catalogue

A. Reading Responses
B. Summaries and Abstracts
  1. Summaries
  2. Academic abstracts
  3. Executive summaries
C. Bibliographies
  1. Simple
  2. Annotated
  3. Mock

D. Reviews
  1. Of performances
  2. Of research literature
E. Data Analyses
F. Lab Reports
G. Research Proposals

Reading Responses

We use the term "reading responses" to cover a wide range of short, more or less informal, writing assignments in which you react to something you've been asked to read for the course. Sometimes reading responses, or "reflections," as some professors call them, will take the form of prompts for your journal: *"For next time, write in your journal about Machiavelli's principles of leadership. Do you agree with all of them? How do or don't you see them working today in the role of the U.S. Presidency?"* Often these are assigned in order to prepare you for a discussion of the material in class.

The educational purpose of such assignments is largely to start you thinking about the material at hand. Professors who assign these are usually more interested in the richness and penetration of your ideas than in the formal precision more typical of the essay. You should write in a style comfortable to you, and you should feel free, as you reflect, to double back on yourself, change your mind, and look at the subject from different angles. As a rule, you can write these as openly subjective, first person reactions—what you think right now, what your impressions are—rather than adopting the more traditional, objective, third person stance. But check with your instructor first.

The characteristics of reading-response papers vary for teachers in different disciplines. A reading response in an advanced course in microelectronics might look quite different from one in an introductory course in history. But to give you some idea of their typical features, let's consider some writing from an actual course. In an introductory course in American literature, a teacher we talked to required his students to write frequently about the readings. Every other class session, students turned in 1- to 2-page reflections on a story they had read the previous week. After using the reflections in small- or large-group discussions, the teacher then collected and graded them. His grading system, which is rather typical for these sorts of assignments, was $\vee$, $\vee+$, or $\vee-$. Sue, one of his students, wrote the following paragraph about Nathaniel Hawthorne's short story "The Birthmark":

I enjoyed reading "The Birthmark." Many feelings arose during the reading (as to the nature of the story). Upon finishing the story I began remembering what we had discussed in class about Hawthorne's character. It made the ideas more distinct and sharp. My immediate interpretation was mans eternal struggle with nature. Aylmer's need to control his environment, his obsession with perfection. This obsession to control nature was apparent in his interaction with his wife, Georgiana. Aylmer's perception of nature's grasp on man, his life, and surroundings is seen through his fear and disgust of the birthmark on his wife's face.

Notice first that Sue feels free to tie her reaction to the classroom situation ("I began remembering what we had discussed in class") in a way that would not be acceptable in a formal essay. She also makes technical errors, such as the lack of the possessive apostrophe in "mans" and the sentence fragment "Aylmer's need to control his environment." And while the writing may be a little more formal than it would be in a journal (as in the phrase "Upon finishing the story"), it's still fairly casual and unstructured. Notice also that Sue is not trying to inform or enlighten her teacher, but showing that she's thinking critically about the material—looking for patterns, meanings, relationships. She is performing, in fact, a sort of sketchy, tentative interpretation; Aylmer's reaction to his wife's birthmark points beyond itself to signify man's eternal struggle with nature. On the other hand, this is not a full-blown analytical paper, either—just a casual pondering, a way of exploring the meaning of the story.

Summaries and Abstracts

Summaries A common form of writing in many courses is the summary. Although a reading response might include some summarizing of the material, a formal summary is usually more carefully written and includes less personal reaction. For most teachers a good summary captures only the gist, or essence, of a reading. Instead of poring over every detail of an article, a summary explains its main points or ideas in brief.

Our suggestions on paraphrase in Chapter One ("Pin down exactly what an author is saying," 13–16) represent the journal version of what we're discussing, and apply here as well.

Despite being short, summaries can be quite demanding. Think back to the last movie you saw. How should you go about summarizing it? What should you include? Where should you begin? How do you boil the film down to its essence? In any summary, you want to cover the main points without burying them in extraneous detail. This is almost certain to take some rereading, some checking back, some review of the work to make sure you're not skewing or blurring your account. A really excellent summary reflects significant understanding and attention.

It also reflects serious consideration of the purpose of the summary. What function is your summary supposed to serve, and for whom? Examine the following summary written by Bill, a student enrolled in Stained Glass, an advanced course in the Department of Studio Arts:

This article focuses on the characteristics and use of the essential tools for creating artistic stained glass. These tools include glass and circle cutters, pliers, scissors and knives, lathkins, lead stretchers, leading nails, drills and brushes, marking pencils, pattern papers, putty, wedges, hammers, and patinas. The most important tool, and the one which requires the most practice to use, is the glass cutter. Types of cutters include ball-ended cutters, carbide cutters, changeable and multiple-wheel cutters, circle cutters, and diamond cutters. Factors that may influence the effectiveness of the cutter include the size of the wheel, the angle of bevel, and its sharpness. The selection and use of cutters and other stained glass tools will depend largely on

the nature of the project; circle cutters, for example, are

not needed in projects requiring only straight cuts.

Notice that in this summary, Bill focuses on the most important of the tools described (cutters), choosing to leave out any discussion of the other tools mentioned in the second line. In most cases, the shape or proportions of the summary should reflect the shape of the article itself: a general introduction to glassworking tools, with a concentration on cutters in particular. If Bill's class, however, was especially concerned with glass cutting, the summary may reflect a deliberate decision to overrepresent one part of the original article at the expense of the others. Every summary has its purpose, and that purpose will determine how you apportion your space and attention.

Academic Abstracts   One of the most common uses for summaries is represented by the abstract. An abstract boils down an article into a meticulously chosen 250 or so words. It then appears in one (or more) of a few possible places: at the head of the article, in the table of contents of the journal carrying it, in an annotated bibliography (see below), or in an annual catalogue of such summaries; e.g., *Psychology Abstracts*. Their purpose is to spare potential readers unnecessary labor. By spending thirty seconds reading an abstract, you can decide whether it's worth your while to dedicate thirty minutes to the work in its entirety. (Or, if it's an especially fine abstract, those 250 words might tell you all you need to know.) If you're ever required to write an abstract of an article of your own, keep the reader's needs in mind. You're providing them a service, after all, and if you remember what they're after, your selection problem will largely solve itself.

Executive Summaries.   A related assignment showing up more and more in courses in science, technology, and engineering is the executive summary. The goal here is to write a brief memo to a business executive explaining the results of an experiment, procedure, piece of equipment (or whatever) which you'd like to see your company adopt. These are sometimes assigned in relation to particular experiments you conduct and write up first in a formal lab report. In this case, however, you're not writing for a fellow scientist or technician. Instead, you need to convince the person whose hands are on the purse strings to adopt your proposal. You really have only one or two paragraphs to do this. And your audience shares little or none of your specific technical background.

What do you say? How do you explain your work to someone without your background so as to convince him or her to support you? This requires thinking carefully about your project from your reader's point of view, with his or her knowledge, needs, and preconceptions, and then selecting and presenting exactly those details that make your case. Which details are those? Given that executives generally think in terms of the bottom line, you'll usually want to present your proposal as a brief, pointed cost/gain analysis. If you're actually majoring in a technical field, you'd better get used to this one; you'll be doing a lot of these throughout your career.

Bibliographies

A bibliography, or list of works on a specific topic, is a common assignment in many disciplines. Bibliographies can take three forms: simple (a plain, ordered list), annotated (which means including a short summary or abstract of each item), or mock (that is, personal and informal).

Simple Bibliographies.   These require you to rehearse at least three intellectual skills. First, you have to develop the necessary search strategies to locate materials in your field. This means becoming familiar with various indexes and resource tools in the library. Second, you need to decide whether any particular work is in fact actually relevant to the focus of your bibliography. Third, you'll have to learn the bibliographic form accepted in your field.

Annotated Bibliographies.   These are somewhat more demanding because they require you not only to read and understand each item, but to write a précis or abstract of the reading that captures its gist. Sometimes teachers will ask you to assemble an annotated bibliography gradually, turning in one item—listing plus summary—at each class session or once a week. Remember in this case to be as consistent as you can; aim for the same general length, style, and format for each entry.

Here is an example of a single entry from an annotated bibliography assembled by Stan, a student enrolled in a junior-level course in Chinese history:

> Hinton, H. C. *China's Turbulent Quest: An Analysis of*
>
> *China's Foreign Relations Since 1949.* Bloomington, IN:
>
> Indiana U P, 1970. Provides a historical analysis of foreign
>
> policy in Peking since the end of World War II. Begins by
>
> examining the place of Maoism in Chinese politics, and
>
> includes discussions of Sino-Soviet relations, Korea,
>
> Vietnam, and the Chinese cultural revolution. Much of the
>
> book details recent Chinese foreign policy and military
>
> strategy in light of China's participation in global politics
>
> and economics. This revised version also includes a chapter
>
> on the outcome of President Nixon's visits to China.
>
> Published in 1970, this is a useful benchmark to measure
>
> more recent changes in Chinese politics.

In this case, it was appropriate for Stan to comment on whether the book was useful. Some bibliographies, however, may allow only factual summaries, not evaluative ones.

Mock Bibliographies.   Actually strings of reading responses, these are also assigned from time to time. In the mock bibliography, the abstracts are personal reactions to the readings rather than crafted summaries, and they can therefore be more informally written. This kind of personal bibliography can be very helpful later in reminding you of material you've read and bringing back some of its details. You might keep one up in your course, whether it's been assigned or not.

Reviews of Books and Performances

A review is an extended description, usually with a heavy evaluative component. Instead of simply writing a paragraph capturing the essence of a work, here you're elaborating on it, sometimes for several pages. You're attempting to move beyond your initial reaction, to a considered judgment of the work. Thus, you have to be able to describe the work; to attend to separate aspects of it; to interpret what it means; and to assess, according to some criteria, how successful it was in achieving its goals.

The range of works you can review is practically unlimited. We think first of book or movie reviews, but you could also be asked to evaluate an article, an act of Congress, an experimental design, a geometric proof, and so on. Because disciplines differ in terms of how they approach their subject matter, you should be familiar with the criteria typically used to judge works in each. The sciences, for example, put a high price on the validity and accuracy of empirical research. A study with a sloppy research design, inappropriate statistics, or unfairly derived conclusions should be reviewed poorly—despite the fact that it was witty, lively, and readable. In art criticism accuracy of factual detail also counts, but here you might focus more on the insightfulness of the author's interpretation of some work, or on his ability to place the work in its cultural, historical, or artistic context. If a book is intended for a general audience, its stylistic color and verve become more important than if it's intended for specialists.

As an example of an academic review, here's an excerpt from a two-page review assigned in an introductory course in social psychology:

Interpersonal attraction concerns the factors involved in

liking or disliking another person. In several chapters

devoted to such topics as the reduction of isolation,

competition vs. cooperation, and the study of proxemics

(how much space people put between themselves), the authors provide a thorough analysis of the factors which influence our attractions to other people. Several case studies, such as an analysis of a boy's camp whose highly competitive structure had negative consequences for interpersonal attraction among the residents, are used to illustrate the more general principles presented in each chapter's theoretical section.

Notice the almost purely descriptive quality of this review, which has the effect of saying, "Here's what the authors did, period." The adjective "thorough" represents the one evaluative comment in the review. In most reviews, however, you will have to go further in evaluating the quality of the work. The style of the review above, in keeping with its formal, academic purpose and audience, is cool and matter-of-fact, with passive constructions and a sophisticated vocabulary. When you are writing as an expert addressing other experts, precision and efficiency of language are at a premium.

In a course in film studies, we found reviews of both popular and artistic films used to help students attend to various techniques of camera work, direction, acting, scripting, and so on. Notice, in contrast to the book review above, how much more evaluative, colorful, and personal is the following slice from a student's review of *Little Shop of Horrors:*

Casting plays a large role in the success of *Little Shop of Horrors.* Rick Moranis does a surprisingly good job as Seymour. One usually pictures Moranis playing the part of an annoying pest, but as Seymour he becomes lovable. Ellen Greene created the role of Audry on stage in 1982 and gives an extremely convincing performance here. Her meek voice, wide eyes, and unassertive demeanor lend credibility to her generally apathetic and unresistant role next to Steve Martin. Martin's part as crazed dentist, as well as the cameo appearances of John Candy, Jim Belushi, and Bill Murray, add a strong note of more basic comedy to the underlying irony which punctuates the film in its more burlesque moments.

The student here is still writing correct, polished English prose, but he has assumed the role of informed movie buff writing for other buffs. The analytical precision of his language is less at issue than the color and verve of his presentation.

Literature Reviews

Teachers will also sometimes assign literature reviews in some area of research. The purpose of a literature review is less to evaluate the quality of any one book or article than to examine an entire array of studies in one subject, in order to assess the state of knowledge within it. You might, for instance, decide to review all the evidence concerning the use of hypnosis as a dental anaesthetic. You would first want to assemble an extensive bibliography of the latest research on the topic. You would then find, read, and assess each study in an attempt to ascertain what each actually demonstrates. And finally, you would synthesize your findings: that is, try to state in a more general way, on the basis of what you found in the articles, what is the current state of our understanding of the use of hypnosis in dental work.

Academic journals regularly carry reviews of literature, usually providing a synthetic overview of research published in the last one, five, or ten years. With researchers all separately at work the world over, every discipline regularly needs to cast a glance over where it has been, what it has established, and what questions still lie open (or have been forced open by previous findings). A review of the literature is also a requirement for anyone carrying out original research on a question. Unless you know what everyone else working in your specific field has done, you may find yourself reinventing someone else's wheel. The articles reprinted in Chapter Six, you will notice, both begin with highly condensed literature reviews in order to define and clarify the questions being researched.

Data Analysis

One interesting assignment we find from time to time is the data analysis (one of many instances in which analysis really means interpretation—a reading of signs rather than an anatomy). In this assignment you're simply given some raw data, usually in a hand-out, with the directions to interpret the data and write up your findings in a page or so. In a course in urban studies, for example, one data analysis assignment provided students with two pages of statistics. The first gave the numbers of crimes reported in five major cities over a three-year period, by weeks. The other provided the average weekly temperatures in the five cities for the same three-year period. Students were asked to examine and analyze the data and suggest a hypothesis to explain them.

A quick inspection of the data revealed a general increase in the crime rate as a function of high temperature. (The crime rate in Seattle, for example, where the hottest average temperature never exceeded 70 degrees, did not rise markedly in the summer weeks.) An even more careful analysis, however, would further examine the types of crimes committed (burglaries, rapes, assaults, murders, etc.), and only then suggest a hypothesis. You might hypothesize, for example, that physical discomfort (heat) leads to aggression, resulting in increases in some kinds of crimes—such as assaults, rapes, and murders—more than others. An astute analysis might also point out other variables not included in the data which could help explain the relationships—for example, that unemployment increases in the summer and might also contribute to the rise in crime.

Data analyses, thus, are primarily interpretive problems: how do you "read" this set of signs? What do these indicators actually indicate? But to arrive at your interpretation requires careful observation, analysis and synthesis. You need to describe the data and note what patterns you see. You need to sort out which factors are affecting what in the data. And you need to pull your findings together into an explanatory hypothesis, accounting for the patterns you've uncovered. Data analyses are found most often in quantitative or empirically-oriented fields like the social sciences, economics, and geography. We've also found them, however, in courses such as political science, history, and speech communication.

Cases

Cases (or scenarios) represent some of the most unusual and interesting short assignments we've seen because they provide a realistic problem to solve in a simulated (or sometimes real) setting. Many years ago, cases were developed for use in the Harvard Business School as a way to help students focus on situations mirrored in actual business settings. Cases are also used routinely in the study of law and medicine, and more recently are showing up frequently in a variety of courses in almost all the fields we've encountered.

A case usually begins by providing you some sort of background information leading up to a problem. Your task is to write a short paper analyzing the important aspects of the case, and perhaps suggesting a solution to its problem or a plan of action. Often, your paper takes the form of a letter or report addressed to one or more of the people in the case. The intellectual tasks involved include interpretation—what does the material in the case *mean*?—and evaluation of various possible courses of action—what might I do, what would that accomplish, and is that what *ought* to happen?

Some cases may be very simple. In a course in Shakespeare, for example, we found a case in which students had to imagine they were Cordelia in *King Lear*. Their task was to think about Cordelia's position and then express her thoughts in a personal letter to Lear. To do so requires a solid understanding of the First Act, which sent many students back into the play a second or third time to be sure they knew what was going on. (Some students also learned quite a bit about Elizabethan language by trying to cast their letters in Shakespearean prose.)

Other cases are more complex, and might include a variety of readings expressing different opinions or perspectives. In a course in genetics, students were asked to imagine themselves as members of an imaginary Court of Medical and Scientific Ethics, something akin to the Supreme Court in status. The students had to read almost a dozen articles on all aspects of genetic engineering, including descriptions of highly controversial genetic manipulation in animals and plants, warnings about the possible dangers of too radically altering the genetic structures of organisms, even philosophical treatises expressing differing views about the prospect of humans playing God by creating new genetic configurations. The final article discussed a controversial process whereby the genes of human test-tube embryos could be manipulated before being transplanted to a woman's uterus. As members of this imaginary court, the students had to write a 5-page paper, using whatever they wished from the readings, to express an informed position on whether this procedure should be allowed.

Because cases usually involve some dilemma or problem, it's always a good idea to take some extensive notes before you write your response, especially if the case presents opposing views. You might, for example, try carrying on a sort of dialogue between two or more voices in the case, or keeping a double-entry notebook, with one set of voices on one side of the page and reactions to them on the other. What main factors are involved in the case? What is the range of possible solutions open to you? What are the pros and cons of each action? You might also try to find connections between the course material, the case itself, and aspects of your own life.

As you respond to the case, remember to put yourself as much as possible into the case's world. This may mean thinking beyond the boundaries of the written case, making assumptions not explicitly dictated by it; but it's preferable to the sort of dull, detached response you'll give if you don't immerse yourself in the problem or take on the persona of people in the case. After all, your instructor has spent time deliberately designing the assignment to involve and interest you and to demonstrate as vividly as possible the difficult problems surrounding your field of study. The problems require careful analysis, synthesis, evaluation and interpretation, processes that are the daily fare of working in the area in which the case is designed.

Lab Reports

Lab reports usually represent an extremely formal kind of written document, with a precisely defined structure to follow in presenting your material. You need to learn what this structure is and follow it to the letter. As a rule, either your instructor will give you the structure in a handout or printed outline, or you will find the form in the front of your lab book. For all that, it may still be an open question how much emphasis your instructor will put on your writing itself and how much on your actual laboratory technique. This is a matter of your instructor's pedagogical purpose in giving the assignment, and, as always, you should check this out.

The standard sections of a lab report usually include the following: a statement of purpose; a description of the physical apparatus used; a narrative account of the experimental procedure; a report of your actual observations; and a conclusion. Some of these, such as procedure and observations, may be combined. Other sections, furthermore, may also be included—such as a data section, presenting the quantitative results in tabular fashion, or a section on error analysis, noting possible problems or limitations in the statistics and results involved. As a rule, the middle parts of a lab report—apparatus, procedure, observations—are straightforward, and almost purely a matter of description. The statement of purpose and the conclusions, on the other hand, might run to any length and require sophisticated interpretation. (You may want to explain your purpose and findings to yourself first in your journal before attempting to explain them more formally in your report.)

Stylistically, lab reports are generally as spare, impersonal, and precise as possible. You will often be required to write in simple past tense and in passive voice: "The beaker was sterilized. . . . The solution was heated for 15 minutes at 85°C. . . ." This is no time to wax lyrical or to meditate on what you felt about the experiment. The object is to produce a report of such detail, precision, and clarity that another chemist or physicist or biologist can rerun your experiment exactly, and verify (or not, as the case may be) your results.

The main intellectual problem here is gauging correctly the level of detail needed to accomplish this. One chemistry professor we interviewed told us that when students do poorly on the procedure and observations section, it's either because they don't explain much at all of what they were doing, or they bury the account in mountains of irrelevant detail. It's either, "I mixed the chemicals and it came out red," or it's, "First I pulled open the second drawer down on the right, gently lifted out the reagent bottle, then closed the drawer and set the bottle on the counter. Then with my right hand . . ." You need to think through precisely what a new experimenter would have to do to produce, for scientific purposes, essentially the same operations that you followed, and then present your account at that level of detail.

In short, the lab report represents a ruthlessly pragmatic text form. It's not intended to have any decorative or literary value. It should have the lean, clean, straightforward, step-by-step simplicity of an excellent set of instructions—the kind you always pray for when you buy a new machine or a software program. Mastering the technical material is not enough; to write a good lab report you must bear in mind—always—your audience and the use they hope to make of your document.

Research Proposals

Though sometimes assigned as an end in itself, the research proposal more often functions as a sort of fail-safe device in courses where you are assigned to do a full-dress research paper. Many professors have found that simply assigning a research paper and then standing aside results in many papers that are poorly focused, vague, or haphazardly developed. The problems in such papers, furthermore, often lie in the way the original research was conceived. The student was researching the wrong kind of question in the wrong way. The research proposal, exactly as the name implies, presents the research project the student proposes to carry out, and gives the instructor the chance to approve it, to suggest alterations, or to veto it entirely if it looks like it's headed into the swamp.

In this case, the student will need either to revise the proposal or possibly even to find an entirely new problem and write a fresh new proposal for that instead. Once the instructor okays the proposal, the student can proceed with greater confidence, knowing that his research problem should lend itself to a good paper.

As a rule, there are three basic parts to a research proposal: the background, the research question, and the method section. The first part outlines the basic area of research, explains something of its importance, and perhaps summarizes earlier studies in the field. It should lead by logical steps to the research problem itself, the precise question you hope to answer. The method section suggests the means you will use to find or develop your answer. This may be, in advanced science courses, an actual experiment or field study. In other cases, the method section might be represented by a tentative or working bibliography, listing examples of the sources you plan to consult.

The background section should convince your reader that your problem is interesting and important, that research ought to be done on this topic. To this extent, it shares the same purpose as the introduction to any paper: to orient and intrigue the reader. Often, after you've completed your research, you can even use a revised version of your background section in the opening paragraphs of your report. To write the background effectively, you need to decide what about the topic attracts you, and then reflect that in a way that will capture the interest of your reader. If you're shrewd enough to begin your work by doing a little general reading in your field, your background section should reflect this.

The core of the proposal, however, is the question itself. This may be only a single sentence, but if ever a sentence merited careful thinking and rethinking, writing and rewriting, it's this one. The more precise and focused your question, the more efficient and interesting will be your research, and the more convincing and coherent will be your final paper. Time put into formulating your question will pay off in spades. If nothing else, every ten minutes put into the careful formulation of your research question will probably save you a good hour of aimless thrashing about in the stacks.

Stylistically, the research proposal should usually be a cool, systematic, analytical piece of work. You want to be as succinct as you can, while presenting your plans as clearly and explicitly as possible. This is no place for either poetry or vagueness. And don't take it personally when, as will usually happen, your first proposal is returned with suggestions for substantial revision. Your professor is probably only trying to save you from a research question that is too broad, too hard to research, or otherwise prone to disaster. One of us assigns research proposals as a regular part of any research-based paper, and returns usually over 90 percent of the first drafts for further narrowing and refinement. It beats drowning any time.

ON THE VALUE OF ARTIFICIAL WRITING ASSIGNMENTS

This catalogue can't hope to do justice to the array of creative assignments you may encounter in your academic curriculum. But then, how inventive do you want your teachers to be in designing assignments? We hear complaints, in fact, from time to time, from both students and teachers, that classroom writing is too often removed from the real world, that it's artificial.

This is roughly comparable to complaining that calisthenics, jogging, weight-lifting, and stretching exercises are removed from playing shortstop, that they don't have any obvious similarities to the motions you make in fielding a hot grounder and winging it to first base. It's true—they aren't at all similar—and this makes no difference at all, as long as the exercise increases your speed, reflexes, agility, or stamina. In the long run, it will all pay off, right there on the edge of the outfield grass.

Precisely the same principle holds true for intellectual development. The artificiality of a writing assignment may or may not have anything to do with that assignment's ultimate educational value. If such assignments encourage you to learn and think, to gain facility in observation, analysis, and selection and use of appropriate evaluative criteria, and so forth, they will have done you entirely as much good as any assignment resembling what you might do on the job. Furthermore, by giving you a chance to be creative, to take some risks, to try out some alternative strategies, such assignments can be a lot less pressured than writing the real thing. Take advantage of such freedom while you've got it. Once you're out of college, your mistakes (or unlucky gambles) become much more expensive.

Chapter
3

The Essay Exam

MANAGING STRESS IN THE FIELD

The essay exam is a strange and sometimes awful writing situation. You rarely get to choose the topic you'll be discussing. Your time is severely limited, which means you're under a lot of pressure. And your audience, the instructor or teaching assistant, isn't reading to learn something new from you so much as to assess what you've learned from him or her. This is hardly a situation most writers would choose to work in, given an option.

Despite the strangeness of the situation, however, some of the same basic principles apply to writing an answer to an essay exam as to writing anything else in a relatively formal situation—short or long, easy or hard, simple or complex. You still need to analyze your writing task and audience, collect and arrange your material, write it down, and, if possible, refine it a bit before you let it go. Your challenge is to find ways to perform each of these under the pressure of a ticking clock.

Given these constraints, many students assume that every second spent doing anything other than writing is a second lost. Through interviews and observations, we've found that many students use the same self-defeating approach. First they sit down and wait nervously for the exam. When it comes, they hurriedly read the question. If they've been given a choice of questions, they just as hurriedly pick the one that looks easiest: *"Discuss the main linguistic changes that the English language underwent between the Old and Middle English periods, providing examples for each."* Then they begin writing immediately, usually by restating something in the question: *"The English language underwent many important linguistic changes between the Old and Middle period."*

And off they go, as if they've won a ten-minute supermarket shopping spree, dumping in anything they can get their hands on as long as it fits in the cart. Forty-five minutes later, their hands are aching and their time is up. One more canned ham goes in just as the bell rings, and they head for the check-out counter, hearts still thumping. Several students usually try desperately to eke out one or two more sentences that might contain that magical bit of information that the teacher, who is now snatching the essays from beneath their frantically scribbling pens, will be looking for in the answers.

For most of us, however, rushing into an exam only yields confusion and frustration, which leads to more anxiety—and a more garbled, disorganized essay. Instead of running down Aisle 1, which contains only canned vegetables, some thoughtful planning might suggest heading first to the meat department. Then you could begin by lining the cart with filet mignon and only bother with the spice section if there's time at the end.

BEFORE THE EXAM

Preparing for an essay exam must always start with an understanding of your instructional setting—something you already have, at least tacitly, if you've been participating in a course. Some teachers readily provide you with context-setting information before the exam—for example, that it will contain six questions of which you'll choose three to write on in 45 minutes; or that it will cover only the history of the armistice negotiations between China and Korea from 1951 to 1953; or that it will ask you to analyze and expand upon the philosophy expressed in one of three quotations by Martin Buber. If your teacher doesn't provide such information, though, it never hurts to ask for it during or after one of the class sessions.

What's the Purpose?

In practically every case, your main purpose in answering an essay question is less to educate or amuse your reader, or to agree with or refute his or her personal beliefs, than to demonstrate your own understanding of the material. This doesn't mean simply regurgitating what you've been taught. This is one of the most common myths surrounding essay exams, leading no end of students down the garden path to unnecessarily poor performances. An essay exam is not simply a test of memory, of your ability to pour forth with reckless abandon anything and everything you happen to remember about the topic of the question. There's a name for that. It's called a *snow job*. It's certainly an improvement over a blank page, but it's also no indication of mastery. And your teacher knows it.

You're being tested on your learning, as this is evidenced in your ability to write about some domain of knowledge defined by the essay question. Without that learning, you can be the best writer in the world and it won't do a bit of good. Sadly, the reverse is also true. You might have a head full of knowledge, but without a carefully planned and written essay, it won't show.

To understand a subject means not only to know the facts about it, but to know what those facts mean, to know how they relate to one another, what they logically add up to. An answer to an essay question shows this command of the subject by a sharp focus on the exact question asked, by a thoughtful selection of the facts presented, by the logic of their arrangement, and by the insightfulness of the conclusions drawn from those facts. A sensible, clear, and well-organized answer, rich in appropriate supporting detail, and revealing original thought and consideration of the subject matter—that would be a success by anyone's standards. In-depth development, perfectly accurate quotations, stylistic elegance, a captivating title—these are just bonus points.

Using Your Journal to Explore and Rehearse

As we suggested in Chapter One, an informal academic journal can become a kind of intellectual forum ideally suited to
preparing for exams (in essay or any other form). In addition to
simply freewriting about the subject of your upcoming exam,
you might also try writing in your journal as if you're actually
taking the exam, perhaps in response to mock questions. Give
yourself an hour and follow the procedures we outline in the
rest of this chapter. You should also pay some attention to the
style of your writing. Unlike your freely written, casual journal entries, here you'll be using a more formal, precise dis-
course of the sort we've described in Chapter Two, perhaps
punctuated with the language of the field. In your Introduction to Independent Film course, instead of writing, "A whole
bunch of independent films are trying to make political
points," you might aim for a more formal, precise statement:
"In its origins in underground political activism, much independent film may be classified in the genre of protest, favorite
targets being war, segregation, military brutality, and the
American status quo."

These two statements are not synonymous; the second
demonstrates a fuller understanding of the subject matter and
the language capable of describing it. Knowledge (facts, examples, concepts, etc.) and language are connected. As we
pointed out in Chapter One, *not* writing or talking about a
subject actually diminishes your knowing it. If you wait until
the day of an essay exam to write about what you know, you
may feel you know too little to write well. (And you may be
right.)

Learning and Studying Together

Before the actual testing situation, it's helpful to collaborate
with your colleagues. In addition to writing informally in a
journal or notebook, the next best way to think about any
material is to talk about it. Educators know that you never
really learn a subject until you've taught it. So teach each
other your subject. Review the material with friends. Draft
anticipated or mock essay questions and develop lists of

points you would use to answer them. You'll find that by making learning more social and collaborative, you'll not only enjoy the process more but engage in it more deeply as well. If your teacher provides you with a review sheet or organizes small-group sessions before the exam, so much the better. But do it anyway, on your own, and you'll find yourself a great deal more assured when you walk into the room on the day of the exam.

DURING THE EXAM

Budgeting Your Time

If, when you receive the exam, you immediately dive into the first question, you may write a wonderful essay only to find yourself with three questions to go and five minutes remaining in the period. Instead, when you get your test, put your pen down and restrain yourself. Read the entire exam first. Note how many questions there are, which require essays and which short answers. Note how much each question is worth. Then figure out a budget for the 45 minutes or two hours you have to work.

Common sense would tell you to leave the most time for the questions carrying the most points; teachers don't assign values to their questions at random. You might even jot down on the test itself roughly when you should be starting or finishing each question. Then stick to it. A string of what seem to you like "B" answers is much safer than one long "A" and three short "F's."

Keep in mind that your first impressions of the exam may be strongly influenced by the content of the questions. Just because you're less confident about answering the second question than the first shouldn't mean that you avoid it until the end (or that you devote all your attention to it). Your teacher expects a certain amount of text in response to each question; allocate your time accordingly. When you begin responding to a question you feel apprehensive about, give it the time it deserves. You may find that with some preliminary brainstorming (which we'll discuss in a minute), ideas and perspectives will open up for you.

Understanding the Question

We want to stress again, as we did in Chapter Two, that your first step should be to read the question and *read it carefully.* Many essay answers receive poor grades simply because the writer discussed something other than what the teacher had asked about. You need to answer *the exact question put to you,* not a close approximation or reasonable facsimile.

A thorough, detailed, carefully organized explanation of Francis James Child's distinction between the folk ballad and the traditional broadside ballad will hardly satisfy your teacher, if the question asked was to discuss the influence upon Child of Svend Grundtvig's 1853 edition of Danish ballads. Nor will the teacher be happy with a detailed and well-organized *description* of Child's collecting and indexing system if what the question calls for is an *evaluation* of this system's strengths and limitations.

The example demonstrates two major ways to miss the mark when responding to an essay exam. You can misfire either by writing about a different issue or topic than the question requires, or by responding to the correct topic but performing the wrong task with it. If your question asks you to contrast the styles of Renoir's *La Toilette* and Cezanne's *Bathers,* and you describe instead the historical conditions under which each was painted, you missed the point. If, on the other hand, an exam question asks you to describe the process of mitosis with reference to the mitotic spindles originating in the cytoplasm at prophase, your simple description of mitotic spindles and their arrays of microtubules, polar fibers and kinetochore fibers does stick to the topic, but it still doesn't really answer the question. It shows that you indeed know something about mitotic spindles, but not that you can explain how they function in mitosis.

Topics and commands　To guide yourself in responding to an essay question, try this. First *underline the subject matter* and then *draw a circle around the "command,"* the word or words that tell you precisely what the teacher wants you to do with the subject. This will force you to be more aware of what precisely the topic and task actually are. Here are a few examples taken from essay exam questions in different college courses:

(Trace) the <u>main events that led to the bombing of Hiroshima.</u>

From the data given, (evaluate) the <u>importance of soil zinc in raising pineapples.</u>

Some historians claim that <u>the American Revolution hardly qualified as a "revolution"</u> at all. (Attack or defend) this thesis.

Sometimes you may receive a double-barreled essay exam question, in which there is more than one subject and/or command. In this case, it's even more important to distinguish between *what* you must write about and *how* you should write about it. You need to decide whether you'll tackle the subjects together or separately, and whether you'll tackle them in the same way. Here's an example:

(Define) <u>the technique of *in medias res* plotting</u> and (compare) <u>its use by Homer and Dorothy Sayers.</u>

In this question, you're being asked to perform at least three tasks. First you must provide an adequate definition of *in medias res* plot technique, and this alone may involve some references to certain writers or traditions. Then you need to show how two different writers use this technique in their works (and here you must choose which works to focus on). Along the way, you also need to compare the use of the technique by writers who lived almost 3,000 years apart. As you can see, the simple procedure of identifying the subject and command of the question can lead to important decisions about the content and structure of your answer. Consider, for example, the following alternatives:

STRUCTURE #1
    I. Definition of *in medias res* plot technique.
   II. How Homer uses the technique in *The Odyssey*.
 III. How Dorothy L. Sayers uses the technique in *The Nine Tailors*.
 IV. Important differences in these two uses of the technique.

STRUCTURE #2

I. How *in medias res* plot technique is used to create suspense and drama.
   A. Sayers' use of the technique in her mystery novels.
   B. Homer's use of the technique in *The Odyssey*.
II. How and when background information is provided when a work of literature begins *in medias res.*
   A. How Sayers supplies details as a result of Wimsey's investigations.
   B. Homer's use of Odysseus' story telling to provide background.

Each structure, of course, could be further elaborated with references to specific works. How complex an outline you need depends on the amount of time you have to write your answer. Structure #1 might be more appropriate for a half-hour essay, while Structure #2 would require more time. Yet each essay answers the question as posed. Obviously, there's a multitude of possible answers to any exam question, but the options are always constrained by the phrasing of the question itself.

The problem of implicit commands   Many essay-exam questions tell you something first and then ask you the question. In such cases, the question itself may not include any explicit command:

> Hitler's fascination with what he called the "folkish state" and its preservation of those racial elements that create the purest and most dignified culture had an important influence on his political agenda during the creation of the Third Reich. How were his beliefs, as put forth in *Mein Kampf,* expressed in his political moves during the early days of the Third Reich?

There is no obvious command for writing here. The prelude—on Hitler's beliefs about the folkish state—serves to narrow the range of possible focuses for answering the question. This at least suggests the appropriate content of your answer. For the command, however, you have to read between the lines of the question itself. Since the question turns on the relationship between belief and action, and since in this case the belief precedes the action, the question is really asking you to *trace,* or *describe the development of something.*

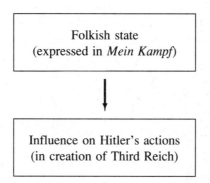

Supplementary questions may also be tagged onto full-fledged, seemingly independent writing tasks that do contain clear topics and commands. In these cases, the supplementary questions may either narrow or expand the focus of the task. An example of the first type is a question from a course in American literature:

> Compare and contrast the characters of Holden Caulfield in *Catcher in the Rye* and Huckleberry Finn in Twain's novel. Is there any truth to the claim that Holden is a twentieth-century Huck?

Here the supplementary question casts a special light on the essay topic. The astute writer will compare Holden and Huck in the context of the respective novels, while simultaneously focusing on Huck's character as a possible antecedent of Holden, or his influence on Salinger as the creator of Holden's character. Less sophisticated, perhaps, but still certainly acceptable would be a straight comparison of the two characters, with a section at the end evaluating the claim in the supplementary question. Given the limits of time, the first option would seem more effective since the focus would be narrowed from the start.

An example of a supplementary question that *expands* the focus of the topic comes from a philosophy course titled Evolution in European Thought, a course which includes a strong emphasis on moral and religious controversies surrounding evolutionary theories:

> Explain why Stephen Jay Gould presents the panda's "thumb" as clumsy workmanship on the part of nature. What is the appropriate use of such biological data in religious controversy?

In contrast to our first example of supplementary questions, this one asks the writer to explain something fairly specific first and then to generalize from this (and perhaps similar specifics) in discussing wider implications. Again, there are several choices for organization, depending on the time allowed for the essay and the amount of background information that has been studied and learned, but the content and question itself do give you some leads.

Sometimes an essay-exam question is extremely general, lacking in any clues to narrow down your options. In that case, you have to assume that the instructor values a certain freedom in the development of the topic, as if to say, "Use anything you've learned to answer this question as long as you do so in an intelligent manner." One question from a course in sociology reads like this:

> Comment on sociobiology as an extension of Darwinism.

Now that's pretty vague. Sociobiology? Darwinism? These are mighty broad concepts. And "comment"? What does *that* mean?

On the one hand, the question does give you a wide field in which to pursue those leads most interesting to you. The question gives you free rein to discuss the origins of sociobiology in the work of Edward O. Wilson and his studies of insect colonies, some of the recent research on sexual infidelity, or even theoretical explanations for altruism (concern for others) and xenophobia (fear of strangers). And what sort of purpose, thesis, and structure you adopt for your comment is equally yours to determine. Each of five hundred students is likely to find a unique approach to this question. When faced with such open-ended questions, however, it's still important not to stray from the stated topic or meander aimlessly within it. No matter how open-ended the question, you're not excused from producing a focused, coherent paper. "Many things go" is still a long way from "anything goes."

Finally, some essay-exam questions may take the form of miniature case studies or may include supplementary information (tables of data, excerpts or quotations, etc.). In certain areas, such as the arts or medicine, it's common to be shown slides of blood cells or paintings, or to be played short segments of musical compositions as part of the exam question. In all such cases, it's obviously crucial to read, reread, and analyze the additional information (or study it carefully if it's in visual or auditory form) before making decisions about the content and form of your essay answer. Again, *slow down.* Study the map a bit first. Don't just hop in the car and go careening off down the road.

Defining the Command Verb Precisely   In reading essay questions, pinpointing the topic of discussion is usually fairly simple. The subtler part of the task lies in knowing exactly what the command requires you to do. Verbs that might appear to be closely related (explain vs. analyze, describe vs. evaluate, compare vs. illustrate) actually assume quite different thinking and writing processes. Consider, for example, the following two questions:

> Explain Robert E. Lee's military tactics as leader of the Confederate Army.

> Evaluate the success of Robert E. Lee's military tactics as leader of the Confederate Army.

In the first question, you might want to discuss the military situation facing Lee, outline his options, describe the tactics that he finally chose, and why he chose them—and then stop there. In the second question, you're required to go further. The question calls on you to assess how well Lee's tactics actually worked. How often did he win? Against what odds? With what kind of casualties compared with McClellan's or Grant's? Was the fall of Richmond inevitable, and if so, did Lee's tactics forestall it longer than another general's might have?

Answers to these questions might, of course, overlap somewhat. To evaluate Lee's tactics, you'd have to explain them at least briefly. And even if you were only asked to explain them, you could always end up with a brief statement about their success. But the difference in the main focus of each answer should be apparent.

The following command verbs show up regularly on essay questions we've examined across the undergraduate curriculum. We've glossed these with brief notes on what each typically requires in a successful essay.

TRACE: This is a very specific verb, usually found in phrases such as "trace the development of . . ." or "trace the process by which . . ." The question implies that some sort of chronological scheme is called for. How did something come about or change over time? What causes what else to happen? Your answer will often take the form of a narrative (*A* happened, causing *B*, which in turn caused *C*), with some explanation of how the events or processes fit together:

Trace the development of the concept of the gene up through the work of Watson and Crick.

Trace the stages by which the nations of Europe were drawn into World War I.

EVALUATE: The key to understanding "evaluate" is another, smaller word buried within it: *value.* To evaluate means simply to assign a value to something, to tell how much of some worthy or positive quality the thing has. Courses in art, literature, theater, film, and the like frequently require evaluations of specific performances:

Evaluate the relative merits of Olivier's and Branagh's movie versions of *Henry V.*

To evaluate an argument, on the other hand, means to judge how sensible and well supported it is:

Evaluate Margaret Mead's analysis of puberty rites among the Lugbara of Uganda.

Evaluate Hamilton's and Jefferson's arguments for and against the establishment of a national bank.

COMPARE AND CONTRAST: If these two verbs appear together, the task requires you to show what two things have in common and what differences exist between them:

> Compare and contrast the visions for Black Americans expressed in the works of W. E. B. DuBois and Booker T. Washington.

If *contrast* turns up by itself, you show only the differences. If only *compare* appears, show both similarities and differences; in that case, it's functionally equivalent to the longer "compare and contrast."

DESCRIBE: Technically, to describe something means merely to present the details of its appearance in some coherent order. You don't need to evaluate its worth or explain its functions. But when the term appears in an essay exam question, you're probably being asked to do more than that:

> Describe the process of human fertilization from intercourse through the first cell division.

The more precise command verb here would be to "trace" the process, exactly as explained above, and that's obviously how you should approach the essay.

Often, "describe" will be used in a topic which has an attached supplementary question:

> Describe the process of human fertilization. What factors in our environment have been shown to inhibit the natural progress of fertilization?

You now have a somewhat more complex intellectual task on your hands. First you must, again, *trace* a process, and then list and explain each of several inhibitory factors.

DEFINE: If "*con*-fine" means to hold something in, "*de*-fine" means to separate it out. A definition should describe something in such a way as to distinguish it from everything else. "A large, four-footed animal" partially describes many creatures but defines none of them. "A large, carnivorous feline, with yellow and black stripes" qualifies as a better definition, since it can only refer to a tiger.

Definitions, of course, may be elaborated. "Define a tiger" could yield one line (as above) or an enormous treatise, depending on the breadth of description. There may be numerous studies on the precise characteristics of even a tiger's claws: their size, growth, retractability compared with other felines, and so on. "Defining" a tiger then might involve several pages at a much greater level of detail. To "define a position," on the other hand, may mean to "present in outline the major principles and arguments" of the position.

DISCUSS: This is a relatively unhelpful (and extremely common) command verb meaning "write about." You're on your own with this one. Look for clues in the rest of the question, and then try to choose a suitable focus for your answer. Since the question doesn't give you a structure, you'll have to design one on your own. But make sure your answer goes *somewhere.* Whatever "discuss" means, it doesn't mean what you do at a crowded cocktail party.

ANALYZE: Strictly speaking, to "analyze" something means to break it down into its component parts, to show what elements it's made of. But like "discuss," this term, when used in essay exams, can mean almost anything. If it *does* seem to mean "break into parts," do that. But read the rest of the question before deciding. It very often means "interpret"—to figure out what some communication or body of information (e.g., a poem, an advertisement, even a collection of data) means from some angle.

Analyze the imagery in Keats' "Ode to a Nightingale."

Analyze the following data from a study on weather patterns in the Pacific Northwest.

In both these cases, the word "analyze" seems to mean "interpret"—in other words, "make sense of."

This list is only a beginning. There are, of course, many such terms—assess, illustrate, attack or defend, examine, argue, show, consider, enumerate, list—used in varying degrees of precision. We can't define them all, and most of them you already know. But the point is to think carefully about what such terms do and don't actually mean when you find them in a question. If the recipe says sauté, you sauté; if it says slice, don't mash.

Finally, as you analyze the precise wording of the essay exam question, don't forget to think about the context of your classwork. When teachers read a batch of essay exam answers, they see each answer *in terms of* the question they asked. They want to know, "Has the student learned enough about the topic to address the question adequately?" In other words, the question is a way to focus your attention on some aspect of the subject you've been studying so that your ability to describe characteristics, express relationships, analyze causes and effects, and the like can be assessed as part of your accumulated knowledge. As a result, it's critical for you to keep in mind how the question relates to the *specific material you've been studying.* If you stray too far from this, the first thought that's likely to enter your teacher's head is that you don't really have sufficient knowledge from your course to answer the question, and are trying to be evasive just to get by.

At the same time, teachers can be especially impressed when, in addition to the obvious way to answer a question, a student also weaves in less familiar examples or cases, or makes connections that might not occur to everyone. If, for example, an essay question in the history of science and technology asks you to relate the central medical discoveries during the Middle Ages to the gradual reconceptualization of the notion of the four humours, a brief nod in the direction of the church and how it factored into that relationship might suggest that you are thinking more actively and deeply than someone who simply sticks to the most obvious and direct answer. In this respect, it helps to think of your response as an answer you might give to an interviewer during a job hunt. If you keep answering the interviewer's questions with "yes" or "no," or give the flattest response you can muster, your interviewer probably won't think much of your abilities. If, on the other hand, you can *do* something with the questions, you might show yourself to be intelligent and well prepared. Your teacher wants—indeed, sincerely hopes—that you can take a question and do something with it that demonstrates your knowledge and ability to work with the material you've learned.

Gathering and Arranging Your Material

Dozens of teachers we've consulted, in courses all across the curriculum, complain that they can't follow the train of their students' thoughts in essay-exam responses. That's because instead of even briefly planning their answers first, many students use the writing itself as a way to come up with ideas. As we pointed out in Chapter One, this is a wonderful way to explore a topic, ideally suited to journal writing. But here you do have an audience—the teacher—who may have reached your exam at midnight after already grading thirty others. An essay organized associatively—one idea leading to another, with no sense of an overarching structure—will probably not leave a strong impression on his weary mind.

It practically never happens that the order in which you remember or think of something proves to be the best and most logical way to present it. And though teachers don't require great elegance and style on an essay exam, they do want answers that are cogent, sensible, and well organized. You don't want to discuss platelets, capillaries, mitre valves, and pacemakers all at once, or jump at random between Normandy, Ypres, and North Africa. You'll want to collect your material into coherent packages, and present those in a sensible order.

This order might be chronological, in a question about the history of something, or about a technical process. It might be from most to least important cause, in a scientific or sociological question. It might be from similarities to differences in a "compare and contrast" question. For any given question, there will be several possible arrangements, any of which will work well. Writing down everything you know at random, on the other hand, will not bring home a trophy.

Instead, you need to jot down—on the top, back, or margin of your paper, or on another sheet—at least a few ideas first, to make sure you cover your topic with sufficient thoroughness. You don't need long passages of reflective, exploratory writing; the time will be up before you even start your actual answer. But, somewhere or other, you should jot down key words that will help you hold more of your material in mind in order to get it into your response.

Once you've jotted down the main ideas relevant to your question, ordering them hardly takes another minute. There are several quick ways to decide what sequence to present them in. You can, for instance, simply draw lines between the various facts and ideas that go together.

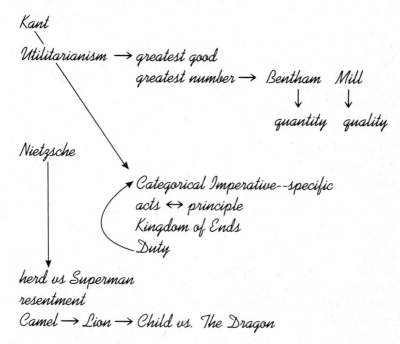

Or, you can sketch a very brief outline (or tree), with only the main headings or a few subheadings.

I. Kant
    --Cat. Imp. -- spec. acts ⟷ Principle
    --Kingdom of Ends
    --Duty as motive
II. Utilitarianism
    --g. good for g. number
    --Bentham: quan. of pleasure (pushpins)
    --Mill: qual. of pleasure (Socrates & swine)
III. Nietzsche
    --herd morality vs. Superman
    --resentment → herd morality
    --Camel → Lion → Child vs. The Dragon

Or, quickest of all perhaps, is simply to list your ideas as they occur to you, and then to number them in the order you want to present them.

Kant (1)
Util'ism (5)
Kingdom of Ends (4)
Cat. Imp. (3)
Nietz. (10)
Greatest good for greatest number (6)
Mill (8)   Bentham (7)
quantity vs quality (9)
resentment (12)
Camel, Lion, Child (13)
Duty as motive (2)
herd morality (11)

Keep in mind in any case that your essay may only contain a few paragraphs. An outline of five points, each developed in a single paragraph, will keep you writing for at least 30 to 45 minutes.

One final caveat: don't, under the pressure of time, forget about *detail*. Many teachers tell us that the broad, sweeping generalization unsupported by specific facts is the single worst problem in the essay exams they read. If you're trying to cover too much ground, you're bound to lose sight of the specifics. Instead of trying to get from Los Angeles to New York in 45 minutes at 35,000 feet, fly a little closer to the ground and aim for Denver. You'll see a lot more of the land and still end up covering some distance. During your brief planning stage, you may want to jot down some specific details beneath the main sections of your outline.

The following notes illustrate this sort of plan. They come from the essay exam of a student in a course in the history of opera. The question asked students to define *opera seria* (literally, "serious opera," a form of Italian dramatic opera characterized by frequent use of recitative, or alternate singing and speaking) and to illustrate the range of its use. Here are one student's notes:

I. Early trad of *opera seria*
   A. noble actions & feelings nobly born; 17th-C. Venetian operas (Sartorio, Legrenzi, etc.)
   B. singers relate direct to audience; arias not part of flow of the drama;
      Handel's mixture—comic & serious
II. Reform of *op ser*
   A. Jommelli and Traetta
   B. Gluck
III. Later revitalization
   A. Rossini's early career (revival of *opera buffa* & *op ser*)

Note that although there are three main sections for the student's essay, the level of detail varies from section to section. Because *opera seria* was more important in early Italian opera, more time is spent discussing its variety up through the age of Handel than during the career of Rossini. The outline, however, shows how much more effective this essay will be than one which simply defines *opera seria* and describes what it involved in operatic performances.

Drafting

The most important sentence in an essay-exam response is the very first one. Get that one right, impress the hell out of your teacher immediately, and the rest of the essay will follow more or less of its own accord. This doesn't mean you should write a flowery or high-flown first sentence. Your first sentence may be—probably should be—plain and simple. But it has two big jobs to do. One is stating your thesis. The other is to orient your reader—and by that, we mean not *just* your instructor.

Here's the test: suppose your essay exam were to blow out the window, across the campus, and land on the steps in front of the library. A student walks by, sees it, picks it up, and idly starts reading it. Question: *Will she, from the very first sentence, know exactly what it is you're talking about?* If the answer is no, your opening has problems. Consider the following first line:

The major difference is that the one is more of a journalist, a story teller, while the other is a more analytical, almost scientific historian.

Can you tell what that's all about? Could you, on a bet, reconstruct the question this was written in response to? It's a fine, lucid sentence—but it's not a good *opening*. This is better:

Whereas Herodotus, describing the wars of the Greeks and Persians, is more of a journalist or story teller, Thucydides, in his account of the Peloponnesian Wars, is a more analytical, almost scientific historian.

Now you know exactly what the essay is about. You know the precise topic—the relative styles of two particular ancient historians—and you know how the student sees their major difference. He orients you to the topic and states his major thesis in thirty-three words. Quick work!

His instructor, of course, doesn't *need* such orientation. It was his instructor, after all, who asked the question in the first place. But providing such an orientation still makes for a most impressive beginning. It demonstrates at the very least that *you* know exactly what you're talking about. This isn't at all clear in the first opening sentence above. Moral: *Don't draft just for the instructor; draft for an intelligent student with a very basic knowledge of your subject.* It's a ruse, but a useful one. It forces you to show what you know and makes for a more readable, interesting, effective essay overall.

When you actually begin writing your answer, remember two things: one, your evident mastery of the subject counts for more than your prose style; and two, you'll have little or no time to revise. The sage counsel to be derived from these observations is to write quickly, write simply, and work from generalizations to specifics in each section of the essay. On the whole, keep your sentences fairly direct and uncomplicated. Your odds of getting them syntactically straight the first time will be higher. A rough, somewhat choppy style on an essay test is excusable; sheer bad grammar or garbled syntax is liable to cost you. Don't be fancy, be informative.

Of course, it's impossible to write at all without thinking, and thinking might lead to ideas you didn't consider during the brief planning stage. If your new insights relate to sections you've already written, don't try to weave them in where they're not relevant. If they're not crucial, toss them; if they are, go back and try inserting them as footnotes in your earlier text. Although this sometimes bothers teachers, especially when such notes are extensively written at all angles in the margins, they are evidence of a mind at work.

Revising

Substantial revision on an essay exam is pretty much out of the question. Your time is better spent generating and arranging your ideas and drafting the best possible answer the first time than skimping on these with the idea of redeeming yourself in a rewrite. If you're ahead of schedule as you approach the second question, spend your time planning for that one rather than revising the first.

Having said that, we would still argue that there is a place for revision of a restricted sort. Plan to spend a minute or two at the end of the exam to reread your answers for the obvious errors, omissions, words left out, silly misspellings, and garbled or nonsensical statements. Don't waste time poring over the complexities of your argument or the sheer number of facts and details you use to support a claim. Time is fleeting. Correct the howlers and turn it in.

COMING HOME TO ROOST

A problem both students and teachers have brought to our attention is what happens after an essay exam is turned in, graded, and handed back. Many students simply glance at the grade and then throw the exam away or file it in a drawer (this is also true, unfortunately, for many other kinds of academic writing). In most cases, the teacher spends a good deal of time reading and assessing the exam and writing some comments on it, but these play no role in the student's further thinking and learning.

It may seem to go without saying that it's important to review your essay exam and think about the comments on it. But it's worth repeating. Often, after the heat of the contest, you may forget exactly what you wrote. Use the opportunity, no matter how well you may have done, to reread and review the question, your essay, and your teacher's comments. Note the structure you chose, and think of alternative organizations. Note places where you might have woven in more details, or places where you should probably have moved on to the next angle on the topic. If you don't see exactly what your teacher was driving at with her comments, or if you're just curious about what the teacher understood the questions to be calling for, make an appointment to sit down with her and discuss the test.

Above all, dive back into the material of the exam topic, and use the occasion to restudy and rethink what you've learned. The essay exam may, frankly, never become a pleasant experience—but you might as well exploit all its potential for learning instead of letting it exploit you.

Chapter
4

The College Paper from Start to Finish

THINK OF WRITING IN STAGES

In this chapter, we want to focus on longer, more complex college writing assignments. Such assignments come in many forms, styles, and lengths. Their aim is not solely to assess your knowledge (like the essay exam), nor solely to help you learn (like journal work). Teachers generally assign longer papers for several reasons: to help you focus on and grasp more fully some specific material in your course; to assess the depth of your learning; and to develop your writing itself. In turn, you use the writing as an occasion to learn, and in the process try to present that learning in as convincing, stylish, and effective a way as you can.

Because of the greater depth and complexity of longer papers, your approach to writing them will differ in important ways from what you do to write a short focus paper or an essay test. Longer papers require more reflection, reading, and thought. The question you answer tends to be more complex, with various perspectives needing attention, more sophisticated relationships to be understood and assessed. You also have more freedom in how to present your answer—which means you have to give careful consideration to how to organize and present your response.

Because longer assignments tend to be fairly complex, you'll usually have several days, a week, perhaps several weeks, to write them. If you use this time well, you'll be able to work up, write, revise, and polish a fine piece of writing with comparatively little stress. But this doesn't mean sitting down late one night and trying to bat out the paper all at once. You should do a lot of work before you even begin to draft, and a fair amount again between your rough draft and the version you finally hand in. Unlike the kind of writing we discussed in Chapter Two, where you think hard and hammer it together in a couple of days, here you'll be returning again and again to the task, measuring it up from different angles, making sure the joints are glued tight, sanding it feathery soft before turning it in (and, along the way, perhaps even rebuilding parts of it when they don't fit well the first time).

In this chapter, we present and explain the logic of techniques you can use from the moment you're handed the assignment through the finishing touches. These techniques are designed to do two things: 1. keep the writing task from becoming completely overwhelming at any point (that is, to spread out the load more evenly over time); and 2. help you produce the richest, sharpest, most intelligent paper you have it in you to write on your topic.

To give you some idea of where we're going, here are the steps of the writing process we cover:

- *Exploring your material.* What are some ways to get started on your paper? What techniques have proven useful to writers for asking a question, setting a direction for their papers, finding out what they know and need to know? Are there any strategies for working with concepts before trying to set these down in well-crafted prose?
- *Finding the heart of the matter.* How can you move from the messy, exploratory, initial stages toward a well-considered plan for your paper? What's a thesis, and why is it important? How do you distill and arrange initial brainstorming notes and freely written ideas for presentation?

- *Drafting*. Can *anything* help out in the often nerve-racking, difficult process of producing a rough draft? How does your audience figure into your drafting process: should you forget about your audience or keep them in mind?
- *Revising*. How can you make the best of a draft that may represent only a rough, preliminary form of your paper? What should you focus on first, and why? What techniques help to encourage productive revision?

EXPLORING YOUR SUBJECT

If you've had any experience writing informally, especially in a journal, we don't need to persuade you of the benefits such writing can have for expanding your paper. When writing more formal papers, however, you may want to experiment with some of the many techniques that writers have developed over the years for exploring a topic systematically.

Freewriting

As touched on briefly in Chapter One, freewriting is a technique ideally suited to getting started writing. It's especially good for avoiding procrastination, that old bogey of writers usually provoked by the anxiety associated with writing "for keeps." In freewriting, you simply begin writing—wandering, really—until you get somewhere. Put your pen to the page and write, as quickly as you can, even if you end up writing the same things over and over. Eventually your mind has to begin working out new ideas, and those ideas lead to more ideas . . . until you're actually writing, without feeling as if you are. The mess you create will have to be heavily revised or even tossed out later, but at least you've begun thinking through your topic.

Freewriting can take two forms: *unfocused* or *focused*. In the unfocused variety, you have no specific topic or area of thought in mind when you begin. Many writers use unfocused freewriting like a warm-up exercise before running or swimming. In focused freewriting, on the other hand, you begin writing anything that comes to mind, but about some particular idea or topic.

Frank, a student in a course titled Utopian Politics, was presented with the following assignment:

> Please write a position paper of at least 5 pages in which
>
> you assess the kind of socialism adopted by the Kaweah
>
> utopian colony that started in California in the 1880s. How
>
> important do you think the issue of land claims was to the
>
> success of the Kaweah colony?

In order simply to get his mental juices flowing, Frank tried some focused freewriting on the topic; he began spinning out ideas about the Kaweah colony in his journal, in whatever order they happened to occur to him. His writing rambled from details about the colony's history to personal opinions about its leaders' ideals to questions concerning the colony's downfall. After a short session, Frank felt less worried about writing his paper because he had already started it. His preliminary exploration gave him ideas, and even some usable text, for the paper. And, since he hadn't yet read enough about the Kaweah community, his freewriting smoked out all those murky and unspecific areas in his knowledge, and showed him what else he needed to learn before beginning his draft.

Freewriting is perhaps the most flexible and adaptable of brainstorming techniques. It makes no requirements with respect to form, so you can do almost anything with it, as you see fit. You can, for instance, engage in dialogues in your notebook, writing in a question-and-answer format. You can create different fictional lawyers, as it were, to argue the case from all sides, in order to see what might be said from different perspectives. You can try explaining your material in a letter, either to a friend or a younger sister or an expert in the field. You can write a long set of questions, and come back later to pick out a few to answer in full.

You might also try doing your freewriting for different lengths of time. Focused freewriting, if it's going well, can take it out of you. Try writing for fifteen minutes, take a break, and then come back later. At that point, you'd want to sit

Lawead paper —

That I want to do here (I think) is to explore some of the historical and political dimensions of the Lawead colony first and then really focus in on why it failed as a colony part of that failure has to do with the relationship of L. to the Federal Gov't — and there's a nice analogy to all sorts of other conflicts ~~be~~ between "alternative societies and the U.S. of A. — ~~Indian~~ ~~reser~~ pre- (and past) reservation, hippies (with local housing ordinances) preventing tree houses in Big Sur, etc.) — and so on. The L. colony land claims are an important part of that whole relationship. Another issue is of course the internal structure of the colony. I want to do some more reading on Gronlund to see where the compartmentalizing came from — that's a typical feature of some communal systems, a kind of over-structured orderliness that somehow always ends up failing. all these bureaus and parts — and then the power structure is important down, read over your earlier notes, and mark anything that strikes you as interesting or curious or worth pursuing further. Using that as a seed, write again for ten, fifteen, twenty minutes and see what you turn up. By constantly referring to your old notes, you can avoid repeating yourself, and cover more ground as a result.

Freewriting works especially well when its episodes are spread out over time on a single project. Freewriting as soon as you receive a three-week assignment or description of a course-long term paper will help you at least begin analyzing the topic and raising possibilities. Then, as you continue to freewrite every few days, you'll find that not only does your focus begin to sharpen and a plan to materialize, but also that your earlier notes (which inevitably contain some useful ideas and speculations) can become good starting points for each subsequent writing episode. The more you write, the more light is shed on your developing paper—and the more secure you begin to feel.

Don't, however, let yourself get too secure, if that means closing down on your possibilities. Students often find that freewriting leads them beyond their original plans and ideas to open up entirely new vistas, which in turn permit entirely new papers. Feel free to follow up any odd hunches and digressions; they may lead you to a more interesting paper yet. And if, in fact, you want to return to your original plan, it'll always be there in your notes. In short, don't be married to your original plans and purposes. Part of the beauty of freewriting is the freedom it gives you to record your first hunches, then leave these safely behind to go off and scope out new terrain.

Listing

Listing is a kind of abbreviated freewriting. Instead of stringing together sentences of prose, you simply record key ideas or concepts. Soon you begin noticing patterns and relationships between and among the items on your list, and these in turn lead to a deeper and more extensive analysis.

To illustrate the power of listing, let's consider a simple writing task. Imagine that you're getting college credit (perhaps towards teaching certification) by volunteering to help out in a community summer activities program for children. The administrators have asked if you could plan to do a couple of short presentations for 7-9 year olds in the "Learn About Nature" series, an educational program reserved for days when the weather is too bad for outdoor activities. You agree. You learn that the next scheduled topic is "The Exotic Panda Bear." Now, you're hardly an expert on pandas, but the point of the program is just to pull together enough material on pandas to teach the children something and spark their interest.

In order just to see what you know, and perhaps what you might want to find out, you begin by listing. Your first list might consist simply of random things you already happen to know about panda bears:

cute, cuddly
endangered species
eats bamboo
Chinese
newborns are tiny
hard to breed in captivity
shy
Ling-Ling and Sing-Sing (Washington Zoo)
black and white
small, round ears
kids love them
hard species to classify (bear? raccoon?)

As you think about the pandas at the Washington Zoo, you remember that they were a gift to President Nixon from the Chinese government. That leads you to add the item "diplomacy and foreign affairs" to the list. "Newborns are tiny," "hard to breed in captivity," "endangered species," and "shy" all remind you that Ling-Ling sat on her newborn baby by accident and killed it. Then you recall that the destruction of Chinese forests has led to a depletion of bamboo, the staple diet of pandas. You recall some other details, but these are half-formed, so you begin raising questions for yourself:

> *Are they marsupials? Heard they're related to dogs or raccoons . . .*
>
> *How dependent are babies on mother?*
>
> *What are babies like when first born?*
>
> *How are they fed in captivity?*
>
> *Any successful artificial inseminations?*

If after creating a first list, nothing much happens for you conceptually, try starting new sub-lists in chains to probe your thinking further. For example, you might start a sub-list by writing "black and white," then list more details about the appearance of pandas. The item "large paws" might then lead to another list focusing on the number of claws, the uses to which pandas put their paws, the panda's "thumb," or the danger of being swiped by a panda. "Danger" might lead you to think about the behavior of pandas in captivity and in the wild. "Behavior" might lead to speculations about why we idealize some creatures (in toys, storybooks, etc.) like pandas and koala bears, and not others like jackals or toads.

Of course, when it comes time for your presentation, you won't use all you have. But a lot has happened in your mind from creating a few simple lists in your notebook. And that can greatly reduce anxiety, even while compelling you to do some harder, deeper, more critical thinking.

Notice as well in this example how the purpose of your writing (in this case, in order to do a verbal presentation for young children) can develop and evolve from your brain-storming. Since your time is limited, you could focus on just some aspects of panda bears. An *environmental* focus might lead to a presentation that helps sensitize the children to the need to preserve and protect our natural surroundings, since one part of the ecosystem (panda bears) can be threatened by the destruction of another (bamboo forests). A *political* focus might show children how animals can figure into world affairs (panda bears being one example). A *social* focus might raise children's consciousness of the difference between the public's conception of animals (anthropomorphized in cute toys marketed to millions of people) and the more biological nature of the animals themselves. Each new wave of ideas can lead to new possibilities for the more specific purpose of the presentation.

Conceptual Maps

Many students' greatest fear is dealing with language—specifically, not being able to find the right words for their thoughts. But the problem may not lie in the verbalizing as much as in the thinking. The language isn't there because the thinking isn't ready for it. Conceptual maps are diagrams of sorts that reveal relationships between ideas, using minimal language. There are several types, but two of the most useful are clusters (below) and tree diagrams (which we discuss later, as an organizational technique).

In clustering, you place at the center of a blank sheet of paper a single idea or concept:

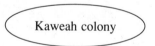

As you begin thinking about it, you attach related ideas to it in a cluster:

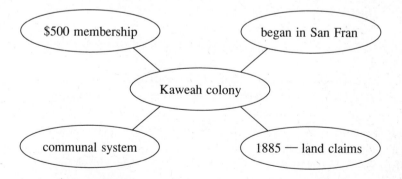

Like listing, each piece of the cluster can be further elaborated. For example, the item "communal system" refers to the political agenda of the Kaweah colony. But what sort of communism was advocated?

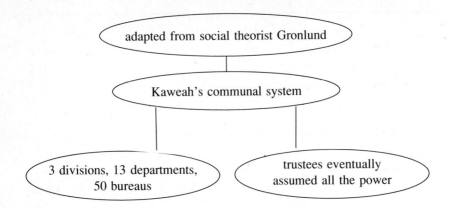

Extensions of this cluster could be made from each of these three elaborations of "Kaweah's communal system," and interconnections between ideas in different parts of the cluster can be indicated with connecting lines. At this stage, however, you're less concerned with the organization and overall significance of your material than with simply getting it down on paper *somehow*. Don't worry about doing this right; just do it quickly and fully, and see what you have to work with.

It's important to stress that during the early stages of pre-writing, if you become anxious or confused, you should try focusing on the subject itself, rather than on your audience or the eventual form of your paper. Follow your subject wherever it leads. Neatness and order shouldn't be issues for you at this point; if you can make sense of your scribbled notes and cryptic phrases, they're orderly enough. A rich, mushrooming flood of ideas, information, and insights should be the aim of this early work.

Nor should you ever stop developing and expanding your ideas. Throughout your writing, you should keep your notebook handy. New insights and information come up all the time when you're writing, and you should be ready to receive them and get them down on paper. Even if questions and thoughts occur to you that have no place in your present paper, you might note them down for future reference. It takes very little time, and you never know when they might prove useful.

FINDING THE HEART OF THE MATTER

Now that you've spent some time exploring your material, you have to start considering your readers, what you want to tell them, and how you want to present what you know. This entails getting a grasp on your material as a whole. What does it all add up to? What does it really mean? What have you learned? Where's the heart of the matter? It might help you to reread the original question or assignment. What are you really being asked? What do your readers primarily want to know?

Sorting your material may itself require more notebook writing. You might do well to take one page—no more than that—and describe for yourself the main import of your material. Try to complete this sentence:

If I've learned one thing about all this, it's . . .

Then go on to this one:

The main things that make me think that are . . .

If you can answer those, you demonstrate a sound hold on your subject. But you may still not have a paper. To decide if you do, you need to complete one more sentence.

All of this is important because . . .

These sentences reflect the issues you face in presenting your material to your readers. Your readers want to know what you think (obviously), but they also want to know your reasons for saying what you do, laid out in order, so they can grasp each idea separately and see how it reinforces or qualifies the others. Readers want to see the importance of what you're telling them. Why should they care? What difference does it make?

Think of the separate ideas in your notes as so many individual testimonies in a trial. Obviously no one would gather witnesses in the first place unless doing so would help to *prove* or *document* something. In a sense, all of your brainstorming has gathered together a room full of testimonies of all kinds. But unlike a court proceeding, where the problem is already established, here your job is to listen to all the testimonies and *then* decide what you want to prove or document. There's no judge (yet), and just one trial attorney (you) and mounds of facts and opinions. Having decided what the case is all about, you can then select those testimonies (from your readings, jottings, etc.) that most fully and persuasively prove your point. In our travels far and wide across the college curriculum, the single most popular term used for that point is the *thesis* of your writing.

Developing a Thesis

What exactly is a *thesis*? The term has a long and venerable history, but most teachers define it as the central organizing idea or argument in a piece of writing. If you were to state the overarching idea in your last paper in a single pithy sentence, that would most likely be the thesis of the paper. A paper without a thesis is like a set of directions which lead to an empty field in the middle of nowhere. In formal academic writing, a paper without a thesis looks like a jumble of ideas and facts with nothing to tie them together, no main idea or organizing point which this information illustrates or extends or supports in some way.

Because developing a thesis is so important in academic writing, let's consider in more detail how a writer goes about developing one in the context of the loose, exploratory writing we've been describing so far. Alec, a senior majoring in public affairs, was assigned to write a major term paper in a course on minority issues. The paper had to involve some sort of primary research (gathering and analyzing actual data from the public, from organizations, and so on). It also had to be written as a report with recommendations for action. Being part Ojibway, Alec decided he wanted to focus on the problem of student retention among Native Americans at his university. It was well known that the number of Native Americans enrolling at his school was fairly low to begin with, but they also had the highest dropout rate of any minority group. Yet no one had bothered to ask why. What circumstances led so many of that population to attend for a while and then quit?

After six weeks of interviewing students and faculty, examining statistics from the department of admissions, talking with leaders in local Indian communities, visiting reservations, reading research on student retention, and surveying various minority populations at his school, Alec had lots of fascinating and useful material. At this point, without a careful synthesis of all the data, Alec would be unprepared to develop a claim, or thesis, in his paper. All he could say by way of introduction would be, "This paper tries to understand why student retention among American Indians is so low at Bristol State University." And, without a sharper analysis of the problem, Alec would be hard pressed to provide a recommendation for change.

After carefully examining all his material, Alec concluded that student retention was linked in a complex way to several factors, including a lack of financial support for Native Americans. But the most important of these, something that surfaced again and again in his interviews with students and faculty and on his trips to nearby Indian reservations, concerned the idea of academic role models. Of over 1,000 faculty members at his university, only four were Native Americans, and one of them taught courses mainly at the graduate level. Native American students who had taken courses with these teachers had a higher retention rate than the rest of the Native American student population and reported feeling greater satisfaction from their academic experiences. After locating several research studies supporting the power of role models on students' feelings about learning, Alec believed that he could make an excellent case for a relationship between low numbers of Native American faculty and high dropout rates among Native American students. From that case, he could extend a strong recommendation that his university should hire additional Native American faculty and staff and set up an American Indian counseling center. He had, in other words, found a *thesis.*

A *thesis,* note, is much more than a simple *topic.* A *topic* represents the specific entity you're discussing; a *thesis* represents your topic *and* the central claim you're making about it. Your thesis comprises the *subject and predicate* of your paper as a whole. A topic by itself doesn't say anything, doesn't go anywhere. It just sits there. You need a predicate, a claim about the subject, to move it along, to set it in motion, so that it becomes a real addition to knowledge.

"Eggs," for instance, may be a legitimate topic, but in itself it can't be a *thesis*. It doesn't *say anything about* eggs. It *makes no claims* for eggs. A paper "about eggs" but without a real thesis will probably collapse into a mere jumble of "Interesting Facts About Eggs"—and who wants to read that? If you want eggs as your topic, fine. But *claim something about them*.

You might, for instance, state: "Despite the place eggs have long held as a staple in the American diet, recent evidence suggests that they are more harmful than beneficial to one's health." Now, there's a thesis. Eggs are harmful. It might be true, or it might not. Someone else might take on eggs as a topic but defend the opposite thesis: "Despite the scare stories recently spread by the media, there is no convincing evidence that an egg-rich diet adversely affects health." Both theses go beyond the mere topic of eggs to assert, or predicate, something definite about them. Both theses, furthermore, are plausible. You could imagine either one being true—though, when all the facts are in, one of them will have to prove false or be modified.

In the most basic terms, then, any given "X" can be a topic but not in itself a thesis. "X = 5" is a thesis. A claim (=5) is being predicated about a subject (X). And, as a claim, it might or might not be true.

In Alec's case, his *topic* is retention rates of Native American students at Bristol State University. His *thesis* is that the rates are critically affected by the numbers of Native American faculty at the University. As a claim, this is literally debatable (as a good thesis should be). Someone else might claim that the number of Native Americans on the faculty is irrelevant, and that the real cause of the poor retention rates has to do with the lack of financial support, weaker college preparation as a result of poorer high schools in Native American communities, or the dispersion of Native Americans across dormitories (preventing their forming a cohesive body on campus). But Alec's review of his information convinces him that, in fact, it *is* precisely the lack of Native American faculty that results in the low retention rate. So that's his thesis, and in his paper he will bring forward the necessary evidence to convince us of its validity.

As a general rule, your readers will be looking for a thesis in one of two places. The most common site is at the end of the introductory section: you introduce your *topic*, provide sufficient background to convince your readers of its importance, and then state your *thesis*, the claim you're making concerning your topic. This is a fairly traditional way to place a thesis, and you won't go far wrong if you follow it.

A second common location is in the *conclusion* of a paper. In this case, you use your introduction to set up a specific *problem*, then review the evidence, explaining its significance as you proceed, and finally draw all the threads together into a definitive answer—your thesis—at the end. This is the academic-paper-as-detective-story approach. It can be a little tricky to manage, and not every paper lends itself to it, but if this structure does work, your paper will probably do a fine job of holding your reader's attention.

The process of deciding on a thesis is likewise varied. Some experts advise you to know your thesis before you begin writing; others will suggest that you write your way into one. We've done it both ways. Sometimes an idea will be so clear from the start of a project that it can safely lead you through the whole writing process, from gathering information to finding a structure to revising for style. A truly open-minded approach to your topic, on the other hand, will almost always suggest some modifications of your original thesis; in this case, sticking too rigidly by it may lead to confusion or frustration. There's no pleasure in battling the facts.

Imagine, for example, that after writing a full draft of his paper, Alec had discovered some new statistics on returning students at his university. By matching the names of these returning students with enrollees who had dropped out (sometimes years before), Alec learned that many Native American students simply took longer to complete their degrees because they left for a time to earn more money for college. Alec's earlier thesis would have to be modified somehow to accommodate this new information. He might still argue forcefully for his role-model theory, but he would have to acknowledge that the financial exigencies of Native American students also contributed to the low retention rate. He might, in fact, argue that the problem of retention may be exaggerated because it is being defined at his university by how many students complete their degrees in four years rather than in six, eight or ten. Simply ignoring the new information would be foolish, since an astute reader might ask why it hadn't been considered. Worse still, it would be intellectually dishonest.

It should be clear, then, that developing a thesis, or focus, for a paper doesn't always happen in the same way at the same point in the writing process. But once you've managed to articulate something like a thesis, however tentative it may be, your next problem, organizing your material, will become much simpler.

LOOKING FOR PATTERNS

In reality, you can't ever fully separate the tasks of formulating a thesis and organizing your material. The tasks involve each other so completely that they effectively blend. In both cases, you're working with the material you've gathered to find the patterns that underlie it. You examine your material, turning it this way and that in your mind (and on paper), to see both what it tells you about your topic—that is, what *thesis* it suggests—and what patterns you can arrange it into for presentation to your readers.

As a rule, you start into the research and reflection on a paper armed with at least a vague sort of question, as did Alec. Keeping your question in mind, you seek out, collect, and study the relevant information on it. The evidence you uncover in turn leads you to an answer to your question. Then, when you go to present your findings on paper, you reverse the pattern. You begin with the answer—that is, with the conclusion you came to, now formulated as your thesis—and you lead the reader back through the evidence that supports it.

In developing your thesis, then, you move from your question through your material, to your answer, like so:

In presenting your findings, you lead your readers from your thesis through your supporting evidence:

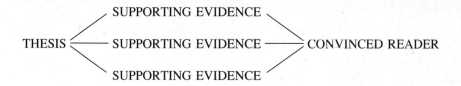

The problem is to decide how best to present your material to your readers in order to convince them of the validity of your thesis. Like a good lawyer, you have to decide how to marshal your evidence.

We'd like to present here three techniques which have helped writers in the past to sort out and arrange their material for presentation to their readers. The problem of organization itself is twofold. You have to gather your material from a sprawling, shapeless, inchoate mass into discrete, unified portions—almost servings—and you have to decide in what order to present these. The techniques offered here—trees, outlines, and sketches—move from the most visual, schematic, spatial arrangements of information toward more linear, prose-like forms. You can use these separately or in conjunction with each other, and in any order. And you may find them useful at various points in the developing of your ideas and your paper. You should try them all, and discover for yourself how they suit your purposes.

Organizational Trees

You can understand the logic of an organizational tree if you think of diagrams you might have seen of the Federal Government or of the various animal species. In each case, some large entity (government, animal kingdom) is broken into smaller units (executive branch, legislative branch, judicial branch; vertebrates, invertebrates); and each of the smaller units broken down in turn (House, Senate; amphibians, reptiles, fishes, birds, mammals).

You can use such trees to organize almost any body of knowledge. Trees help you sort your material into its major components and see the relationships between them. They don't necessarily suggest the final arrangement of your ideas in linear English prose, but they can move you closer to the goal.

The trees in Figure 4.1 demonstrate the basic logic involved. The first could represent an early sorting of your material for an astronomy paper. You're writing about the various objects found in space, and you've chosen to divide these according to location: whether they occur within the solar system or beyond it. The second might help you organize an essay-test answer in abnormal psychology: "Discuss the major causes of psychotic disorders and explain how they're related." You start by sorting the causes into genetic factors, family and social dynamics, and the influence of drugs. Obviously, this doesn't answer your question, but it does give you a framework to build on. The third might help you organize a memo for a corporate executive. You've been asked to analyze the workings of the purchasing department and to suggest ways to improve its efficiency. Even before starting your observations, you realize that you can organize your findings according to (1) who is doing the work, (2) what they have to work with, and (3) how they are going about it.

Obviously, these are simple examples. If you were writing more than a page or two, you'd probably have several pages of brainstormed material, which would lead to a more complex structure. The tree used to organize the psychology essay, for instance, might be revised and developed in greater depth for a term paper, as in figure 4.2.

You'll notice a few things about the tree right away. As you proceed from top to bottom, the categories become smaller and more precise. Your large, general entities stem straight down from the main topic. Each level down contains more nodes, representing smaller subtopics, arguments, or ideas. Your most fine-grained supporting facts, statistics, examples, etc., are arranged along the bottom. Furthermore, along any horizontal row, the abstractness of the ideas runs about on a par. Nodes at the same level are about equally general or specific, abstract or concrete. Finally, each idea supports the idea directly above it. In drawing your organizational tree, these are the ideals to aim for.

It doesn't take especially deep reflection to see the logical problems in the tree in figure 4.3. The writer, organizing his material on the causes of the Northern victory in the Civil War, gets off to a sound start. He divides his topic into Political Advantages and Economic Factors—two categories of a high and equivalent level of generality. Under Political Advan-

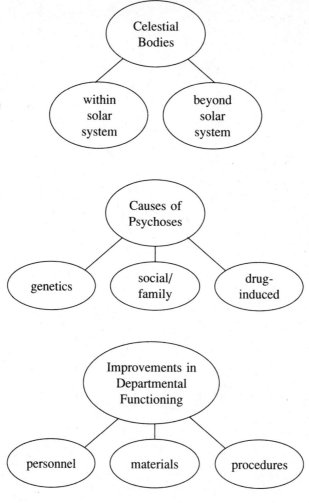

Figure 4.1

tages, he continues to sort his information sensibly. He divides Political Advantages into Leaders and Policies. Under Leaders, he discusses the President and two highly influential cabinet members. He divides Policies into Internal and Foreign Affairs, and under the latter discusses U.S. relationships with two important European nations.

When he reaches Economic Factors, however, his arrangement falls apart. He places Military under Economic Factors—and straight across from Robert E. Lee and the Monitor! Geographical Advantages is buried even deeper, though in terms of generality it about equals Political Advantages or

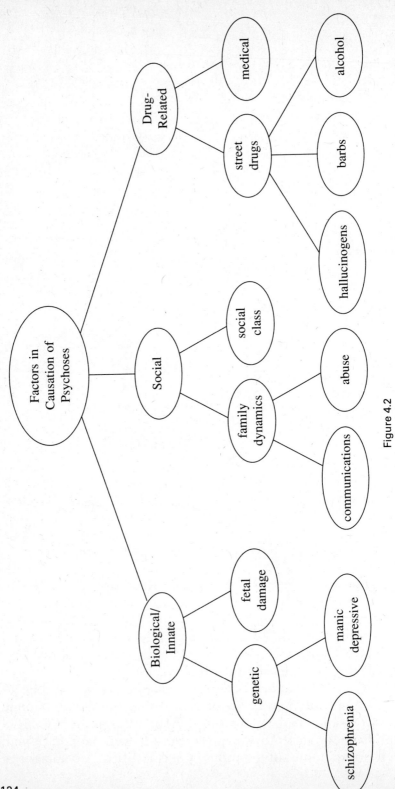

Figure 4.2

Economic Factors. He places four generals under Copperheads—which is a political designation—and he drops Atlanta Burning, Slavery, and the Gettysburg Address into his chart almost at random. If he bases his paper on this tree, the first half will be clear and easy to follow. From there on, however, the reader will be swimming. Fortunately, this is still only the organizational stage. He hasn't written anything yet, and revising his tree will require only minutes (at least, it will once he has a good night's sleep followed by a cup of strong coffee).

Before developing your tree in depth, you should experiment with a variety of ways of sorting your material at the highest, most general level. Draw no more than the top node and the first row beneath it—the main topic and major concepts—but do it several times and in several different ways. You may find that your material lends itself to a variety of organizations, each of which suggests a paper unique in significance and approach. If you're looking for the best slant on your material, sketching several different trees, all quite short, may lead you to it.

Suppose again that you've been studying the psychoses. You've compiled copious notes on them, but you're not sure where to begin your paper. You might draw a number of small trees to explore different approaches, as in the example in figure 4.4.

The first would compare previous myths surrounding the psychoses with our present understanding of them. The second suggests a three-part paper, noting first the demographics of psychotic disorders, then examining the causes of them, and then describing the various treatments currently in use. The last focuses on a smaller topic within the general field. Instead of covering the psychoses in general—an enormous topic—you decide to concentrate solely on their genetic aspects. You explain first the various methods of genetic research, and then the findings of such research, organized perhaps by disorder (schizophrenia, depression, pre-senile dementia, etc.). You could draw any of these trees in less than a minute. And by trying out these options, you stand a good chance of finding the most interesting and coherent central thesis and organizing structure.

Trees can also help you forecast the shape of your paper before you draft it. You should be able to tell just by looking at your tree whether your paper will move along at a good even

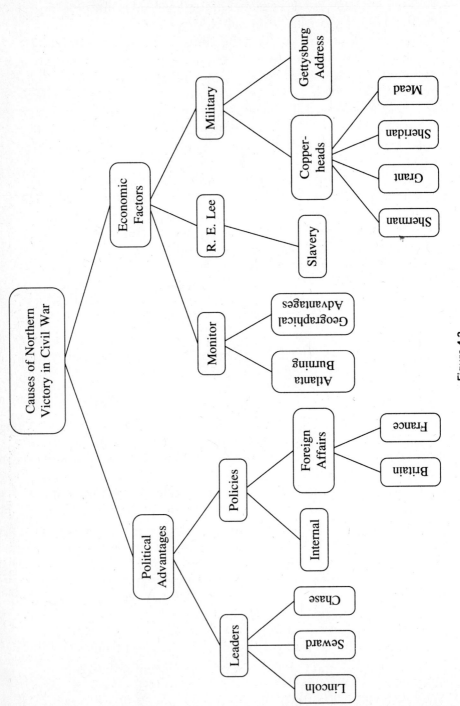

Figure 4.3

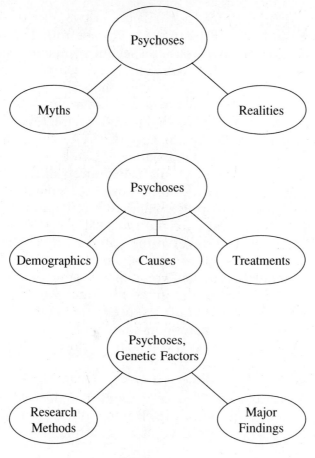

Figure 4.4

pace, or whether it will be choppy, long-winded, or unbalanced.

Consider the trees in Figure 4.5. Either of these, if written up in its present shape, will produce a structurally weak paper. The first tree shows a long string of topics, with no attempt to sort them. Nothing in the chart suggests which topics belong together, which support which, or which are more important than others. The tree suggests the writer will touch on each topic briefly but develop none in detail. The paper is liable to read like a string of headlines or news briefs.

The second tree suffers from a different problem. The writer has divided her material into three broad categories. Under two of these categories, however, she has little or nothing to say. Only under "II" does she have much information;

and even here, the bulk of it falls under two further subdivisions, "A" and "C." If she drafts her paper from this tree, the inequalities between the parallel sections will annoy and disorient the reader. The writer will seem garrulous at some points and positively tongue-tied at others. Since the writer is clearly most interested or knowledgeable in Part II, she might just drop Parts I and III from her design completely and focus on her best material. Within Part II, she might either drop section "B" or flesh it out to balance "A" and "C." Obviously, any of the changes would result in an entirely different paper, constructed to defend a different thesis. She's not just moving a few bones, she's creating a whole different animal.

Organizational trees are the quickest and easiest way to experiment with and develop the patterns in your material. They do a splendid job of keeping you from getting bogged down in detail before you've seen the general shape and extent of your subject. But since they are two-dimensional diagrams, you still need to transpose them to one dimension before you draft. Fortunately, standard outlines provide a convenient bridge between the planar world of trees and the linear world of prose.

If we label the nodes of the tree (Figure 4.6) with the standard heading markers we were all taught in fifth grade, the tree practically shuffles itself into outline form. This tree converts itself automatically into this outline:

Thesis

    I. Major Argument
      A. Supporting Argument
      B. Supporting Argument
      C. Supporting Argument
        1. Detail
        2. Detail
    II. Major Argument
      A. Supporting Argument
      B. Supporting Argument
    III. Major Argument
      A. Supporting Argument
        1. Detail
        2. Detail
      B. Supporting Argument

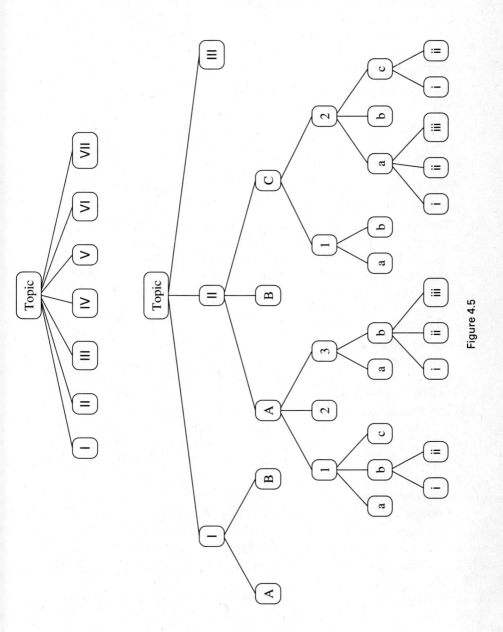

Figure 4.5

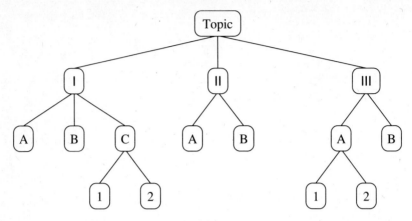

Figure 4.6

As the example suggests, turning your tree into an outline gives you only the body of your paper. The outline still lacks the Introduction and Conclusion. But that's all right at this point. You know where they go, and it's too early to worry about them now in any case. (We discuss the writing of Introductions and Conclusions in some detail below; see pp. 147–149).

Outlines

Few American children escape having to learn to do outlines in elementary school. Even fewer ever understand what they were all about, much less care to use them thereafter. Few of us would have believed it if our teachers had told us that the purpose of outlines was to make our lives easier. They never did. We all wrote the paper first, then struggled through the business of turning the paper back into the formal outline it was (supposedly) based on.

Yet the only valid purpose of outlines is to make writing easier, and used wisely they can. What interfered with their usefulness was the stiff, formalistic way we understood them. What we learned was Proper Outline Format. Every line was indented a certain amount and prefixed by a symbol: capital roman numerals, capital letters, Arabic numerals, lower case letters, and perhaps—for the real obsessives—lower case roman numerals. The structure looked like this:

Title

I. Major arguments
    A. Minor, supporting arguments

1. Smallish arguments or supporting facts
   a) Little tiny supporting details
      i) Incredible minutiae

And saints preserve us if we mixed these up. The other Inviolable Rule was that under no circumstances could we have only one subheading at any level. If you had an "A," you had to have a "B." If a "1," then, whether your material justified it or not, you'd better come up with a "2." One of us recalls being so frustrated by this that he used the words "Because it's required" for a second heading. The teacher, needless to say, wasn't amused.

Actually, this was all worth learning. It reflects principles of organization which the writer really does need to understand. Though the details of all this can go by the board, the underlying logic is sound. Divested of some of its pedantic stiffness, the method can help a writer to work more swiftly and easily, and to produce more coherent prose.

Writing Topic Outlines Outlines are meant to accomplish the same ends as organizational trees. They present a visual analog of which things go where—which details belong together, which concepts subsume others, what order the material goes in, and so forth. They let you sort and arrange your material so that you can present it to your reader in a fashion she will follow and remember. If your outlines help you achieve this, you're doing them right.

The most useful way to begin an outline reflects its tree-like logic. Don't start at the top and simply plough your way through the entire outline, filling it out to the fourth-level little letters as you go. That's a confusing, frustrating way to work, and it gives you small room to maneuver if you change your mind about anything. Instead, to begin with, write the briefest, most general outline possible—only the major headings. Get the big pieces in place before proceeding further.

Once you've tried a number of arrangements at this level of generality, you can go back and flesh out each heading one more level down. Again, don't get ahead of yourself. Get your second-level headings—your indented capital A's and B's—in place, before working down any further. Your mind should be filled at this stage with your Grand Design.

Having worked your way through the outline to one or two levels, the rest of the development is optional. You might work it all out further yet, to the third-level 1's and 2's and on down. You might work out only certain sections of it, and plan to keep the details of the other sections in your head as you draft. Or you might stop cold at two levels. The only criterion is what serves your own purpose. The larger the paper, the more levels and details you'll probably need in your outline. For a short paper, two levels may do it. For an essay question or a memo, the main headings alone may be enough.

In Alec's case, he had already decided that the broad focus of his paper would be the causes of low retention among Native Americans at Bristol State. His earliest outline— several main conceptual headings—reflects the nature of his data, and so became a kind of investigative plan for his research:

   I. Admissions data
  II. Student interviews
 III. Faculty interviews
 IV. Site visits to reservations
  V. Site visits to community centers
 VI. Library research

At this point, it would have been impossible for Alec to progress in writing the outline because he hadn't yet conducted his investigations. As a plan for his research, he might have moved one level further in the outline, at least for one or two of the main headings:

I. Admissions Data
  A. % of Native Americans, past 10 yrs.
  B. Drop-out rate, compared
  C. Academic preparation, compared
  D. Purpose statements???

Until he actually sat down with personnel in the admissions department, however, he wouldn't be sure whether these sub-categories would provide useful data (or whether, for that matter, he could even have access to information like "academic preparation"). He questions "purpose statements" because at this point he's not sure whether all students write a purpose statement for admission to the university; nor is he sure what he'd do with them once he got them.

As Alec moves along in his paper, however, his outline

begins to reflect less the process of his research and more the organization of information in his final report. At first, until he develops the sharp thesis we described earlier, his outline mirrors some of the linked causes of low student retention:

I. Lack of financial resources
II. Little motivation in native communities
III. Cultural disenfranchisement
IV. Lack of adequate role models at university
V. No counseling/advising center
VI. Discrimination
VII. Inadequate academic preparation for college

Since these categories contribute disproportionately to the problem, Alec needs not only to decide what sequence he should discuss them in, but also whether they are all worth discussing in the first place, or whether some of them could be consolidated into a single, higher-level category. His next outline changes as he begins to focus on the role-model theory:

I. Theories of role modeling's effects on motivation
  A. Sanspirizo (1974)
  B. Rogers & Darnon (1978)
  C. Emile (1985)
  D. Brown (1988)
II. Retention rates at Bristol State
  A. Whole population
  B. All minorities
  C. Native Americans vs. whole population
  D. NAs vs. other minorities, singly & summed
III. Faculty role models
  A. Current stats. on NA faculty
  B. Past record; projected likelihood of increase
IV. Recommendations
  A. Student counseling center for NAs
  B. Increase hiring of NA faculty and staff

For purposes of a rough draft, this outline serves Alec well. Later on, however, he recognizes that his draft begins too abruptly with the results of research on role models and also doesn't adequately synthesize the mountains of data from his surveys and interviews. His final outline reflects the final organization of his report, which includes in part III a substantial section summarizing his interview data, and also shifts to that section the research material from his library reading:

   I. Introduction and Problem Description
      A. Retention Rates at Bristol State
      B. Admissions Data
      C. Academic Preparation
  II. Disproving of Possible Causes
      A. Financial Dimensions
      B. Discrimination
      C. Preparation
 III. Role Modeling as Key to Retention
      A. Theories/research of role modeling and motivation
      B. Interview data: students and mentors
      C. Present status of role modeling at Bristol State
  IV. Recommendations
      A. Revising Hiring Agendas for Next Decade
      B. Student Counseling Center for NAs

As should be apparent, we're hardly advocating doing an outline in the old high school sense. One black-tie-and-cummerbund Formal Outline rarely helps much with the rough-and-tumble of getting your thoughts straight. We're recommending instead a series of outlines, of different arrangements and degrees of detail, and perhaps with separate smaller ones for each major section. By the time you're through your ten-page report, you may have written a dozen or more outlines, and thrown out most of them. They will still have served their purpose.

Sentence Outlines   There is, finally, a variation on the standard format many writers find helpful: the so-called sentence outline. Instead of headings of only a word or a phrase, you write complete sentences at each numeral or letter. The following two outlines—one the standard variety and the other a sentence outline—reflect a student's efforts to organize a paper on Albert Camus' novel *The Stranger*. The student, in reading the novel, had become aware of an ironic reversal in the way the different characters symbolized life and death for the main character, Meursault. The student's thesis was that

Meursault's mother, whose death is announced in the first paragraph of the book, becomes in time the most powerful life symbol for Meursault, while his apparently "livelier" young friends come to represent death. Having arrived at her thesis, the student then needed to distill and arrange her evidence from the novel into a coherent presentation for her readers.

Her first quick outline looks like this:

Symbols of Life and Death in Camus' *The Stranger*

   I. Mother = death
  II. Friends = life
 III. Friends → death
 IV. Mother now = life

She then expanded this into a sentence outline as follows:

Symbols of Life and Death in Camus' *The Stranger*

   I. In the opening scenes of Albert Camus' *The Stranger*, Meursault's mother, recently deceased, represents Meursault's first major experience with death.
  II. By contrast to his mother, the stranger's friends, especially Marie, represent the pleasures of, and desire for, life.
 III. Though his friends represent the joys of life to Meursault, it is through his interactions with them that he brings about the death of the Arab, and hence his own.
 IV. While he's in his prison cell, awaiting his execution, Meursault comes to understand his mother's own great appetite and feeling for life. She has come from representing death for Meursault to being his primary life symbol.

This kind of outline takes longer to write than the others, but it has the advantage of translating into a draft with great ease. The sentences in your outline can often be transcribed with minimal alteration straight into your draft as topic sentences. You then flesh out each paragraph or section one by one, and you're well on your way to a working draft.

Since it does take more work than the standard format, you might use the sentence outline as a transitional stage between short, sketchy outlines and a full draft. Do your collection of short outlines. Develop the best one a level or two. Then go back and write sentences at each line. Your drafting should be comparatively easy after that.

Sketches

A sketch is essentially an abstract of your paper written before your paper itself. It's a sort of pre-summary of your paper, a short overview of the whole, compressed into one paragraph or page. Setting all your notes and outlines aside—and we mean, clean out of sight—you try to say what it is you have to say in one breath. As with trees or outlines, you stand to benefit by trying this several times.

When you do this, the real core significance of your material becomes apparent. The important ideas and information crop up in all your sketches; the secondary material is only sporadically present or not at all. You're able to separate the ore from the slag. With each attempt, furthermore, the central claim you wish to defend will become clearer. Finally, in explaining your paper, you will often intuitively arrange your material in the most logical order. If you set yourself the additional goal of selling your idea, you will clarify for yourself its real importance.

Basically, you're writing your report in miniature, making something akin to an architect's model of it. As with trees or outlines, you're working out your thesis and organization in a quick, painless way to head off major structural problems and revisions later. If by writing a few paragraphs, you can find your core message, its importance, and its form, you can start drafting your paper with much greater confidence and ease.

DRAFTING

There is an interesting anecdote about the French playwright Racine that tells something about the business of drafting. Racine came to a party one night in extremely high spirits. A friend asked him what he was so happy about. Racine answered, "I have just written a wonderful new play! Now all I have to do is add the dialogue!"

Now *that's* a man ready to start drafting.

Drafting is that part of the writing process most people think of as actually writing their paper. This is unfortunate. It puts too much stress on one phase of the process, raising the stakes (and the tension), and making it harder as a result. It's better to think of the whole process as writing—everything from the first brainstorming to the final editing—and to use the word "drafting" to denote the business of getting your material down in paragraph form.

When people try to accomplish too much with it, drafting often gives them trouble. Many people have fond hopes that they can sit down without having given their topic any careful thought and grind out one good solid draft to turn in. Thus, they're trying to develop and arrange their ideas, write their paper, polish their prose, and even check mechanics and spelling, all at the same time. They pay for their hubris both in agony while writing and in embarrassment when their work is returned.

To draft most efficiently, you need to relax a bit and lower your expectations of what drafting can accomplish. You need to depend more heavily on both earlier and later stages of writing to help you produce the paper you want. We've already discussed journal writing, brainstorming techniques, and various ways to organize your material. The more thorough your work in these early stages, the better your draft will go. You should come to drafting with a considered blueprint of what you want to say and the order you want to say it in. You shouldn't have to stare out the window for your ideas. They should already be there—as notes, trees, sketches, or whatever—beside you as you write.

Drafting also grows easier as you learn to depend more on revision, the careful reworking of your paper's content, structure, and style. You can think of revision as a sort of safety net. You don't have to write a perfect draft if you're going to rework it anyway. Your revision is your chance to shoot retakes.

Most writers agree that drafting is generally harder than revision. As a result, you can afford to spread the burden. If, while you're drafting, you see a change you can legitimately make for the better, go ahead and make it. Many writers revise frequently as they draft. But if your self-criticism takes on a carping, strident, negative, defeatist tone—*defy it*. Write over the noise. You're already committed to a revision, so if your paper does have weaknesses (and it probably does), you can fix them then. Your job for the present is to get words down. Sheer page-count is of the essence.

The late great E. B. White, legend has it, kept a sign over his desk at *The New Yorker* which read: *Don't get it right, get it written!* Sound advice from an old major leaguer.

Drafting for the Right Audience

Whenever you get writer's block, you don't so much feel that you can't write *anything* as that you can't write *anything good*. Every sentence you write strikes you as stupid, clumsy, and empty: "I can't write that. I sound like a jerk. What kind of grammar is that? What a stupid, trite, hackneyed idea for a paper anyway!" The more determined you are to write well, in fact, the more danger you run of hearing this voice. You're not blocked, exactly. You're just frozen with fear at the prospect of your audience reading your work. You've got stage fright.

If you can draft for your actual audience—your instructor, your boss, your colleagues—well and good. But if you find that audience too demanding, you may want to back off and draft for the nearest approximation to that audience you're comfortable with. If your history professor intimidates you, imagine yourself writing for your more casual philosophy professor or your graduate student teaching assistant, or your brainy roommate. You may even abandon your audience completely and fall back again on writing just for yourself. Some writing teachers advise doing this as a matter of course. They suggest you explain your material on paper first to yourself, and only then try to explain it to someone else. The version for your own benefit is called a zero-draft or writer-based draft. With that beside you, you can then focus more confidently on your audience, and write your reader-based draft.

Semidrafting

If drafting still causes you to freeze up, think of it as a mere transitional phase between a well-developed outline and a working revisable text. Your goal is no longer your paper; it's something you can rework into a paper, like a potter's ball of clay. If the attempt to write a standard draft hobbles you, you can back off and adopt a series of shortcuts and half-measures that may let you get at least something down on paper.

You can also, if it helps, skip writing your material in full declarative sentences. You may, for some paragraphs, write only a sentence or two and then simply draw in brackets and set your thoughts down in short notes. Later on you can come back and expand your notes into real sentences. If you're writing a paper based on research, you can draw brackets and list the statements or data you plan to include without yet quoting them in full.

Your paragraphs, thus, will be a mix of standard prose and assorted fragments, something like the following:

The Greenhouse Effect results from the way different forms

of radiation pass through the atmosphere. Light rays from

the sun pass easily through the various gases in the earth's

atmosphere. They then strike the ground—[explain this

briefly: short waves, long waves, which move easier. Effect

of CO2 on heat transmission. Analogy with glass

greenhouses. Quote Jenkins, page 37, top. Note increase in

global CO2 and causes thereof.] As a result, the average

temperature of the globe may soon start to rise, with

catastrophic results. As one scientist put it: [Reinhardt,

229, middle]

On the one hand, the writer is obviously not as close to his goal of a final, presentable paper as he would be if he had written out his material in full. On the other hand, it has taken him perhaps one-fourth the time. In the long run, his shortcut may well pay off.

One final use of semidrafting is to help bridge one day's work to the next. A paper of any length often requires several sessions to write. As a rule, each session follows the same pattern. It begins with a still, tense, concentrated preparation phase, in which you arrange in your head what you want to say in a particular section. Then you have a period of moderately steady writing. Then you stop, usually with some idea where you're headed in the next passage. The next day starts all over again with another period of tense mental effort, while you regroup your thoughts before continuing.

Since starting the sessions almost always takes the most time and energy, you can help yourself by jotting down notes at the end of your day's work, capturing your thoughts about the upcoming section. Write a sketchy, broken, semidraft of the next few paragraphs at the bottom of the page. When you sit down the next day, you can start by simply writing out these passages in full, and that often gives you the momentum you need to draft efficiently for the rest of the stint. At the end of that session, jot down your thoughts again for the next bit of writing, and so on.

If, for example, we had been drafting the paragraphs just above, and had been forced to stop for the day, we might have semidrafted a bridge to the next day's work as follows:

One final use of semidrafting is to help bridge one day's

work to the next. A paper of any length often requires

several sessions to write. As a rule, each session follows the

same pattern.

—concentration; arrangement of thoughts

—moderately steady writing

—stopping, some idea of future direction

—whole thing over again

—how semidrafting helps get started each session

—other points?

The next day, we would flesh out each of these ideas in turn, and then continue on drafting from there. It works. Try it.

Drafting generally goes best when you keep a mild, even pressure on yourself to produce. Stay calm and businesslike, and push your sentences steadily and deliberately across the page. If you stall, you won't gain much by stepping on the accelerator; you probably need to release the brake. As one writer suggests, if you can't hit the ball across the net, lower the net; if you still can't do it, lay the net on the ground and roll the ball over. Get something on paper you can live with. In the next stage, revision, you can make it over into something you can be proud of.

REVISING

The same people who have inflated notions of what they can accomplish drafting tend to underestimate the need for careful revision. They hope to produce a near-perfect draft the first time, and limit their later work to fixing minor problems in spelling, grammar, and mechanics. The most effective writers reverse the emphases. They tend to write their drafts more quickly and freely and then spend greater amounts of time rewriting them.

They are the ones taking the etymology of revision seriously: *re-vision*, to see something a second time. They look for more from revision than just getting the bugs out of an otherwise adequate draft. For them, revision represents the full, systematic reworking of one paper into another richer, sharper, better one. They don't strive simply to make their rough draft less rough, but to develop a stronger, more interesting piece of writing altogether.

To revise, you review all that you know about your actual, real-life audience, in terms of age, education, reason for reading your work, dominant attitudes and preferences, and so on. You then assume precisely those characteristics, and then you confront your draft as if you had never seen it before. Here you are, robed in all the mental garments of your reader, and here is this piece of writing. Now, how does it look to you? The more thorough your self-transformation, the more accurately you will diagnose the strengths and weaknesses and possibilities of your paper, and the more constructive your revision will be.

To arrive at the most objective and useful idea of your draft possible, there are two things you can do. For one, you should put your draft out of sight as long as you can afford to before beginning to revise. Drafting itself brings you too close to your work to see it accurately. When you look it over, you're too likely to see what you *intended* to put in, rather than only those things *actually captured by the words on the page.* You should shelve your draft for a while—at least overnight and preferably longer—and come back to it with a clearer, fresher mind. You'll be better able to read as a newcomer and to see where you've left gaps or repeated yourself.

Your other best bet is to ask someone else to read your draft and tell you what she gets out of it. Don't ask her whether it's good or bad. That's not a useful question; neither answer helps you actually do much to improve your work. Ask your reader instead to summarize it for you, to tell you the main ideas of it, the main points you were getting across, and to do all this preferably without looking at it. Find out what sticks in her head. Then find out where she could follow your paper, where she was confused, what entertained or annoyed her, and so forth.

Few people are naturally observant and articulate critics. You'll need to guide them. Ask them specific, answerable questions about whatever aspects of the draft concern you, and simply note their answers. You don't need their *advice.* You don't need their *encouragement.* You simply need their *feedback* as readers. You're on a fact-finding mission. What you do with the facts is the question you have to answer back at your keyboard. Above all else, *never defend your work.* You'll only alienate your helpers and probably reinforce your own worst literary habits. If the criticism seems misguided or unjustifiably hostile, take note of it and move along.

Top-Down Revision: Content

You don't revise your paper best by starting at the first word and grinding through, dotting the i's and fixing commas as you go. *You revise most effectively by working first with the whole paper, then with the separate sections, then with smaller and smaller details.* Such matters as correcting spelling and fixing punctuation, though important, should not concern you until all the larger matters have been attended to.

Something we've repeatedly stressed and that's relevant again here is the degree to which *writing teaches the writer.*

You learn about your subject in brainstorming your ideas, you understand it better as a result of organizing them, and you find out still more as you draft. Many times, in fact, we only discover, in drafting the conclusion of a paper, what it is we've been trying to say all along. We half express our ideas, half discover them as we go. By the time your draft is done, you will probably be more knowledgeable and have a deeper understanding and insight into your material than when you started. As a result, you should now be able to write a more intelligent paper. As you revise, then, your first concern should be with content and purpose: what you actually said in your paper and why, and what you plan to say in the next edition.

To start, read your paper straight through, without so much as touching your pen. Read it end to end without stopping, as you would any article or story. Put it down again, out of sight, and try to summarize it, perhaps writing your summary on the back of it or on another sheet. Ask yourself the questions we suggested you ask your reader. What does this say? What are the main points being made? How does the whole thing strike me? Then start thinking about how you can use the material in this draft to write a new paper based on what you *currently* know about your topic, the new insights you came to as a result of actually drafting it. How can you make a smarter, more interesting, better-informed paper out of what you already have? What else do you need?

Ask yourself which parts of your paper stick most clearly in your mind. What parts of it seem most alive and interesting? Is your original focus in the paper—the thesis or question you had in mind when you started—still the strongest part of it? Or has the center of gravity shifted? Has an apparent side issue risen up to dominate the work? If so, should you focus on that when you rewrite it? Do you even agree with what you said the first time, or have you changed your mind? (A changed mind is, after all, usually an improved mind.)

These are the kinds of questions that motivate meaningful revision. What do I really want to say? What have I really said? How do I use what's here to say what I want in the final draft?

Write down your critical observations and your tentative revision plans for when you actually start your rewriting; that is, compile a set of revision notes. Don't try to hold in your head all the changes and developments you plan to make in your draft. Writing down and referring to your revision notes guarantees that your critical insights will actually pay off in terms of an improved final version.

Structure

As a rule, the more carefully you shape your material before you start drafting, the more coherent the draft will actually turn out. This is consistent enough to merit the time you put in at the beginning, but it's not foolproof. There are always surprises when you draft. One line of your outline suddenly takes three pages to explain; another whole section dries up in a couple of paragraphs. Furthermore, unless you're remarkably self-aware as you write, the version that winds up on paper will not fully represent the understanding in your mind. It will be shot through with gaps, digressions, and redundancies that will be invisible as you draft but will jump out at you when you reread. So, having read through your draft once to check its content, it's time to go through it again and assess how it actually hangs together.

In any kind of expository writing, the question of organization can be asked in terms of the reader's informational needs at every point in the essay. As you read through your paper, ask yourself repeatedly: Does my reader have all he needs to understand this paragraph, this sentence, right now? Have I prepared him to understand and appreciate this material when he arrives at it? Or will he feel as if I have towed him out to sea and cast him off without a compass?

There are two basic ways you can assess how close your draft comes to accomplishing all this. You can read your draft through, attending to its *subjective flow*. And you can stand back from your paper and discern its *objective shape*. These provide you different but complementary kinds of information on your draft, and make your revision of it more effective.

Subjective Flow   To assess your draft's flow, sit back, relax, and read it through again, from end to end, as you did when you were evaluating its content. Only this time, keep the pen in your hand. Read the draft fairly quickly; don't stop to mull it over too much. And as you read, keep track of your own reactions to the words on the page. As a newcomer to this paper, one who has never seen it before, does it make sense to you at every point? Do the ideas develop for you in a sensible, clear, and interesting fashion? Does it move along at an even, steady, pleasant pace?

Wherever you find the paper moving steadily, clearly, and pleasantly along, note it in the margin; a check mark will do. But, of course, you should also be on the lookout for other reactions as well. Do you feel the paper jarring or bumping anywhere? Do any passages confuse or surprise you? Does the draft seem to be wandering off course anywhere, losing its bearings, or even just losing steam? Where is it repeating itself, or even contradicting something it said elsewhere? Do any paragraphs seem as if they belong somewhere else, in another part of the paper? Do you find yourself wanting to skim over parts of it (a sure sign that something needs the axe)? Finally, where is the draft most urgent and engaging? And which parts leave your mind wandering?

It's not essential that you know what you plan to do about your draft at this point, only how it affects you. This is the diagnosis phase. Record the symptoms; note your reactions in the margins, as well as in your Revision Notes. You'll perform the surgery presently.

Objective Shape   Though reading your draft through in this manner often tells you all you need to know about your structure, sometimes the results are confusing or ambiguous. With longer papers especially, you may find it difficult to form a clear picture in your mind of how your draft fits together; in which case, you need to form a picture of your draft on paper. You need some sort of visual analog of your draft's structure, a diagram of its objective shape. So here's how you get one:

Step One: number your paragraphs. Step Two: write "1" on the first line of a fresh sheet of paper, read your first paragraph, and in just a few words write down its main theme or idea. Then write "2," read your second paragraph, write its main theme (next to the "2" of course), and so on. You should end up with a list of all the paragraph topics in your paper.

If you were to do this for the discussion on "Structure" so far, you might end up with something like this:

Structure
  1. Need to assess how coherent the draft is.
  2. Readers' informational needs.

3. Subjective "flow" and objective "shape"
Subjective Flow
  1. Read and note your reactions.
  2. Note smooth and bumpy passages; note in margin.
  3. Purely diagnosis; revision comes later.
Objective Shape
  1. Sometimes need a visual analog: shape.
  2. Numbering paragraphs—example.

If you find a particular paragraph especially difficult to summarize in a few words, you've probably already found one problem. If a paragraph goes in too many directions or touches on too many topics to capture its main theme in one line, you've probably got enough material in it for two separate paragraphs, or even more. You should consider dividing up your material into shorter, tighter units.

Once you're satisfied with the paragraphs individually, look at their overall arrangement. Have you really put all the apples with the apples, the grapes with the grapes? If the same topic shows up in several lines, you may be repeating yourself or leading your reader in circles.

Ask yourself if it's clear which topics are major and which are minor or supporting. Can you draw brackets in the margin, marking off major divisions in your material? Do these major divisions follow each other in the best order, or might you gain by moving Part Three up between Parts One and Two? Within each bracketed major section, do the paragraph topics seem to flow in some sensible order? Or should you rearrange subtopics within one part or another?

The acid test is the attempt to write these topic listings into standard outline format. Is it clear which topics deserve the roman numerals, which the capital letters, and so on? If organizational trees work better for you than outlines in designing your paper, you can use them here instead. Once you've worked your paragraphs into either an outline or a tree, you're in a position to see the shape of your paper as a whole and to consider restructuring it. Is the outline or tree you came up with the best possible for your material? Or, given the way your understanding of your topic has changed over the course of drafting, should you now rearrange the parts, shuffle the headings, and try a different structure?

Once you've assessed your draft's subjective flow and its objective shape, draw lines and arrows and boxes and diagrams to show how you'll stitch it together in your final version. Drawing these right on your draft will usually be sufficient. Otherwise, you might revise from a new outline or tree. Or you may even take scissors and tape to your draft, cut it into pieces, and stick it back together into something resembling its final form (or make the appropriate block moves if you use a computer). You still have all the finegrained matters to attend to—sentence style, grammar, spelling—but these will prove easier once the larger considerations are taken care of.

INTRODUCTIONS AND CONCLUSIONS

We bring these up now because this is the point in the writing process to deal with them—not sooner or later. Introductions and conclusions require careful work. Much stands or falls on how evenly and smoothly you lead your reader into your paper, and how cleanly and memorably you usher her out. Because they are so difficult and so important, they can paralyze you when you're trying to draft. Introductions especially, coming right at the beginning, can stall you before you even get started. Furthermore, what exactly an introduction needs to say usually can't be determined without reference to the paper as a whole. Since any major change in the draft will force changes in the introduction, you don't have the information to write it correctly the first time anyway.

In terms of procedure, then, our advice is to sketch your way through the introduction quickly on the rough draft, and get it behind you. Get it done and go on, and don't let its half-baked condition distract you. And do the same for the conclusion. Then, once you've reworked the content and organization of your paper, you can return to the opening and closing of it, knowing what you need to in order to do these right.

Writing Introductions

The introduction attempts to negotiate a sort of contract with your reader: If you, O Reader, will peruse this paper, I will reward you with such and such. You need, first of all, to let your reader know what you have to offer. State clearly the question or thesis you intend to pursue.

Your contract should also suggest the order in which you present your material: "The three groups most important in settling the American West were miners, farmers, and people in trade." You should, obviously, go on to discuss these groups in that order in your paper. How you present your material is also, in part, a matter of attitude or tone. If you're writing an angry editorial, strike that chord from the start. If you handle your material more lightly, let the style of your introduction reflect that.

Finally, your introduction needs to sell your paper. This doesn't mean indulging in all the vulgarities of TV advertising. It means showing in your introduction the real importance of your subject matter. What about this material makes you want to write about it? Does it revolutionize our thinking about some topic? Does it confirm old wisdom? Are you discussing a scientific principle capable of making major improvements in future medical technology? Are you presenting an ecological problem that, if not fixed, will increase rates of cancer in the next twenty years? If so, say so. Make it clear from the start why what you have to say is worth knowing, worth investing the time to read about.

As we've mentioned, over the course of drafting you often produce a paper different from the one you had planned, and usually a better one. As a result, your original introduction often no longer matches what you wrote. You have, obviously, two ways to correct this. You can stick by your original commitment and rewrite your paper to satisfy the contract. Or you can rewrite your contract to match your new product. The latter is always easier and almost always wiser.

Writing Conclusions

Whatever lasting effect your paper has will be determined in large part by its final one hundred words. The question you need to ask yourself here is: What do I want my readers to carry away? If you're writing a difficult, technical paper in a complex field, you might use the conclusion simply to summarize your arguments, to help your readers get your ideas straight one last time before stopping.

Most of the time, however, you can get more mileage out of your conclusion than that. You can suggest what new questions arise as a result of the material you've presented. You can note useful directions for future research. You can plant a question in your reader's minds. You can remind your readers again of the social or moral consequences of your topic. You can call for vigorous action of one kind or another.

If your conclusion is too conclusive, oddly enough, it may have a leaden, dulling effect on your readers. Like a *too* satisfying meal, it may put them to sleep. If, instead of just wrapping it up, you can introduce some new, interesting, provocative element into your conclusion, it may keep your ideas alive for your readers just that much longer.

SPIT AND POLISH

Revision, then, entails far more than just rephrasing your sentences. It means rethinking your content, rebuilding your structure, reworking your beginning and ending. But when these are more or less in place, revision still means a certain healthy amount of sandpaper and varnish. A rough, bumpy, jarring style—a meandering bog of long, twisty, verbose rivulets of language—a diffuse, hazy cloud of bureaucratic abstractions—any of these, by offending your reader and obscuring your meaning, can render all your previous efforts futile. You owe it to your reader, your subject matter, and yourself to write as clearly, smoothly, and straightforwardly as possible. As any professional can tell you, that requires a startling amount of effort.

Your best guides in stylistic revision are your voice and ear. If you read your draft out loud, you'll hear most of what you need to fix. Don't trust yourself to pick this up by reading silently. The actual sound of your words will indicate better than the marks on the page where your sentences are too choppy or where you've rambled on too long at a stretch. Also, don't expect to accomplish this task in one sitting. Read through your draft several times, separated by other activities.

Writing clean, straightforward, lucid expository prose has often more to do with integrity of intention than with skill. The writer who allows his love of his subject matter to excite him, and who desires sincerely and intensely to share this subject with an open-minded, benevolent reader, will contrive to write good sentences. He'll avoid getting fancy or stiff or overly sophisticated, and he will present his material in the clearest, most engaging way possible. If, on the other hand, the writer's primary goal is to present a particular, flattering portrait of himself—as an in-charge bureaucratic type or an ever-so-scientific sort or a hyper-sophisticated literary wizard—his prose will quickly become unendurable.

Another way to write badly is to fear your audience. Academics and politicians are especially prone to this. The effect on academic prose is to render it vague, elusive—at once towering and empty. You'll find sentences filled with qualifiers such as "could possibly be the case that" and "it has often been thought that" and "it could perhaps be argued. . . ." It looks at first like laudable precision, but it's really a failure of nerve.

As a point of honor, you should write in such a way that if you're wrong about something, you'll be caught immediately. Ignorance is forgivable (even largely curable). One hundred years from now, most of what we think we know will be stood on its ear. Your job is not to have the final, unchallengeable, unassailable word on anything; it's to advance a discussion. Being wrong in such a way that someone else can set you right does that. Wrapping your weaker arguments in an impenetrable haze of language does not. The sentence that can't be pinned down won't really inform anybody of anything. If you *can't* be proven wrong, how will you ever prove that you're *right?*

If your intentions are straight and you genuinely desire to share your ideas with your reader, stylistic revision will usually be a matter of cleaning and tightening—throwing away material more than adding it. Throw out redundant passages. Combine sentences with overlapping or repeating phrases. Rearrange your unwieldier sentences into subject-verb-object format. Strip out the unnecessary adverbs, adjectives, and qualifiers. (Scratch out all your "as we can clearly see" type phrases.) Exchange arcane polysyllabic jargon for common English words. You'll almost be able to see your ideas gain richness and color as they slide into better focus.

After the varnish comes the final touch-up and cleaning. Proofread your work end-to-end one more time. Now is the time to consult the dictionary, the grammar handbook, the punctuation guide. Make it perfect.

A GRAIN OF SALT

The model for brainstorming, organizing, drafting, and revising we've offered here represents the experience of thousands of writers, writing teachers, and editors. Most effective writers work in some fashion resembling what we've described. But they each also adapt the model according to their own situations and personal preferences (not to say eccentricities). The solid bedrock principle is this: *Do the job you're ready to do.* You can't revise something you haven't drafted. You won't get far outlining before you have something to say.

Within the broad boundaries of that one principle, though, writers have worked out for themselves an enormous range of approaches for getting the right words down on the page. Some do freewrites over and over, slowly refining their conception and their language, until they've freewritten themselves into a paper. Others outline with great care, so that drafting is short and sweet, and the emphasis in revision falls largely on stylistic matters. Some write entire drafts at breakneck speed, then spend hours (even days) cleaning up the wreckage. Others draft and polish each paragraph in turn, incapable of proceeding if the work behind them seems at all shabby. Experienced writers even vary their procedure for different works. The importance of careful blueprinting, for instance, rises with the length of the work you're doing.

The less experience or confidence you have as a writer, the safer you probably are following closely the model we've presented. On the whole, it will produce the best work for most people most of the time. It represents a sort of expert systems approach to writing, suitable for immediate adoption. But don't feel constrained by it. Keep track for yourself of what works for you and what doesn't, across a range of situations. Whatever works, keep doing it. Your course log is an excellent place to observe and record your results.

Above all, recognize that good writing both causes and requires *hard thinking.* Writing isn't the luxury of the power yacht, it's the labor of wrestling with mainsails and jibs, coming hard about, hoisting the spinnaker. The end result will be at least some blisters, a bit of windburn, and a few aches in the joints. But the experience is always, always worth the effort.

Chapter
5

In Search of Research

IT ALL STARTS WITH A QUESTION

Around three hundred years ago, Sir Isaac Newton formulated the principles of gravitational attraction that accounted for the movements of the planets. For this he was widely celebrated. His own account of his work, however, is telling. "If I have seen further than other men," Newton said, "it is because I have stood on the shoulders of giants." Research means standing on other people's shoulders (whether giants or not). It means making the most effective use of the experiences of others to answer a question of your own.

This doesn't mean copying or imitating others. It means formulating a question, deciding what information would be needed to answer it, finding out if anyone has that information, then assessing long and hard exactly what the information you find actually tells you about the question at hand. The dynamic impulse must be yours from the start. *You* start with a question, something *you* want to know, even if the general area has been chosen by someone else. You make the question your own; you *will* its solution for yourself.

From the very start you'll be writing in your notebook to think through the details and significance of your question.

Later you'll return to your notebook to record and analyze the information you find. Finally you'll present for a new reader your own best considered judgment on the issue in light of what you've discovered. Research should feel like detective work, like sleuthing. The more you experience the Holmesian sense of pursuit, the eagerness to hunt down the clues, assemble them into a pattern, and reveal the truth to your readers, the more vital and useful your research will be.

In this chapter we offer you strategies for planning and carrying out research on your particular question (whatever that may be), and for presenting an answer to your question making use of what you've found. This is not quite the same thing as "teaching the research paper." Our interviews with teachers make us doubt whether there even *is* such a thing as *the* research paper, or if those teachers who assign one all mean the same thing by it. Furthermore, much of what writing a research paper entails we have discussed in other chapters and will not be repeating here. Chapter Two, for instance, discusses at length how to read and understand an assignment, and Chapter Four presents strategies for developing, drafting, and revising longer papers. You may want to look through those now, if you haven't already.

If we're not sure about the status of The Research Paper, however, we are quite certain about the practice of research itself. It is still absolutely central in college education. Textbooks on any subject will only take you so far. They present the central, established, agreed-upon findings of a discipline, but they stop before reaching the borders. Outside the topics covered in a standard textbook lies The Beyond, the living, growing edge of a field of study, the Unknown toward which the field is striving. Sooner or later you will be asked to explore this zone for yourself. You will be asked to seek beyond the range of textbook and encyclopedia knowledge and examine the state of knowledge closer to the leading edge of exploration, where the conclusions are still in doubt and the most informed of scholars still disagree.

What we present in this chapter, then, are the general strategies and tactics for conducting research and using what you find. To start, we discuss in detail the importance of, and methods for, developing an interesting, useful, and workable research question. Then, once you've formulated what it is you're trying to learn, you need to find the most relevant and useful sources. Having found them, you must read, assess, and bring away from them whatever essential ideas and information they have to offer. You have to synthesize for yourself what all the material you've gathered adds up to, what it means for the question you originally set out to ask. And, finally, at the end of much labor, you need to present for your readers your best considered judgment on your original question in the light of what you've learned. You argue your case, calling the most useful witnesses in the most effective manner. These represent the basic steps of research regardless of the field of study or the type of paper you're writing, and they can all be done more efficiently with a little thought and a few suggestions. We can provide the suggestions.

What Kind of Question Are You Asking?

A crucial stage in developing any program of research, and one that is perhaps most often overlooked or given short shrift by students, is the formulating of an interesting, precise, workable, and appropriate question for research. There are, after all, an infinite number of excellent questions you can ask but that emphatically would not lend themselves to research. What is the truth about China? How do extraterrestrials breed? What is two plus two? What are the major themes of the lost plays of Sophocles? Or, as Bill Cosby's philosophy majors used to ask, "Why is there air?" These are all fair questions about real (or at least possible) entities, but for obvious reasons, as questions for research they would only lead you to despair.

Though few students would tackle any of these particular questions, they often attempt to research problems not much more workable. A grim percentage of student research papers run into trouble by virtue of a question that's too broad, too vague, or otherwise inappropriate. Arriving at an appropriate question for research, fortunately, is not just luck. Mostly, it's knowing what to look for. The criteria for determining the usefulness of a research question are largely a matter of common sense, but it may help you to have them spelled out here before going any further. Having presented a few guidelines for research questions, we will then outline a procedure for developing one.

Is Your Question Empirical?   Can your question be settled on the basis of some external, verifiable evidence? Can you answer your question by *looking at something?* No matter what the field of inquiry, and no matter how empirical evidence is defined there, writing a research paper involves an investigation of some sort. The opposite of an empirical question is an "armchair" question—one that can be settled without getting up from your Naugahyde recliner, one that you can simply think about to answer.

There's nothing inherently wrong with an armchair question. Mathematical questions often take this form and so do some questions in philosophy. Every empirical question, furthermore, also has several armchair components. Before even starting to search for evidence, you have to decide, for example, what counts as evidence to begin with, where to search for it, and how it might be useful in your research. You'll probably want to work out some of the answers to these questions from the desk in your study.

A research question, however, clearly requires you to *find something out.* If your question doesn't lend itself to such a process, if the whole question can be settled by chewing the intellectual cud, then no matter how excellent a question it might be in other ways, it probably doesn't lend itself to a research paper.

Is Your Question Interpretive?   Though your question should be empirical, it should also have an interpretive component. It can't, in other words, be "just the facts." Facts by themselves mean nothing. If someone shows you a table of numbers and says, "Isn't this incredible?" you're more likely to wonder if he's taken leave of his senses than to gasp in amazement.

Questions of the "true/false" variety or the "name that year" sort don't make especially interesting or compelling problems for research. The question, "When was John Brown born?" is certainly empirical—you can trot off to the library, locate a book, and find the answer—but having done so, you're still faced with the most critical question ever asked of a researcher: *so what?*

On the other hand, you could ask, "How did John Brown reconcile his violent attacks on bigots, some of whom he slaughtered in cold blood, with his compassion for black slaves before the Civil War?" There you have a question that still requires evidence for its answer—in the form of letters, diaries, trial proceedings, newspaper stories, retrospective accounts by friends and acquaintances, and so on—but that also requires careful analysis and interpretation of the evidence, once you've got it. These accounts, furthermore, may not all suggest the same answer to your question—which makes the research process all the more challenging. Your job is not only to dig up information relevant to your question but also to make sense of that information.

Does this mean you're "supposed to give your opinion?" Well, yes, in a sense, you have to. Your information simply won't add up to an answer on its own. With any piece of information you will have to ask, "What does this tell me about my research question? What does it contribute to an answer?" It's your job to review the cases for the prosecution and defense, consider the testimony of the witnesses, study the evidence of the ballistics and fingerprint experts, and finally determine "who done it." Merely heaping up your evidence and slipping out of the court room won't do the job.

Is Your Question Actually Researchable? While your question may be empirical, it may still not be researchable, at least in your lifetime. Much will depend on your time, background, and resources. If you're a professional researcher a short car ride from the Library of Congress in Washington, you can tackle grander and more specialized questions than if you're a student working under the constraints of a tight deadline and a small-town public library.

This matter of feasibility shouldn't be taken lightly. Bite off too much and you'll be panicking all the way to your "Incomplete." Here's an example: Among some patients who have suffered minor strokes, there's a strange and very rare affliction which is called "foreign language syndrome." Apparently, these few patients, soon after their strokes, speak their native language with a distinctive and authentic foreign accent. Speakers of English have been known to sound exactly like Polish, French, or German immigrants, even though they have never learned these other languages, have never visited the countries where they're spoken, have no relatives or friends who speak the languages, and so on. Soon after recovery, their foreign accent disappears as mysteriously as it developed. No one, not even the best of experts, knows for sure what causes this syndrome.

If you chose for your research the question, "What causes foreign language syndrome in stroke patients," you'd be joining hundreds of professionals in neuropsychology and psycholinguistics who continue to shake their heads in wonder over this affliction. But unless you were a professional in one of these fields, it's unlikely that you could either conduct experimental research or read and understand other people's research well enough to begin answering the question. So while such a question is empirical, it's just not practical to set out to answer it in the context of a typical college research paper—at least, not until further evidence has accumulated.

Does Your Question Interest You?   Nothing else is as important as your motivation for the research. Answering a question that bores you will make uncovering every book and article like digging sewer lines in a cold rain on Monday morning. Ask yourself, "What draws me, interests me, intrigues me?" When your research is really interesting, you won't even notice the midnight oil running low. Moreover, since research projects take a while to accomplish, you'll do yourself a favor by finding a topic you can live with, day in and day out for most of the semester, without wanting to shoot yourself. (It's very important in research that you not shoot yourself.)

Moving from Hunch to Developed Question.   You want to arrive, then, at a question for your research that is:

- Empirical (answerable on the basis of external evidence);
- Interpretive (requiring careful analysis of the evidence you find);
- Researchable, given your actual time and resources;
- Genuinely interesting to you.

Such questions don't usually just fall out of the air. They are the result of careful thought and reflection. Here are some steps you can follow to develop as interesting and appropriate a question as possible.

List Major Areas of Interest.   Many people's almost automatic response to having to find a research topic . . . is to go completely blank. If this happens to you, a good first step is simply to list all the topics you can think of—good or bad, dull or clever, interesting or boring, appropriate or off the wall. It doesn't matter. Put 'em all down. Sometimes ideas silly in themselves lead to excellent ideas down the road. Suppose you're in a senior seminar on Technology and the Human Spirit. A beginning list of topics for your paper in the seminar might look like this:

Technology—Televisions—Telephones—
Communications Technology—Medical technology—
Organ Donation—Birth Control—The Printing Press—
H. G. Wells—Jules Verne—Weapons systems—
The Atomic Bomb—Word Processors—
Environmental Problems—Air Safety—Science fiction—
Respirators and the Right to Die—Cryogenics—
Nuclear Energy

There's no telling where any of this is going yet. Your final question may develop from any of these topics, or you might need to do more listing still before hitting upon something that engages your interest. In fact, we can pretty much guarantee that more than 90 percent of this listing will end up in the round file. But if it gets you—finally—to a topic you'd like to pursue, then it's been worthwhile.

Consider What Subfields Your General Topic Area Comprises.   Break out your topic into its major divisions, as if you planned to write an enormous volume on the subject and these were its main chapter titles. Then break those down further, producing a deeper tree (see pages 121–130) or outline (see pages 130–136) or table of contents for the topic. Keep on dividing the topics at each new level, longer than you think you need to.

Early Russian Tribes;
Russia during the Middle Ages;
Russia under Catherine the Great;
Nineteenth-Century Czarist Russia;

The Revolution;
Stalin, Khrushchev, Brezhnev;
Gorbachev and the Liberalization.

Each of these in turn could be subdivided even more. The "last chapter," for instance, might yield:

Gorbachev's Early Struggles;
Glasnost;
Perestroika;
Changes in Central Europe;
The 1989 Revolutions;
USSR and US Relations;
Relations with the Third World;
Russian Journalism.

And, of course, each of these potential chapters could be further subdivided yet. In time you should move from such global topics as "Russia" to much more specialized areas, such as "Glasnost and Modern Russian Journalism." Or you should get from "Geology" to "Slippage Rates along the San Andreas Fault," or from "National Economics" to "ICC Regulations and Inflation in 1990-1991."

In James Joyce's *Portrait of the Artist as a Young Man*, Stephen Dedalus writes the following on the flyleaf of his geography textbook, to identify himself:

Stephen Dedalus

Class of Elements

Clongowes Wood College

Sallins

County Kildare

Ireland

Europe

The World

The Universe

You want to do something akin to this, but in reverse.

You've chosen, say, to research something about African tribal communities—Great, we say, but don't stop there.

Okay, so you narrow it down to tribal rituals.—Very good, but don't stop there either. Can you choose a particular tribe?

All right, you answer, how about the Lugbara of Uganda? —Keep going; what sorts of rituals?

Well, the most intense are the puberty rites.—Good, keep going.

Maybe particular aspects of the rites could be examined in greater and more precise detail: dancing, blood letting or ritual scarring, the functions of sexuality.—*Now* you've got something like a focused topic!

When you're doing this, you might want to consult either the *Library of Congress List of Subject Headings* or the index of any good encyclopedia. There you will find thousands of topics already broken into subtopics, and this might direct you in finding a suitably narrow focus of your own. (How many of us, after all, just happened to know about the Lugbara of Uganda off the top of our heads?)

In any kind of research, depth is more impressive than breadth. Only by aiming to be a specialist in your field can you dig deeper than encyclopedia-level generalities. You should define an area narrow enough for you to become a genuine expert in. Your material, in any case, will almost certainly expand as you develop it.

Review What You Already Know About Your Topic. Sketch a summary of your current knowledge. If this strikes you as an impossibly huge task, you're probably dealing with too broad a topic. *What do I know about the social consequences of the Vietnam War in the U.S.?* To answer that would take you pages of scribbling and would be far too broad. *What do I know about the lives of Vietnam War veterans in the U.S.?* This is better; but if you're in a course focusing on Vietnam, you might still find yourself able to fill up several pages on your own. *What do I know about the success of interracial marriages between Vietnam War vets and the Vietnamese lovers they returned to find and bring back to the U.S. after the war?* Now you're getting there. What *do* you know? Probably, even in a course on Vietnam, not much. This might be pay dirt.

Transform Your Suitably Focused Topic into a Live, Interesting Question.   A topic by itself is a dead, inert, stiff sort of thing. "Glasnost and Modern Russian Journalism." There it lies. Well, what about it? What is it you want to know?

You might start by asking yourself the "so what" question. What about your topic interests you? Who's affected by it? Why are you interested in Glasnost and modern Russian journalism? Does the topic primarily interest you as a chapter in the history of journalism, the history of Russia, or the career of Mikhail Gorbachev? Or does some theoretically interesting point about communications theory or international politics hang on the answer? What makes your topic more attractive than others you might have chosen?

A vague enthusiasm won't help you here. You need to articulate your answer on paper. Don't trust yourself to just sense why your topic is interesting. Write it out. Answering this question gains you two things. It will help focus your efforts later when you're actually doing your research, and the words you write in your notebook now may very well find their way into your introduction when you draft. By, in a sense, *introducing* the topic to yourself, you'll find it easier to introduce it to someone else later.

Once you know what interests you about your topic, go on to specify your exact research question. If you think a bit, you can cook up several quite different questions about the Russian journalism topic:

- How have the policies of Glasnost actually affected the reporting in the two newspapers, *Pravda* and *Tass?*
- What did Russian journalists have to do with bringing about the adoption of the policies of Glasnost in the first place?
- How did Russian journalists cover Glasnost itself during its development and inception?
- How has Glasnost affected the underground press in Russia?
- What is the actual degree of freedom of the press in Russia, and what are the chances of its surviving or collapsing?

These are all questions you could derive from the topic "Glasnost and Modern Russian Journalism." But each requires you to find different sources of information, and to interpret and present your material in different ways. Your research will be much more efficient if you know which question you're actually out to answer.

Develop a List of Subsidiary Questions. Whatever your main research question, the answer to it will probably not be a simple Yes or No, or a single name (Guy de Maupassant), or a single figure (47 percent). If it's the sort of thing that requires a written report, it will actually be a composite answer to a number of smaller questions. Once you've formulated your main question, you should spend some time brainstorming as many of these subsidiary questions as you can.

Suppose, for example, you're involved in a group project in your business course and you've been assigned to assess the feasibility of implementing flextime scheduling at a fictitious stereo components assembly plant. Having formulated your question and written some notes about its importance, you might continue by asking yourself, and writing down, questions such as these:

- What exactly is flextime? How does it compare with other scheduling options (like permanent part-time)?
- How has it been implemented at some real companies?
- How has it affected productivity at places where it has been used?
- What schedules prove most popular with employees?
- What administrative problems does it cause?
- How do employees on flextime perform in comparison with straight time employees?
- How would we have to adapt our equipment and procedures to handle differing numbers of workers at different hours?
- What is the feeling about flextime among our workers?

All of this early work on a research problem is strenuous but probably one of the most interesting and useful parts of the process. It may feel easier to sleepwalk into the library and start randomly "looking stuff up." But in the long run, the present approach not only produces a more focused, intelligent paper, it's more efficient as well. Any effort put in at this point saves a great deal of time later. This all, again, is the armchair component of your empirical research project. This is where you study the travel guides, pore over the maps, and plan and revise your itinerary. Only then will you pack your bags and head off for the mountains.

FINDING THE BEST SOURCES AND GETTING THE MOST FROM THEM

Suppose for a moment that you're working on your Ph.D. in marine biology. Under the direction of your adviser, Dr. Elliott, you've decided to study the rather elaborate feeding habits of *ansoniae culinaris* (known to collectors as the "Glittering Gourmandizer"). *A. culinaris* can only be found schooling along certain parts of the Great Barrier Reef in Australia, and the fish has been only very little studied till now. You have applied for and received a grant to travel to Australia, gather live specimens of the Gourmandizer, and return to your university, where you plan to breed the species in captivity, and try to make sense of its remarkable nutritional preferences. So you fly to Australia, gather your nets and your live traps, and then have to decide how most efficiently to find and capture enough specimens of this elusive species.

After pondering the problem, and discussing it with other collectors in the area, you break the problem down into a series of steps which, if followed with care, should result in your capturing enough good specimens for study. You synthesize your strategy in your notebook as follows:

STEP ONE: Explore broadly and freely the various coral reefs and other biologically important waters around Australia. I want to get the general lay of the land (or, in this case, water). Develop a general picture of what kinds of fish occupy what areas. This should stand me in good stead, whatever I run into.

STEP TWO: Make use of whatever advice or guidelines I can find to help me decide what waters to cast my nets in. Since I can't cover the entire Barrier Reef, and I don't already know exactly where *a. culinaris* schools, I need to pick the likeliest waters and cast my nets and set my live traps there.

STEP THREE: Once I've found the more promising waters, I need to cast my nets and set my live traps in them as widely and evenly as possible.

STEP FOUR: Release immediately all fish that a mere glance will tell me *aren't* Gourmandizers.

STEP FIVE: Anything that clearly is *a. culinaris*—capture and put into holding tanks immediately. If in doubt about positive identification, put in holding tanks to be safe. If, upon closer inspection, the fish does prove to be *a. culinaris*, great. If not, release it then. Better safe than sorry.

STEP SIX: Return with sufficient genuine *a. culinaris* specimens to the lab. Begin formal study of feeding habits.

This would, in fact, almost certainly be the best approach. Find the likeliest waters, spread your nets, capture your fish, sort out Gourmandizers from others, study the Gourmandizers at more length.

It's also very analogous to how you organize and conduct research, once you've developed an interesting, focused research question. You don't simply dive into the stacks and start thrashing about. That would be like diving into the Barrier Reef anywhere, netting whatever swam by, and hoping for the best. It would take an extraordinary amount of time to gather anything, and it still wouldn't really be what you were after. Yet many students behave in exactly this fashion.

Instead, you want to apply the very sensible search strategy you used for *a. culinaris* to find the most useful sources of information for precisely the question you're trying to answer.

1. Do a little free exploring (in the form of background reading) to develop a sense of the intellectual terrain.
2. Use whatever guides you can to decide where in the library to search.
3. Search widely in the most likely spots and note all potentially useful titles.
4. Divide sources by apparent usefulness; discard the unuseful immediately.
5. Review more carefully the remaining sources to assess which are the *really* helpful and necessary ones.
6. Take those home, in some fashion, to study and analyze in depth.

In the pages that follow, we'll describe each of these steps, and the reasons for them, in more detail. It may sound complicated at times, but the result of our discussion should ultimately both save you time and improve the quality of your work.

The Promise and Perils of Research

Every source, whether interview or written text, has the potential to be a gold mine or quicksand. The greatest danger in conducting research is being sucked under by everything you read, being dragged slowly, agonizingly, paragraph by paragraph across articles that, however little they contribute to your work, you somehow can't get out of. Since every article becomes such a tedious, grinding effort, you'll naturally try to get by with as few as possible. As a result, you don't cover all the ground you need to, leaving broad aspects of your question insufficiently researched.

And even the articles you read don't yield you all that they could. To be sure, you read every word in them, and you perhaps even fill pages with quotations and numbers, but still somehow your memory of the articles afterwards is foggy, muddy, clogged. This is an unpleasant way to work, and it produces feeble results. It's also very easy to fall into.

Most often such problems stem from an overly vague or formless plan of research. If you don't have much idea what you're looking for, you can't ignore or reject or screen out anything. If all you're sure of is that you want to "do some research about AIDS," whole shelves of volumes will require your attention. This is part of why we stress narrowing your topic and formulating a precise research question before going anywhere near the library. The more precise your sense of what you're looking for, the more articles you can actually *avoid* reading, with the result that the ones you do read will be more directly relevant to your topic. One glance at the *Reader's Guide to Periodical Literature* should convince you of the wisdom of this.

Knowing what you're looking for—that is, having a carefully framed main question and rich accompanying list of subsidiary questions—serves a similar purpose for each separate interview you conduct or article you read. In both situations your task is the same: to extract from your source the information you need quickly and efficiently. Take what you need, skim the rest, and move on to the next source. How best to do that depends on the kind of source you're consulting.

Having said that, we want to recognize the person who just asked, "But isn't there something to be said for just browsing around?" Yes. Plenty of time, freedom in the domain of your research, and a strong sense that you'll stumble on something really interesting—all of these do support a more exploratory approach. But let's face it: normally you're under pressure, the term is marching along, and the deadline for the project is looming ominously in your already full calendar. Wandering around in the stacks may be relaxing, but it won't get your paper started.

A more useful kind of wandering happens when you've already settled on a specific question to research and, as you begin digging up material, you learn something you didn't know which leads you off in a new direction. One of us, on a family trip to Arizona, didn't realize that the Hopi Indian reservations held such a wealth of artisans creating unique paintings, pottery, and other works of art. We soon abandoned our plan to drive straight back to Phoenix from the Grand Canyon via the main highway and headed off into the deserts of east-central Arizona in search of treasures—which we found in abundance. When you learn something in the process of your research which strongly tempts you to deviate from your well-mapped route, follow your hunch. Your entire paper could move into richer, more intriguing, more interesting territory yet. Even if it doesn't, you've seen more of the land.

Background Reading (Learning the Waters)

If you've narrowed your topic sufficiently for a well-focused paper, you may still head off into the jungle of literature only to find yourself entangled in a bewildering thicket of complex terms and ideas, thrashing around and crying for a guide. If you've decided to study the migration patterns of South American killer bees toward the southern United States, a quick glance through the general work on bees may help you to develop a context for your work before diving into the article from the *International Journal of Entomological Demographics.* If you're quite new to the subject, in fact, an hour or so spent with a standard encyclopedia may provide you a sort of aerial photograph of the country you're exploring.

Right here, in fact, is where one or more good encyclopedias are most likely to be of help to you. Encyclopedias come in two broad varieties, the general and the specialized. The major general encyclopedias you're probably already familiar with: *The Encyclopedia Americana, Collier's Encyclopedia, The New Columbia Encyclopedia, Encyclopedia International*, etc. These will give you a reliable, broad grounding in whatever you're studying. But for most topics, you should also consult one or more of the most appropriate specialized encyclopedias in your field. Because they devote all of their pages to a more restricted content area, the specialized encyclopedias can afford to go into more detail than the general, though still without assuming more than ordinary previous knowledge on your part. Since you're less likely to be familiar with the startling range of specialized encyclopedias available, we've listed a small fraction of them below:

International Encyclopedia of Statistics

Encyclopedia of Religion

Encyclopedia of Philosophy

Encyclopedia of Crime and Justice

International Encyclopedia of the Social Sciences

Encyclopedia of Education

Encyclopedia of Educational Research

McGraw-Hill Encyclopedia of Science and Technology

New Grove Encyclopedia of Music and Musicians

Encyclopedia of Historic Places

Dictionary of National Biography

Who's Who

Dictionary of Scientific Biography

Even this list, of course, represents only a few of the available resources in a given area. In Religion, for example, there are at least a dozen well-known encyclopedias in addition to the *Encyclopedia of Philosophy,* including *The Catholic Encyclopedia, An Encyclopedia of Religion,* and *The New Standard Jewish Encyclopedia.* The same goes for most other fields.

The decision to begin with something more general, of course, will depend on how familiar you already are with the research literature you're gathering. If you're enrolled in an introductory course in modern art, you may not have a fund of prior knowledge about various research topics, and some general reading could help. If you're in a senior-level course on the history of World War II, on the other hand, you may bring plenty of previous reading with you to dive straight into your work on Erwin Rommel. In either case, don't be tempted to choose a more general topic just because you have a more general knowledge. Be specific from the start.

Locating the Most Useful Sources

Having read enough at the textbook or encyclopedia level to know your way around, you then start gathering leads for the most immediately relevant and helpful sources on your question. You don't need to be reading anything in detail yet. You're just assembling a list of possible leads. As in your search for *a. culinaris,* you want to cast your net in the most promising waters, cast it wide, and draw it back in with as many fish as you can. The more carefully and diligently you do this, the more actual Glittering Gourmandizers you're going to find.

For most of the research you do, you'll depend primarily on written sources, and that means time in the library. Now a library is a magnificent resource, but it can be dangerous as well. A library is like an island of buried treasure, sometimes astonishingly well-buried indeed. As with all buried treasure, you can't dig just anywhere and hope to find it. Most students spend far more time than they need to in a library, only to come away with a fraction of the gold that's there.

As we've stressed, the first thing you need to know is what you're looking for: your core question and your list of subsidiary questions. Without these, you won't be able to tell the fool's gold from the real. You should also develop, if you haven't already done so, a fine working relationship with the librarians. These are the people who know the island well, and even if they don't immediately have the time to show you around, they have plenty of maps.

Thinking About Your Subject Headings (Deciding Where to Fish)

The information in a library is sorted generally in two ways, by subject and by author. Unless you're actually doing research on the writings of one particular person—Mark Twain, Julian of Norwich, Alice Walker, Charles Darwin—you will almost always start searching by subject. Card catalogues, computerized listings, printed bibliographies and indexes—all of these sort knowledge into conventional content categories. This all seems obvious enough but it can raise a curious and sometimes mystifying question: what is your subject *called?* Since relevant information on your topic is likely to be identified by a variety of names, what are the most likely headings under which to find useful sources listed?

Suppose, again, you're researching the question: "How has Glasnost affected the actual reporting practices of the two Russian newspapers, *Pravda* and *Tass?*" Will you look under "Glasnost"? This might work for the most recent sources—readers' guides, bibliographies, etc.—but the card catalogue probably won't list it. Will you look under Soviet, Russia, newspapers, journalism, communications, press, censorship, Eastern Europe or some other subject headings entirely? Where do you want to start casting your nets, anyway?

Or suppose you're researching a question concerning movement of the Pacific Plate and risks to homeowners on the San Andreas fault. The sorts of headings you might look under would include: Pacific Plate, plate tectonics, earthquakes, geology, continental drift, San Andreas fault, California, fault lines, earthquake prediction, Richter scale, seismograph, seismology, seismometer. And who knows? You might also look under houses, house construction, architecture, building, home insurance, natural disasters, etc.

You can start all this on your own. Simply by pondering your question, you can probably intuit a number of likely subjects to search under. You can also consult the notes you wrote in developing your research question. If you started from a broad topic and narrowed it down in stages, you might be able to simply use some or all of the earlier, broader topics as your leads in searching the card catalogues and printed guides.

Once you have a few guesses, however, you should use these to search even further. Go to the library and look up your topic in the index of one or more good encyclopedias. There you will probably find it listed, divided into subtopics, and related to parallel topics or broader ones. You can enter the index of the encyclopedia with two or three reasonable headings and leave with a dozen. And one source you should definitely consult is the *Library of Congress List of Subject Headings.* This is a massive work (in three monstrous red volumes) filled with *nothing but* subject headings. Its importance lies in the fact that practically every library in the country organizes its card catalogue by the headings listed in these volumes. If the *LC List* carries your exact topic, you will certainly be able to find it in the card catalogue. It will also usually list narrower topics, broader topics, and related topics. If it doesn't list your subject as a formal heading, it might at least tell you what to look under. And if your subject isn't mentioned at all, you'll need to guess again at what it might be called.

From Subject Headings to Working Bibliography (Casting Your Net)

The subject headings tell you only where to start looking for sources on your question. They're only categories of sources; they're not the sources themselves. You still need to search these headings in card catalogues, indexes, and readers' guides; find titles of possibly useful books, articles, or pamphlets, and record the information necessary to look them up. Your list of all these titles—the ones that look like they're at least worth laying your hands on—is your *Working Bibliography.* Over the course of your research, you will constantly revising this list. You will find new titles to add. You'll look up a certain number of works, only to find they don't help you, and scratch them off the list. And the final survivors—the works you consult and actually use—will remain as the formal bibliography at the end of your actual paper.

So now is when you actually flip through the card catalogue or run searches of subject headings at the computer screen, finding out what books your library carries under each. Now is when you look in the *Reader's Guide to Periodical Literature* or any number of the other, more specialized bibliographies and indexes, whether in print or on-line. This is when you consult *The MLA International Bibliography, Psychology Abstracts,* or whatever the important listings of publications are in your field.

For each possible source, you will want to write down its title, author, publication, date, page numbers—whatever you'll need to find an actual copy of it. And if there's any other information about the source—a thumbnail summary, précis, or abstract—you'll want to write that down as well. Consider each title in turn, and if it looks relevant, note it. Later, once you have a long list of these, you can drop the ones that sound only loosely related to your topic, and just try to lay your hands on the more potentially useful ones. You're engaging here in poker logic: you draw as many as you can, in order to have the best hand left after you discard. You want a long list of titles, with any other information about them you can find to help you weed out your list.

Though your search for relevant sources represents one of the earlier phases in a research project, it never really stops. The books and articles you find will themselves have made use of earlier sources, and they will frequently have a list of these sources at the end. With every book and article you examine, you should see if it does, in fact, carry its own bibliography. And if it does, steal it. Make a point to search it for any other titles that look relevant to your work, and add them to your Working Bibliography as well. This is not really theft, after all; it's legitimate use (sorry to say), and it's part of what the bibliography is there for in the first place. If you're reading an article directly related to your question, the sources listed in its bibliography have a high probability of being relevant as well.

Reading Like a Researcher (Examining What You've Netted)

Once you've located the most relevant sources for your question, you need to *carry away the most useful information they contain.* This means reading and understanding the material, and then recording in your notes what you will need to have on hand when you actually start drafting your paper. As always, the secret is to stay on the offensive. Knowledge has to be pursued. It doesn't select itself out and imprint itself on the blank, passive mind.

The first thing you should do, once you've decided to give a book or an article or any other printed source your careful consideration, is to make sure you have down in your notes all of the bibliographic information you'll ever need: title, author, publication, date, page numbers, edition, translator, and so on. It's terribly easy to forget to do this; you have to have the information, and you'll kick yourself if you have to make a special trip to the library to get it later. Once that's done, you can then turn to your real intellectual labor.

Search for the Gist. First try to come to an overall understanding of the piece. You might start by reading just the beginning and ending of it and noticing whatever subtitles it may have in between. That should give you a good idea of where the article's going, its main point, and how it goes about defending or illuminating that point. You should formulate some hypothesis about the article's major directions before trying to plough through it. At least try to see the forest before wandering in among the trees.

Read the article quickly, end-to-end, and at this point try not to take any notes. The minute you start writing down interesting statements or paraphrasing ideas, you stand in danger of bogging down in irrelevant detail. Move through the article easily and quickly to try to grasp its main outlines in its entirety.

Write a Summary. Once you've read the article through, try to abstract or summarize it in your notes. Holding the entire article poised in your mind, how would you state in a few pithy sentences what the writer was saying? If you're not sure you can do this yet, glance back over it. Reread the opening and closing sections. The author may have stated her thesis quite directly and simply somewhere. Which one sentence best captures the main gist of the piece? (See pages 66–68 for more detailed directions on how you might set about doing this.)

Bullet the Main Ideas. When you've defined what the author was saying, sketch in the major supporting points and arguments. Try to get down how she attempted to prove her point or how she illustrated it. Did the author rely on experimental procedures, anecdotal evidence, chains of logical deduction, or some combination of these? At this point, you're still examining the article from the author's perspective rather than from the perspective of your own question. What did the author claim and how did she support it?

Now that you've sketched in the thesis and method of the work, you can start thinking again of what in it might be relevant to your own concerns. Without looking back, what do you remember seeing that struck you as useful in trying to settle the question you've framed? Is the author's main point itself relevant to your concerns, or is one of the chains of reasoning? Or were there anecdotes or statistics which the author used for one purpose but which you can turn to another?

Focus on Your Question Again.   Think again now of what it is you're trying to answer: your own question, not the author's. What here is useful to you? Find it, reread it, and then get the pertinent parts down in your notes. Your notes may consist of straight summaries and paraphrases of ideas in the article. Or you might want to get down the precise words the author used. If you do decide to quote directly, you need to transcribe the passage flawlessly, down to the comma placement; or, better still, find the relevant pages and photocopy them.

By now you should have the following material in your notes:

1. The precise bibliographical reference of the material.
2. An abstract or summary of it.
3. An outline of the major arguments or pieces of evidence the author presents to prove or illustrate his point.
4. Paraphrases, summaries, transcriptions, or highlighted photocopies of the passages in the article most useful in answering your specific research question.

Now Stand Back.   You have what you came for. You've found the most relevant articles, and you've preserved in your notes the material in them of greatest usefulness in answering your own research question. Now you want to spend some time thinking aloud in your notes about what the information actually means. Try to answer in your notebook some of the following questions:

- Why is this material important? How does it affect my understanding of the issue I'm examining? Does it support a hypothesis of mine concerning my question? Does it challenge my understanding and force me to rethink my position?
- What is surprising about this material? Is the article itself internally consistent, or does the author contradict himself in different parts of it?
- How does this material fit with other things I have read? Does it reinforce earlier sources? Does it correct earlier sources in some detail or point of reasoning or other? Does it refute outright points made in other readings?
- If the material I've just read does conflict with other sources, is the conflict apparent or real? Can both positions possibly be true? Or is one of my sources necessarily wrong? If only one can be correct, which is it? What makes me say that?

The art of research, again, is emphatically *not* to march forth with a preconceived opinion about something, find some sources that support your position and cite those as experts, and find others that refute your position and debunk those. All that does is to entrench you in your original position, making you more articulate in your prejudice perhaps, but certainly making you no less prejudiced.

Research should be the active attempt to build on the work of other thinkers, observers, and writers in order to understand something *better*—and that means *differently*—than you did before. That's why this brooding phase of the research process is so vitally important. You get nowhere simply collecting facts. You need to think long and hard about what the facts mean. This is where you make your most distinctive contribution, in reassessing what others have learned and thought. This is where you go beyond bagging intellectual groceries to genuine culinary art.

Though this may slow down the research part of your job itself, you'll receive the practical payoff when it's time to draft. You won't find yourself sitting there with a stack of photocopied articles and notes, wondering where to begin to make sense of it all. You'll arrive at the drafting stage of your work with a well-developed sense of what you now know. You'll probably, in fact, find many passages already written in your notebook that you can clean up a little and incorporate straight into your draft. For the rest, even the sections you have to draft fresh will come to you more easily for having given your material such long and careful consideration. And there won't be the slightest danger of turning in a string-of-sources paper. The paper will be yours, not theirs. It will belong to and represent you, not your sources.

PRIMARY VS. SECONDARY RESEARCH

The sort of research we've been discussing so far—"standing on the shoulders of others"—is called *secondary* research. It's secondary because it synthesizes the results of other people's work, who did *primary* research—who looked directly at their object of study rather than merely reading about it. Reading and synthesizing articles about Koko, the chimpanzee trained to "talk" with the use of plastic symbols, is secondary research. Raising a chimpanzee yourself, spending hours a day with it in the lab teaching it what the symbols mean, and observing and analyzing what it does with them is primary research.

Secondary research can be, and usually is, conducted entirely from the resources of a good library. The resources required for primary research vary quite a bit depending on your field. Obviously, the facilities needed for primary research in chimpanzee language learning are difficult to come by. A few universities maintain such laboratories but not many. And it's hardly the sort of experiment you can conduct in your dorm or apartment, even with the most astonishingly patient of roommates. Some sociological research, by contrast, may require only that you write up a questionnaire, distribute it, collect it, and tally and interpret the results. To take yet another case, imagine what's required for radiotelescopic studies of quasars. [Suggestion: if you want to research this, get someone else to pay for it.]

Primary research in some subjects, on the other hand, may still require only a collection of specific texts. A historian, for instance, may be interested in congressional opinions about the sanctity of life in the period from 1850 to 1900. The "raw data" here will be government documents, contemporary newspapers and magazines, letters, and journals. The procedure for finding and analyzing such information and arriving at an answer to her question will not differ significantly from the process of secondary research we've been presenting.

For obvious reasons, then, most research-based papers assigned in college require secondary rather than primary research. Even in some undergraduate courses, however, you may be asked to conduct and report on laboratory experiments, direct observations of events rather than written accounts of them. You may be asked to design, conduct, analyze, and report on an experiment tied somehow to the general content of the course. You may be asked to do a survey of public attitudes about a certain product in an introductory marketing course. You may take notes on a site visit to a developmental hospital in a course in human genetics. Or you might find yourself writing research-based papers in a laboratory course in chemistry, biology, or animal learning. All such assignments pose different kinds of research and writing tasks than does secondary research, though the same general principles apply.

In terms of the effectiveness of your final report, the game is going to be won or lost in the notebook work you do along the way. Any time you set up shop in the laboratory without your notebook beside you, you're probably wasting your time (at the very least, you're overtaxing your memory). The effectiveness of your final report will depend, after all, on two things: (1) how methodically and accurately you describe what you did and observed; and (2) how well you explain the reason for the experimental design and the significance of the outcomes. Regular and careful attention to your notes as you're conducting your research will raise your odds of succeeding at both of these tasks.

Defining Your Question

Just as in secondary research, you want to begin on primary research by defining your question as carefully as you can. What precisely are you trying to answer? It may take you several attempts to state this correctly, succinctly, and unambiguously—but it has to be done. Since you'll need this material in the introductory section of your final report in any case, you might as well get started. Furthermore, if you can't state the question itself with precision, you really don't have any guarantee that the method you're following will answer it. You can't design a sharp, elegant, useful research methodology to answer a vague, ill-defined question.

If you want to be absolutely sure you understand the problem and the logic of your proposed method for solution, try explaining it so that a fairly intelligent high school sophomore could understand it. There's the acid test. Your temptation may be to explain the question and method just well enough for your instructor to figure it out; after all, she's your real audience. But this runs the risk of depending too heavily on her understanding to make sense of your account. It's too easy to get the question sort of vaguely roughed out and decide that your instructor can put it together from there. "He knows this stuff. He'll see what I'm doing." You may just be throwing up a smoke screen of technical jargon to hide the fact (perhaps even from yourself) that *you* really don't understand the logic of what you're doing, after all.

Instead, force yourself to get the logic of your question and methodology as straight and clear as you can from the beginning. The best way to do that, again, is to explain them in your notebook for someone who knows *less* than you do. You might, in fact, show your account to another student outside of your course, just to see how well he or she understands it.

Keeping Up Your Log or Notebook

While you're carrying out your research, take careful, regular notes on what you're doing at every step. Don't get ahead of yourself. It's very difficult to reconstruct accurately from memory the actual steps you followed in any complex research project, especially if the research involves doing something you've done so often that it has become second nature—running a particular computer program, for example, or testing various electronic components. If you're doing something that you can do in your sleep, it will be, oddly enough, just that much more difficult to call to mind and describe all the individual steps involved. In your final report, you'll need to describe everything you did in enough detail that a newcomer could replicate your procedure exactly. This will be easier if you've been recording your actions in detail as you go.

Similarly, you should describe whatever you're observing as you're observing it, or as soon thereafter as possible. This is yet another reason for keeping your notebook with you. Imagine examining a particular bit of plant tissue under the microscope—stained to make the major structures more visible—and then having to wait three days before having a chance to sketch what you saw. You'd never begin to capture the sort of detail you could record if you had your pad and pencil right on the table beside you. The same logic applies to virtually every observational task. Record what you see ASAP—immediately if not sooner.

Reflecting and Analyzing

Take some time every so often to reflect on the significance of what you've observed. What's happening? What do your early findings suggest? What other questions do they raise? What other experiments or field observations would you want to carry out if you could? In retrospect, what flaws might exist in the design of the research? What are the implications of your findings for other questions—perhaps even for other fields? We're not insisting that you brood over the philosophical issues raised by "talking" chimpanzees or the prospect of black holes swallowing the cosmos—though you might want to give these some thought. We're simply suggesting that, as your research progresses, you pause (with your notebook) every now and then to look around you, see where you're headed, and see if there's anywhere else you'd like to go.

After you've finished collecting your data, and before you sit down to draft your report, try to state in your journal what the findings mean, what answer they give to your original question, and perhaps what they suggest for future research. That is, take a little time to think about what you did and the meaning of what happened as a result. Don't immediately dive into technical descriptions of your method and results. Think about the question you defined (so very carefully) earlier in your work, and consider exactly what your results tell you about it. Was your experiment or observational study, after all, the best way to address the problem? Did it give you a definitive answer? Did it leave parts of your original question unanswered or only ambiguously answered? Where might you go from here, or where might another researcher go from here, given the results of your current research?

Not all of this reflection necessarily needs to find its way into your final paper, though some portion of it will, usually in a "discussion section." What you do include should be explained, once more, as if to someone less informed than you are. You may rewrite it for your final report in a way that assumes more expertise from your audience, but if you write it the first time for a complete novice, you'll at least know that *you know* what you're talking about. If you can explain something to a child, you can explain it to an adult. The reverse is not always true.

WRITING THE RESEARCH-BASED PAPER

The process of drafting and revising and editing a paper based on outside sources is not in itself much different from that of any other kind of writing. All that we had to say in Chapter Four applies here as well. (If you haven't read Chapter Four yet, you should. It's very wise.)

Perhaps the one other piece of advice we might offer is this: before starting on your draft put all of your notes away for at least a day and then, without looking at them, write a sketch (see page 136) of your paper. After having spent days or weeks doing your research, you can so fill your mind with the specific pieces of information you've found that you lose the overall sense of what your paper is about. You need to step away from your sources, get your mind clear, review your original question, and then try to summarize for yourself, in no more than a page, what you now believe is the answer. Once you've written such a "pre-abstract" of your paper, you can develop your blueprint—perhaps a tree or outline—from that and then return to your sources to see where and how you'll incorporate them.

The "Default Audience"

How you present what you know will depend heavily on whom you're writing for (see pages 48–49). In professional settings, this issue is usually settled from the start by the actual situation you're working in. You know who your primary audience is, who else might see your report, and so on.

In popular and scholarly writing, the audience is determined by your choice of which publication to submit to. You'll write up your research on genetics and unipolar depression differently for the professional readers of the *Journal of Consulting and Clinical Psychology* than you will for the drugstore magazine rack browsers of *Psychology Today*.

In the classroom, the instructor will sometimes designate a reading audience for you: "Write up your findings on automobile emissions testing as a report with recommendations to the state legislature." More often, however, the audience isn't specified in advance. In that case, you should fall back on what we call the "default audience" (see page 49). If you don't know whom else to write to, write for yourself as you were before starting the research. What did you already know about the topic? What preconceived ideas did you have? Attribute such knowledge and preconceptions to your reader as you write.

Using Your Sources in Your Paper

Many writers have a difficult time knowing just when to draw in an outside source, whether to summarize or quote it directly, how to format it on the page, and when and how to credit it with a footnote, endnote, or parenthetical reference. Some writers are so overawed by the problem that they dodge it completely; you'd never know from their papers that they'd even done any outside reading if they hadn't tacked on a bibliography.

Others defer to their sources continually. Such a writer may be reading and thinking about a particular issue for the first time. He feels like a rank amateur, a total novice, the new kid on the block. Then he starts reading the words of people who have been working on the problem for years and are highly qualified to discuss it. Faced with all of this, the writer panics, doesn't dare offer his own opinion, and simply transcribes quotations of all that he read, glued together with a thin tissue of connecting prose. Instead of standing on other people's shoulders, he's hiding between their legs. The anxiety is understandable, but all it produces is the "string-of-sources" paper. Long reflection, a careful comparison of different sources, and a certain boldness will produce better work—at least give evidence of more active thought.

Your paper should represent your own best considered judgment on your research question in the light of what you've learned. The paper has your name on it, represents your opinion, and should headline your vision of the problem from start to finish. *You lead* in the paper and draw the outside sources in with you whenever you need them.

How and When to Draw In Outside Sources   If you've done your homework, you're going to know far more than you can explain and substantiate in the space available to you. As a result, you need to be efficient. Your first duty is to get across to your reader, as clearly as possible, your final, informed understanding of the issue. Your second duty is to present the most compelling evidence for your position you can. The former may require nothing but your own prose. The latter will more likely require you to draw in passages from your source material to prove or illustrate your point.

Your own writing, thus, must predominate in your paper. Your reader isn't primarily interested in your sources. If he were, he'd be reading their work instead of yours. The reader wants to hear from *you.* You raised the question in your introduction and persuaded him of its importance. Now your reader is going to want to hear *you* tell him the answer. Whenever you can present something as well by yourself as you can by referring to an outsider, go ahead and do it yourself.

Have a positive reason for the inclusion of every summary, paraphrase, or quotation you present. Don't put it in simply because you feel a need to "put in some quotes." There's obviously nothing wrong with their inclusion. But since they require space for their presentation, you should make sure they're carrying their weight. This will help you avoid the pastiche: the patchwork quilt of nothing but the words of other people.

Purposes of Outside Sources   Every source you refer to should have a legitimate reason for being cited. One of the most common mistakes in writing research papers is dropping in references just to show off to a teacher, to prove that you've been "researching." Unless it has a distinct purpose which is recognizable in the flow of your text, a reference is only so much baggage (and conspicuously proclaims itself as such).

Among the various purposes that sources can serve in your writing are these:

Authority　An outside source can speak with an authority greater than your own on some aspects of your problem. Such an "expert witness" might simply supply you a piece of the puzzle. It's still up to you to decide how we should reduce the national debt, but a Washington economist might at least be able to provide authoritative numbers on what the debt is. At other times, the witness might be directly defending the same point you're making, but from a position of greater expertise. If your reader won't believe you on the advisability of arms reductions, perhaps he'll believe a senator, general, or secretary of state. Just be careful in this case that you don't let an outside source do all your talking for you.

Illustrating the Problem　Some sources do nicely as examples of the very problem you're discussing. Popular magazines are especially fond of using a single anecdote to capture the human interest of a broad class of problems. Hearing about the trials of one farm family can convince a reader of the importance of otherwise seemingly abstract questions concerning agricultural policies.

Reflecting Public or Scholarly Consensus or Sentiment　You might, in a similar vein, present an assortment of outside sources to reflect the range of views on some issue. You might cite a statement by one senator arguing that the family farm is economically outmoded and should be allowed to die out. Back to back with that, you might cite a second senator strongly defending government intervention to keep family farms alive. This helps define the problem you're addressing and suggests the variety of viewpoints available. If you choose to hold off your own opinion until the end of your paper, such an opening creates a sort of narrative tension that should keep your reader's attention to the end.

Sparring Partners　You might also cite an outside source as a sparring partner, someone to quarrel with. The full significance of your opinion might not be clear to your reader until he sees a vigorous, articulate statement of an opposing view. Such opposition clarifies and sharpens your own opinion and shows the reader that you're not just tilting at windmills. You want to be careful, however, not merely to set opposing arguments against one another—as if your paper is a boxing match and you're sitting outside the ring, calmly watching (with no opinion whatever) as your sources bloody each other's noses. The early stages of drafting often lead to such a structure, but making up your own mind about the validity of the various points is essential for the conclusion of your research. Saying "there are a lot of opinions about this matter" doesn't help your reader a bit. There are a lot of opinions about most matters.

Summary, Paraphrase and Quotation

Your options for how to include the testimony of your various witnesses are summary, paraphrase, or quotation. Again, the economy principle applies. Present whatever you need to from your source, but do so in the least possible space.

Summary   The most condensed form of incorporation of outside material is, of course, summary. If all you need is the gist of some idea, boil it down into your own words—as few as will do the job—and present that. Your main concern here is accuracy. You want to present the idea or argument or story in its most condensed, crystalline form without distorting or misrepresenting it, a task which is harder than it sounds. Since summarizing is the most space-efficient means of presenting outside material, you should consider it first. If, however, you need more than just the essence of the source, you'll need to move on to paraphrase or quotation.

Paraphrase   A paraphrase is a more complete, thorough, detailed restatement of someone else's ideas. It may or may not, in fact, be shorter than the original. A good paraphrase should reflect not only the core meaning or essence of a passage, it ought to reflect something of its structure, of its subordinate parts and how those are organized. An informational abstract, such as you might find at the head of an academic article, is itself one form of paraphrase. (See also our directions on paraphrasing on pages 15–16 and 173–174.)

The main use of paraphrase is to make someone else's ideas accessible and useful to your particular reader, in the light of your subject matter. This may take a certain effort of translation. For instance, for a paper in political science, you may need to paraphrase the main contents of a recent senate resolution, in order to bring it from legalese into plain, accessible English.

You might, on the other hand, be using something written in one context to illuminate your ideas in another. You might paraphrase the accounts of certain geological studies for a feasibility report on the location of a new office building. Here again, you'd be in effect translating the writings of geologists for business executives interested in a purely practical question. In both cases, you're presenting the structure and content of other people's ideas without breaking the texture or continuity of your own prose. You're using their ideas, but the words are yours.

The greatest danger in paraphrase, in fact, lies exactly here—in keeping the language of the original source from seeping into your text. If you want to use the language of the original source, you certainly may. Only be sure to mark it as a quotation and don't fob it off as a paraphrase. To do the latter constitutes plagiarism—a serious moral and legal offense. In fact, when you're actually writing a paraphrase, you do well to keep the original out of sight until you're done. The language of a paraphrase has to be entirely your own, consistent with the language of the rest of your paper, and not colored by the words of the source itself.

Quotation   If you find the language of the original does tempt you, you probably should consider the third way of incorporating outside material—by direct quotation. You rely on direct quotation when the language of the original offers something you cannot replace in summary or paraphrase, when the words have a special value above and beyond simply the information they carry.

The expression might be so unusually *colorful, pithy, or precise* that no paraphrase could improve on it. Or the words might give your reader a feel for the personality and mind of your source that you couldn't capture any other way. Consider the following statement from *Plain Speaking* by President Harry Truman:

> I fired General MacArthur because he wouldn't respect the authority of the President. I didn't fire him because he

was a dumb son of a bitch, although he was, but that's not against the law for generals. . . .

It's hard to imagine how anyone could paraphrase a volley like that and not kill it: "Truman stated that it was not General MacArthur's lack of intelligence that provoked the dismissal, such a lack not traditionally constituting grounds for dismissive action, but . . . " As the statement stands, it's terse, it's provocative, it's funny, and it has the fingerprints of that tough, no-nonsense Missourian all over it.

You will probably also want to rely more on direct quotation when your source is someone already of interest to your readers than if they have never heard of him. You paraphrase anonymous experts; you quote celebrities, of whatever stripe. You paraphrase articles in physics journals; you quote Stephen Hawking. You paraphrase articles from *Foreign Affairs;* you quote ex-presidents. The direct quotation puts your reader in more immediate contact with your source; the warmth and color of the original personality comes through. If the reader enjoys the closer contact, he won't thank you for standing in the way with a paraphrase when you can throw the door wide open and invite the person into your text with a quotation.

You should also quote when you need to establish with unusual care a point made by your source. If you plan, for example, to attack something one of your sources said, you should quote the statement exactly. If you paraphrase the idea, your readers will suspect you of distorting the opponent's words to make an easier target. To play fair in such a situation, reproduce the source's words, letting the source speak for him- or herself, and then go on with your critique.

The same thing applies if you're relying heavily on the support given your position by somebody. If your case depends on the statement of a particular witness, you'd better give the witness's words verbatim. Here again, your readers may not entirely trust the accuracy of your paraphrase.

How much should you quote? Answer: the minimum that will do the job. Pull out as precisely as possible the words you need and no more. In presenting the statement from President Truman, you might, for instance, blend paraphrase and quotation something as follows:

> Truman claims to have dismissed General MacArthur not
>
> for being "a dumb son of a bitch" but because "he wouldn't
>
> respect the authority of the President."

This preserves the fabric of your prose, saves a little space, and still captures the saltiness of the original.

A Few Matters of Form

In the world of scholarship, words are property. They belong to whoever wrote or spoke them. To present someone else's words as your own, as we noted above, is plagiarism, a form of intellectual theft. You can present other people's words as much as you like, but you need to indicate clearly which words in your text are your own and which originated with someone else. Over the years, codes have been developed to mark the parts of a text that are borrowed. The whole point of quotation marks is clearly to label a passage as belonging to your source and not to you. The quotation marks, in other words, announce: "This sentence is the property of Harry S. Truman."

In the pages that follow, we present the options available to you and the codes required for incorporating the words of others in your own text. We apologize in advance if this is about as fascinating to read as a set of instructions for running a washing machine. But if you want clean clothes, you'll read what you must.

Short Quotations   If you're incorporating only about three lines or fewer of someone else's language, you simply mark the passage with quotation marks and leave them embedded in your own prose.

> In his essay on biography as a literary form, Johnson
>
> writes, "I have often thought that there has rarely passed a

life of which a judicious and faithful narrative would not be useful." Johnson thus rejects the idea that only the famous should have biographies written about them.

Longer Quotations   If the quotation runs longer than three lines, it should be separated out from the body of the text, indented five spaces, and single-spaced:

Though aware of the difficulties faced by one doing scholarly work, Johnson holds out the promise that long, hard effort will be rewarded.

> Every man, who proposes to grow eminent by learning, should carry in his mind, at once, the difficulty of excellence, and the force of industry; and remember that fame is not conferred but as the recompense of labour, and that labour, vigorously continued, has not often failed of its reward.

It would be hard on the basis of such a statement to support the claim that Johnson is pessimistic; the statement is unillusioned rather than disillusioned.

Partial Quotations   You're also free, as we suggested above, to borrow only those phrases you need. You are never obliged to quote passages in full, so long as you indicate any changes you make. You can, for instance, incorporate short scraps of the original language into your paraphrase, provided they are marked:

Johnson insists that scholars should keep in mind both "the difficulty of excellence, and the force of industry" when at work.

Fragments of Quotations   Or you can delete words from either end of the sentence, or from the middle of it, and indicate the deletion by an ellipsis (three spaced periods). If you cut off the end of a sentence, give the final punctuation mark (period, question mark, or exclamation point), followed by the ellipsis.

> According to Johnson, "Every man, who proposes to grow
>
> eminent by learning, should . . . remember that fame is not
>
> conferred but as the recompense of labour. . . ."

Altering Quotations   Sometimes you might find it convenient to change a quotation from first person to third or from one verb tense to another. You can make such changes by altering pronouns and verbs and placing your changes in brackets []. For instance, you might find it more graceful to present an earlier quotation we used as follows:

> In his essay on biography as a literary form, Johnson wrote
>
> that "[he had] often thought that there [had] rarely passed
>
> a life of which a judicious and faithful narrative would not
>
> be useful."

Smoothing Quotations   This example suggests one final principle in the formatting of quoted material, and that is to run your own words and the quoted material together as gracefully as possible. If you splice words from your source into your sentence, keep the syntax consistent and smooth; make the sentence sound as unified as you can.

However you choose to incorporate the words of your source, the same basic principles apply:

1. Use what you need, but don't pad.
2. Mark clearly whose words are whose.
3. Mark clearly any changes you make in the quotation.
4. Make sure that your changes do not fundamentally alter the meaning of the original statement.
5. Splice your own prose and the quoted material together as gracefully as possible.

DOCUMENTATION (Another Exciting Few Pages)

When you incorporate the ideas or words of another into your text, it's not enough just to mark them as such. You need to *state somewhere in your paper precisely where you got them.* You need to provide enough information so that your reader, if she chooses, can look up the source for herself. That is, you need to give the author's name, full title of the book or article, what magazine or publishing house carried it, when it was written, and so on. Since this information usually takes two or three lines, you almost never present it right in your text. Instead, you place some sort of a marker in your text next to the borrowed material and present the source location somewhere else—either in a section at the end of your paper or at the bottom of the page. This is what's meant by *documenting your sources,* or just *documentation.*

Over the years various systems for presenting this information have developed. The system of footnotes and alphabetized bibliography that you learned in high school represents only one among many. Different fields, different publications, different companies, all have their own particular forms and strategies. Rather than present you with details of any one system, we advise you to find an example of something published in your field and learn from that how documentation is handled in your area. In Chapter Six we discuss in detail what to look for in your example in order to master the documentation system you should be using (see pages 206–210).

What do you need to document? To be on the safe side, *document anything that you didn't bring to your paper yourself.* Any time there's something in your paper that you got from an outside source, mark it as such and indicate where you found it. You have to document everything you borrow, whether it's a direct quotation or only a paraphrase. You do not document your own ideas, items of common knowledge, or famous sayings.

Later on, if you're addressing an audience of experts, the rule changes slightly: the most precise principle then is to *document anything that is not common knowledge among your audience.* Thus, you may need to document a fact about Benjamin Franklin for a history class that you could skip footnoting if you were writing for historians of the American Revolution. If it's a fact any qualified expert would immediately recognize as coming from Franklin's *Autobiography*, you could leave it unmarked in your paper. But on the whole, you will never go far wrong by footnoting anything that you had to go get.

You will often find as you write that you have an interesting insight or piece of information or opinion on something that you would like to share with your reader but which doesn't really fit anywhere in your paper. It's a sort of colorful leftover scrap of material you can't quite bear to throw away but which you can't stitch into the quilt either.

This is what a *content footnote* is for. You mark where in your text the scrap should go, move to the bottom of the page, and get the thing out of your system. That way you've put the scrap where the reader (if he chooses) can attend to it, but you haven't disrupted the continuity of your main argument. Since such footnotes are understood to be asides to the audience, you can afford to be less formal in them than in the body of your work.[1]

---

[1] A content footnote is often, by the way, a great place for wry commentary. The footnotes of Gibbon's *Decline and Fall of the Roman Empire* are sprinkled generously with such dry, sardonic one-liners. And, yes, you are indeed now reading a content footnote.

Chapter
6

The Comparative Anatomy of Texts

SPECIES OF WRITING

To take part in any cooperative social activity, you need to learn the language. There's no use shouting "Touchdown! Touchdown! Touchdown!" at a bowling tournament, or discussing a heavy metal rock group in the vocabulary of classical music FM radio ("Notice the romantic, almost sensual, tone of the clanging, twisting metal in the bass line playing in delicate contrapuntal harmony to the breaking of glass and screaming in the melody"). You have to talk the talk.

The same thing is true in writing. Every shared activity, whether it's work or play, develops its own forms and styles of writing; and to be part of that world, you need to learn to write the prose of the shop. A recently graduated M.B.A. needs to be able to read, understand, and write each of the kinds of letters, memos, and reports likely to show up on her desk. A new Ph.D. psychologist, if he enters clinical practice, will need to write testing reports, interview summaries, chart notes, discharge summaries, treatment recommendations—and, of course, billing letters. If, instead of doing clinical work, he wanders into academia, he will probably be writing conference talks, journal articles, and research reports, the form and style of which will depend heavily on what psychological camp he belongs to. A standard APA research report is a different animal from a psychoanalytic case study, an etho-logical field study, or a discussion of different schedules of reinforcement and their effects on behavior. Whichever ap-proach the researcher follows will dictate the form and style of the articles he writes.

Published guidelines, such as style sheets and handbooks, can help you master the text forms and rhetoric of these differ-ent worlds. If there is a style sheet for your subject, you should get hold of a copy—for keeps, not just to borrow. You should sit down with it and thumb through it at random, just to see what sorts of information it contains, what problems and topics it covers. And then you should keep it within easy reach of your keyboard at all times. You never have to *know* much from such a guide; you simply have to know when to grab for it and how to find what you need.

But no matter how up-to-date and thorough your style guide, you dare not rely on it entirely. Not all businesses do their progress reports and year-end summaries just alike; not all scholarly journals, even in the same field, accept articles with the same format, language, and documentation. Worse yet, all of these conventions change over time. New ap-proaches to a subject generate new ways of writing about it. Sometimes, in fact, whole new subjects appear on the intel-lectual horizon, bringing in their wake new terms, new ways of organizing information, new structures for theorizing and observing—and hence for writing. Think of computer sci-ence, for example.

As you can see, trying to learn all the various text forms you might ever need to use would be an endless, frustrating, and horrible job. Fortunately, it's not necessary. You don't have to memorize form after form after form. Instead, you need to develop the ability to examine any particular text, take it apart piece by piece, figure out how it was constructed in the first place, and then use that knowledge when building one of your own. You need to know what parts to look for, how to analyze their organization, and then how to draw a sort of blueprint or schematic of the text that will guide you in your own writing. You don't need a hundred separate rules for a dozen different texts; simply go out and observe the characteristics of the creature itself, so that you can paint one of your own. You need, in other words, a kind of manual of techniques for reproducing what you find in the field—along with a sharp eye and a little patience.

The manual, at least, we can give you.

BASIC ANATOMY: A GUIDE

Rhetorical Environments

In order to understand any particular kind of text, you need to understand the role it plays, the function it performs, in its environment. What does this kind of document *do?* The various academic disciplines and professions have each developed a wide range of documents for different tasks and purposes. Consider, for example, all the different types of writing produced in the process of hiring somebody for a job. There is a job listing, a cover letter, a résumé, perhaps a formal job application, an invitation for an interview, the acceptance of that invitation, the interviewer's report, perhaps one or more follow-up letters, a hiring letter, an acceptance letter, a formal contract, and an official job description and catalogue of employee benefits. Each is a different kind of document, with its own structure and language, and each with its particular bit of work to get done. To write any of these, you would need to understand how it fits into the entire involved business of matching a candidate to a job.

In scholarly fields, as a rule, the paper trail leads through the development, application, and dissemination of knowledge. The development of knowledge usually entails some combination of looking and pondering, so you'll find some works of research, some of theory, some of both. In most fields, furthermore, people will seek to put the knowledge gained to some practical use. You should be able to find works in almost any field on the application of what is known, from clinical or technological studies to how-to writing. Finally, new knowledge is intrinsically interesting. Readers at all levels want to know what's going on in the various disciplines, and there are always experts and journalists ready to explain it to them. One biochemist's work on liver enzymes might spawn three articles in the professional journals, five reports in medical magazines on the development of new techniques

for the treatment of cirrhosis, several brief items in the popular science monthlies, and ultimately take its place in the
"Enzymes" chapter in an organic chemistry textbook.

As a first step, then, in learning to read, understand, and
(ultimately) write any specific kind of text in your field, you
need to survey the types of writing your field generates. Since
you know some of these already—your field could hardly *be*
your field if you hadn't already read something in it—you
should start by reviewing the kinds of texts you're already
aware of. Here are the steps:

Make an Inventory.   List all the kinds of texts related to your
field that you're already familiar with, and decide what function they serve in the field as a whole. If you have trouble
getting started, list the books you're using in class. They
count.

This list will get you started, but it won't be comprehensive. To complete your survey of text types, you'll need to do
some browsing, some if it certainly in the library. There's
where you'll find the research and theoretical works, the attempts at application, the explanations for other experts or for
lay readers—all the books and articles cranked out by the
people who find the subject most interesting. The library is
also where you'll find the bibliographies and indexes and
reference works in your field, which help coordinate the original sources and make them more accessible. (You should
make a point of asking the reference librarians to explain
these to you, beyond the general advice we provided in Chapter Five.)

For most fields of study, you should be able to find examples of each of the following kinds of texts:

- Volumes of theory or research by one author (or a team of
  authors), written as an expert to other experts.
- Collections of essays by several authors, all on one topic,
  and sometimes drawn from a conference at which the
  authors spoke.
- Books addressed to a popular audience (including textbooks).
- Articles in professional journals, presenting the results
  of one expert's (or team's) thinking and research to other
  experts in the field.

- Articles in popular magazines explaining recent ideas and discoveries to nonspecialists.
- Reviews and criticism of all the sorts of books described above.
- Summaries or reviews of the recent research in a particular area.
- Books and articles seeking to apply the knowledge in a particular field to practical problems.
- Encyclopedias or handbooks, sometimes highly specialized, summarizing aspects of the field in short articles.
- Indexes, catalogues, and bibliographic works organizing the publications in the field and guiding the reader in finding them.

Locate Examples.   Go to the library, track down some examples in your field of each of the kinds of texts listed above, and write down their titles. Note where in your library the books and journals for your field are kept, what kinds there are, what they look like, and how to find them again when you need them. Take notes.

Dissecting a Text

Now that you have some sense of the rhetorical environment of your subject, you need to capture and dissect one particular species of text that inhabits it. For the rest of this chapter you will be analyzing, step-by-step, one particular piece of writing. You will sketch the skeleton, find and label the major organs, note how the connecting tissues hold it together, and subject parts of it to microscopic analysis. You will also note its overall color and texture. (You will do this, we hope, on a photocopy of the piece, and let the original go free.) When you're done, you'll be in a position to take one further step— one impossible in the biology classes you've had in the past. You'll be able to make a creature of your own. Once you know how a chemistry lab report, a historical essay, or an article in biblical exegesis works, you can carry on in-depth study in the area, presenting what you learn in such a way as to contribute to the ongoing conversation which is the discipline itself.

  To follow along with us in this process, find an example of one kind of writing in your field. Work from a photocopy, and keep it by you as you read the rest of this chapter. Keep your notebook open and your pencil sharp. Consider yourself writing a sort of lab report in rhetorical anatomy.

The Author(s)   A logical first step in analyzing your piece is to notice who wrote it. In the early stages of study in your field, the author's name may not mean much to you, so go beyond it to the author's credentials. Is the author a professor, some other sort of expert, a journalist specializing in the area? Has the author published in the field before? Don't guess at this. Find whatever evidence you can and stick to it. Is there a college listed under the author's name? If so, you have strong reason to believe the author is a teacher or researcher there. Does the bibliography list other works by the author? Does the journal or book contain a brief biographic sketch of the author anywhere? If so, where? And what does it tell you?

- Write down the author's name and whatever you know about his or her credentials. Also note down where you found this information.

The Audience   Though you are usually given the author's name and credentials, you must infer the audience of an article indirectly. Any time an author is writing, she has before her mind an expected readership, the people she believes are most likely to read her work and appreciate it. How she conceives of her audience will affect her work at every point. Who reads this sort of work? What is their general educational level? What is their level of specialized training in this field? Is this written for general educated readers or for Ph.D.'s doing research in the area?

What kind and degree of interest, furthermore, do readers bring to this work? Does the author have to catch the reader's attention, or can he assume that no one reads about the synthesizing of tadpole liver enzymes unless he or she is already doing research in the field? Does the author hope to find readers both among specialists and the broader reading public?

Some of this can be inferred from the nature of the journal carrying the article or from the publisher of the book. Many professional journals, for example, describe their readership and intellectual mission in a short paragraph at the front of the issue. *Laboratory Medicine* informs you that it is "published monthly by the American Society of Clinical Pathologists" and that it is "devoted to the continuing education of laboratory professionals and publishes articles on the scientific, managerial, and educational aspects of the clinical laboratory." A rather different journal, *Ultimate Reality and Meaning: Interdisciplinary Studies in the Philosophy of Understanding,* opens its self-description this way: "This journal is published quarterly by an association of professors and experts from all parts of the world who have an interest in interdisciplinary research on our effort to find meaning in our world."

Given such information, what can you reasonably infer about the readerships of these two journals? How does that affect the way you write for each of them? Will either one of them be anxious to publish your research on "The Kirby Puckett Story"?

- Describe the expected readers for this piece. Note their educational level, probable specialized training, and why they would be interested in reading this. What are the clues leading to your conclusion?

The Author's Purpose   In a general sort of way, you could describe the author's purpose for a work even before reading it. Authors write to advance the knowledge in their fields, to disseminate what they know to others, to win fame and glory (or tenure), to earn an honest living or raise their chances of promotion—or because, like a few damned souls, they're never entirely comfortable when they're not writing. But here we're looking at something much more specific. What is the explicit, stated purpose of the particular work you're examining? What does the author come right out and say that she's trying to do?

If you're examining a book, you should find the purpose stated in the Preface or Introduction. If you're examining an article, the purpose ought to surface somewhere in the opening paragraphs—possibly in the very first sentence. The purpose will sometimes be stated in the baldest possible form:

"The purpose of this experiment is to . . ."

"What I want to examine here is . . ."

"This study was designed to determine whether . . ."

Sometimes the purpose will be presented as a problem:

"What happens when . . ."

"Though many scholars believe . . . , this leaves unexplained why . . ."

The purpose may, in fact, only be implicit. The author presents a thesis statement, and the purpose of the article becomes to convince the reader of its validity. If there is no explicitly stated purpose, trying to distill into one pithy sentence the major point of the work may be the closest you can come:

> The importance of Sherman's march to the sea lay more in the effect it had on the presidential election of 1864 than on its intrinsic military utility.

> The fact that research on the language of young children in the ghetto has been particularly unrevealing may be explained in part by the laboratory-like, artificial conditions in which such easily intimidated children have been studied.

A business letter, of course, usually states its purpose in the very first sentence:

> I am writing to complain about the service I received at your shop when I brought my Honda 50 Elite motorscooter in for repairs last week.

The author's statement of purpose is the one sentence most likely to help you grasp the significance of the piece overall. Pinpointing the statement of purpose also constitutes your first major piece of anatomical observation. Notice *where* the statement appears in the work and what form it actually takes. You need to notice how and where it is placed in this particular rhetorical animal, so that you'll have at least some knowledge of the conventions when you write your own version of this kind of text.

- Find the author's statement of purpose and copy it *verbatim* into your notes. Then write down where it was located—in what part or what section of the piece. If it was labeled or marked, make a note of that too. If there is no explicit statement, write down in your own words what you think the author is trying to achieve. This may be simply convincing the reader of the validity of his central thesis, whatever (and wherever) that is.

The Title The title of the book or article is a sort of calling card or invitation. Its purpose is to seek out an appropriate audience and introduce it to the written work. As a result, the style of the title depends on the nature of the readership the author is seeking. For an article trying to catch the eyes of busy or frustrated shoppers waiting in line at the supermarket, the title has to be sufficiently catchy, intriguing, or even puzzling to lure the readers to the first paragraph (or make them toss the magazine into the cart): *Guacamole in the Boudoir? Liz Tells All!*

In academics and business, on the other hand, most of the reading we do is work-related. We already bring to the situation an interest in a very specific kind of content: the behavior of electrons in a magnetic field, the application of Rawls's theory of justice to medical ethics problems, the causes of the 1987 stock market crash. If an article covers the area we're interested in, we read it almost automatically; we don't really need a sexy title to arouse our interest.

The titles of academic articles and business reports, therefore, tend to be long, detailed, and rather colorless when compared to popular writing. This doesn't reflect a failure of creativity; it's simply a convenience. What the reader wants is as thorough, explicit, and precise a label on the article as possible—not "Beautiful Crested Birds with White Plumage Show Their Passion Even in Public," but "A Study of the Mating Behaviors of Australasian *Calyptorhynchus* in Zoo Environments." Of the columns of articles listed in a bibliography, he wants to pick out and read only those most relevant to his own research. The reader of an article on photosynthesis in saguaro cacti will probably first make contact with the title in a bibliography of some sort. He wants, in effect, a statement of the article's ingredients: "The Effect of Differing Levels of Soil Silicon Content on Photosynthesis in *Sereus giganteus*."

Some titles, especially those in the humanities and social sciences, attempt to combine color and thoroughness. The main title will tend toward the snappy or engaging. This is followed by a colon and a subtitle, with the subtitle doing the actual business of labelling the contents. Thus you may get something like this: "From Victim to Bride: The Changing Status of Princess Katherine in Shakespeare's *Henry V*," or "Measuring Things in Words: Language for Learning Mathematics."

- Copy into your notes the title of the article you're examining. What kind of work is the title doing? How thoroughly does the title present the major topic of the article? Does it make any attempt to sell the piece, above and beyond simply listing the ingredients?

The Skeleton   By the skeleton of an article, we mean the structural framework it's built on. The most obvious evidence of this lies in the subheadings that divide it. In articles on literature or history you may find no subtitles at all—at most, perhaps, sections marked with arabic or roman numerals, or merely divided by an extra blank line. In other fields, however, articles will be carefully sorted into different labeled sections: e.g., Introduction, Method, Results, Discussion. These structures, furthermore, are often standardized. Journals published by the American Psychological Association expect to see their contributors' articles sorted into the sections and labeled with precisely the subtitles above. If you label your sections "What the Problem Is," "What I Did," "What Actually Happened," and "What I Make of It All," you'll only annoy your readers and offend the editor. Other works—such as this textbook—make heavy use of subtitles, but don't follow any standardized rhetorical format, though their physical layout is dictated by the publisher's style guide.

Besides the name and arrangement of the sections, you also need to take note of the placement and capitalization of the subtitles. How does this article distinguish major sections from minor? Where do the various subtitles go (centered or flush left or indented)? And what words in them, if any, are capitalized? Are any of the subheadings underlined or in italics, and if so, which ones?

- Examine the title, major subtitles, and minor subtitles of your article, and from these construct a formal outline of it. Also describe how each level of subtitle is indicated: position, capitalization, special markings, etc.

Major Organs Whether or not the text you're studying has an obvious, explicit skeleton—subheadings, numbered divisions, etc.—it always has an *organization.* That is, it has *organs,* interworking parts, interrelated components. It is not a mass of pure, undifferentiated prose—a sort of rhetorical bowl of yogurt. It is constructed of different sections, each with its own purpose and meaning, and each depending on the others to give the article its full significance. The results of a study mean nothing without a statement of the problem. A book review without at least a brief synopsis of the book's content is incomplete; it simply doesn't *work.*

If there are subheadings, these obviously will delineate and possibly even describe for you the major organs of the piece. But even in the absence of such labels, you need to locate and identify them. Before reading the article in detail, glance it over quickly. Read just the opening paragraphs of each section. Then read the opening sentence of each paragraph. Try to find the logical breaks in the work. Where does it finish one task and pick up another? Where, for instance, do you find transitional sentences moving you from one topic to the next:

> With this understanding of Bultmann's notion of 'demythologizing' to build on, let us turn briefly to his notion of 'kerygma.'

Once you've located the major parts, read each one over quickly and try to decide what kind of work it's doing. Is it defining a problem? Reviewing past research? Summarizing another writer's position? Refuting an argument? Outlining a method of research? Reflecting on the broader significance of the author's conclusions? Surely it's doing *something.*

- Locate the major parts of your article and analyze what each one is for. Mark on your article where each section starts and stops. Draw a diagram or schematic of this organization in your notebook. Then try to state as clearly as possible the different function of each organ. What is each section of the work *doing?*

Minor Organs: or, Even an Article Can Have an Appendix   Locating and noting the function of the major parts of a book or article may give you a complete schematic of it. Then again, it may not. It may, in fact, miss a number of smaller parts not included in the body of the work. Books, for instance, almost always have title pages, publication information, sometimes a dedication, a Preface, a Table of Contents, perhaps a List of Illustrations, and then, after the final chapter, an Appendix, Bibliography, and Index. Many articles have an Abstract wedged in between the title and the Introduction, while others have key word lists, author's credentials, and a list of Works Cited (or References) at the end. As with the major organs, you need to find these, notice where they are, how they're formatted, and what useful work each one does. And you must articulate all this for yourself, clearly and thoroughly, on paper. The point of all this, again, is not simply to comprehend the article better, but to see how writing works in the field, and to be able to cast your own observations and thoughts into this kind of format.

- Find and describe in your notebook the minor organs, the small parts of the article or book not included in the main body of it. Note their placement, format, and function. Be able, from your notes, to create these when you try to write a similar document.

How Outside Sources Are Used   We discussed in the previous chapter why you might sometimes paraphrase or quote in your own text somebody else's work. The knowledge in any discipline is built up slowly, brick by brick, with every researcher studying the work of her predecessors and then going beyond it, adding to it in some significant way. It's this kind of continual mutual borrowing that allows a discipline to grow, to explore new areas, to test and verify its claims. Because it is so essential, each discipline has found standardized, systematic ways for writers to incorporate and comment upon each other's work in presenting their own.

To take part in the ongoing conversation of your field, to write the kind of text you want to write, you need to know how this is done. Specifically, you must understand *why* outside sources are cited, and *how* they are worked into the fabric of the text itself.

Find the places in your text where the author has summarized, paraphrased, quoted, or even just mentioned the work of a previous writer. Note first how many such references there are. Does the author perform a fairly thorough review of previous research, make just occasional mention of other scholars, or not bother with them at all? (Any of these may be appropriate.)

Note also where in the article these occur. A brief review of research in a scientific article will probably appear early on, in the introduction. On the other hand, if you're reading a review of a recently published collection of Winston Churchill's correspondence, you'll probably find quotations from the letters scattered throughout.

How much of each previous work was used? Are the references to the work of the earlier writers actual quotations, or only paraphrases and summaries? If they are quotations, how long are they? A phrase here or there? A few sentences? Or does the author sometimes quote passages at length? Sometimes, you'll find strings of authorities cited to make one point, as if the writer were conducting a poll on the issue: *Other researchers, however, have found just the opposite (Baker, 1978; McCarthy, 1981; Urbaine, 1984; Winslow, 1987).*

Once you've charted all this, you should be in a position to answer the really vital question: *why* is the author pulling in these previous works? If we assume that the author is trying to make a case, to convince us of something, we need to ask what purpose *each* citation serves. To turn the question another way, how would the author's case be weakened if the material were missing? What does it add, above and beyond what the writer can tell us herself, in her own words?

A few purposes such borrowed material can serve are the following:

1. It can offer direct testimonial support for the main point the author is making. "Jones, in her 1983 monograph, reaches similar conclusions."
2. It can prove or illustrate some point. "An example of this comes from the work of Farnsworth. . . ."
3. It can act as a "straw man," a representative statement of a position the author is attacking. "The logical flaw in such a stance appears clearly in the following passage from Schaeffer. . . ."

4. It can help define the precise nature of the problem the author is trying to solve. "Though Jones (1982) believes that . . . , research by Hendrix (1987) suggests. . . . My own study is designed to test Jones's hypothesis under more tightly controlled conditions than Hendrix was able to achieve."

• Find all the places in your article where the author makes use of the work of previous writers and scholars. Describe in your notebook where you find these, how many you find, how extensive they are, what form they take, and what purpose each one serves.

Giving Credit Where Credit Is Due   Every time you pull the work of a previous writer into your text, you are of course morally and legally obliged to give the writer proper credit. You have to mark for your reader precisely which parts of your text are your own and which you borrowed from someone else. You may borrow as much as you need; just give credit where credit is due.

You do this not only out of fairness to your source, but as a service to your reader. Some portion—sometimes a very large portion—of the readers of any scholarly article are themselves researchers in the field, working on and writing about problems similar to that discussed in the article they're reading. If a source has proved important to you in your research, the odds are very high that it will be valuable to your readers in theirs. Thus, your readers will want to know exactly where you found your material. They will want to be able to go to their own libraries, hunt down the journal or volume you used, and read the source in its entirety for themselves. Part of your job is to make this possible, by giving full bibliographic information for every source you use.

The assigning of credit and providing of such bibliographic information in your text is what documentation is all about. Over the years (centuries even!) different disciplines have evolved different conventional ways for doing this. And—you guessed it—you need to master these conventions in order to carry on the written dialogue in your field. Much of this strikes everybody as incredibly picky. But the fact is, you can cause your readers a great deal of trouble if you don't give your documentation careful attention. Try looking for an article sometime when the lead you've been given has the wrong page number or year. (And bring your aspirin with you.)

Placing the information   Since the information a reader needs in order to locate the book, chapter, or article cited in another work is often pretty extensive, you don't find this in the body of the text itself. You just don't see anything like the following:

> As Todd and Palmer have noted (Todd, G., and Palmer, B. "Social Reinforcement of Infant Babbling." *Child Development,* Vol. 39 (1968), pp. 591–596), social and vocal reinforcements seem to increase the amount of an infant's babbling. Dodd and Nakazima, however (Dodd, B. "Effects of Social and Vocal Stimulation of Infant Babbling," *Developmental Psychology,* Vol. 7 (1972), pp. 80–83; Nakazima, S. "A Comparative Study of the Speech Developments of Japanese and American English in Children." *Studies in Phonology,* Vol. 2 (1962), pp. 27–39) disagree.

This would obviously be too cluttered and obtrusive. Not only that, if you decided you wanted to look up Todd and Palmer's article, and the piece you originally found it in was a long one, you'd have to spend a lot of time just relocating the bibliographic reference in the mass of prose surrounding it.

Instead, virtually every discipline relies on a system of markers in the text referring the reader to full bibliographic information somewhere else, out of the way. The markers can be something like asterisks (*) and daggers (†), or, more often, raised numerals. These point the reader either to the bottom of the page or to a list of notes at the end of the article, chapter, or book.

Lately, however, more disciplines are using parenthetical documentation. The marker in this case is a pair of parentheses containing very little information—just enough to allow you to find the source in an alphabetically arranged list of them at the end of the article. *There* you can find the rest of the information you need to locate the source. This does away with the need for a separate list of footnotes or endnotes *and* a bibliography. The alphabetic bibliography alone does the work of both.

For instance, if you see a reference such as the following:

Identical twins proved concordant for schizophrenia at a rate four times that of fraternal twins (Kendall, 1979, p. 246).

It becomes a simple matter to find the appropriate article in the bibliography (under Kendall), jot down the full reference, locate the work at the library, turn to page 246, and check out this piece of information for yourself.

- Find where in the article the author gives the full bibliographic information for the sources he cites. Note if these are footnotes, numbered endnotes, or an alphabetical bibliography, or some combination. Then notice and describe the system of flags or markers used in the text to point you toward the fuller citations.

Form of the Full Citations Once you've figured out the pattern in your article for where the full bibliographic information is given and the system of textual markers to point you there, you have one task left: to work out the exact pattern of bibliographic references themselves. For *this particular discipline or journal,* you have to know what information is required in a footnote, endnote, or bibliographic listing; you have to know what order the information goes in; and you have to know how it's to be punctuated. This calls for precise, almost microscopic observation. It's not fun, but it's necessary.

In any such reference, you can count on having to give the full name of the author(s) exactly as given in the original source; the exact title and subtitle (if any); the publisher or journal carrying the piece; the date of publication (and if it's a book, the place); and, if it's an article, the numbers of the pages it appears on. If the source is a speech, a pamphlet, a broadcast, a film or some other less usual form, you'll need to provide different information. How all this is to be arranged and punctuated you can learn by studying examples from the article you're reading.

To do this right, you'll need to boil these entries down into something like schematics, showing in a precise way what information is included and how. For an article you might, after examining the references in the article you're reading, work out a schematic like this:

Name, Author's. "Name of Article." *Name of Journal.* Issue # (year): xxx–xxx.

"Name, Author's" means here *author's name*—but reflects the pattern of last name first (e.g., Einstein, Albert).
For a book you might come up with this:

Name, Author's, and Co-author's Name. *Title of Book.* Nth Edition. City: Publisher, year.

Here notice that the first author's name is reversed but the second author's name is left in the normal order (e.g., Addison, Joseph, and Richard Steele).

Since the incorporated material can come in any number of forms—books, articles, encyclopedia entries, interviews, government publications, unpublished papers, television documentaries, etc.—you may need to draw a number of such forms. Your schematics will pay for themselves later, when you need to write your own bibliographic references.

- Study the footnotes, endnotes, and/or bibliographic listings in your article. For each *type* of listing (government document, speech, etc.) work out in your notebook the schematic showing what it contains, how the information is arranged, and how it's punctuated.

Note: Some disciplines have arrived at a fair degree of uniformity on these matters across their various journals and books. All the journals put out by the American Psychological Association, for example, use what is called "APA format." Most journals of literary studies use the "New MLA format" developed by the Modern Language Association. "New MLA"—a system of parenthetical documentation—is so called to distinguish it from "Old MLA"—a system of raised numerals and endnotes (plus bibliography)—which was how this group handled documentation until a few years ago. Both of these organizations, furthermore, publish style guides or publication manuals which explain their documentation systems (along with many other matters of form) in exhaustive detail. Other fields publish style guides as well. You should check to see if a style guide exists for your area and, if it does, keep a copy by your desk. A good default guide is the *Chicago Manual of Style*. (You want to see *thorough?*)

Use of Graphics   These may not be an issue in the article you're reading now, but they will come up at some point and you will need to give them close attention. You'll need to look at where they're used, how they're constructed and labelled, what purpose they serve, and how they are coordinated with the author's prose text.

Location   Where are they used? Largely in one section (Results) or throughout the article? How heavily does the author depend on them?

Construction   How are they constructed? Are they tables, graphs, electronic schematics, flow charts, maps, exploded diagrams? What's on the "X" axis and what's on the "Y"? What special symbols do they use? Are these standard or idiosyncratic?

Labeling   How and where are they labeled? Are they all figures or are some of them labeled "Table" or "Diagram"? Does the label appear above or below the figure on the page? Is there anything else on or around the figure, such as a parenthetical reference if it's borrowed, or a caption if it requires some explaining?

Purpose   What purpose does the figure serve? How is *this* picture worth a thousand words? Could the same information be given in prose? If not, why not? (A major skill in learning how to write is knowing when *not* to write, when you'd actually do better to *draw*.)

Integration with Text   What does the author say about the figure in the text? Sometimes the writer will simply mention the figure in passing and assume it's self-explanatory. Other figures require careful introduction, some explanation of how to read them, and a careful discussion of what they illustrate for the purposes of the author's argument. This will, of course, depend on the complexity of the figure itself, and at least somewhat on the audience the author is writing for.

- Examine the figures in your article, if any, and answer the questions asked about them above. (We have labeled the steps for your convenience.) Write the answers in your notebook and save them for future reference.

Coloration To return to our biological metaphor . . . . By now you should have a thorough account of all the rhetorical inner workings of the article you're studying. You've examined its environment, its skeleton, its major and minor organs, and put its documentation under the microscope. Your notebook should contain a comprehensive anatomical description of the beast. You now have one final observational task and then you're through. You need to examine the overall prose style of the work—what we've dubbed its *coloration*.

Prose style can best be considered in terms of the writer's *persona*. Your persona is the image of yourself you project to another person (the word originally meant "mask" in Latin). Whenever you speak to somebody, you communicate a message, some piece of information, *and* you try to make the other person see you in a particular way. This isn't a form of fraud; it's simply inevitable. And you do the same thing in writing. The persona you adopt as a writer manifests itself in the style of the prose you produce.

As a rule, someone writing in his or her discipline is writing either as an expert to other experts, or as an expert to a lay audience. If a biologist, say, is describing her research on octopus intelligence to other biologists, she won't preface her report with a humorous account of her childhood collecting sea creatures in the Florida Keys. Her professional colleagues, reading her article with an eye toward advancing their own research on the higher mollusks, won't be interested—not right then, at any rate. If, however, she's writing for a popular magazine—*Smithsonian,* say, or *National Wildlife*—her readers might be happy to have the weightier scientific material broken up with her personal reactions and anecdotes.

The same audience considerations will control her prose style. To her colleagues she will write formal scientific prose; she will present herself in the *role of* a fellow scientist. To the readers of *National Wildlife* she will write more casually; her prose will sound like intelligent, succinct, lively speech. She will *sound like* a bright, fun person with a consuming interest

in animals—a sort of energetic, likable nextdoor neighbor—
who just happens to have a doctorate in marine biology. Note
that neither persona is "false"; she *is* a scientist, and she *is* a
smart, fun collector of animals. Her choice is simply which
side of herself to present.

The first thing to notice about the prose of your article,
then, is how professional vs. how casual it is. You'll probably
see this first in the level of formality of the writing. Is it
business suit prose? Lab coat prose? Or does it suggest a
sweater and slacks, as (we hope) this book does? (Your notebook is one of the few places where cut-offs and a tee-shirt are
welcome—or, for that matter, nothing at all.)

What constitutes professional dress, furthermore, differs
from one field to the next. The prose of an art critic, for instance, is often colorful and impressionistic, full of metaphor
and imagery. Anthropological studies of various cultures' religious ceremonies may be richly descriptive but in a scrupu-
lously objective way. A mathematician uses prose only to glue
together the strings of abstract symbolic notation that do her
real work. As a result, her prose is austere, precise, often
wonderfully clear, but suggestive of nothing beyond the exact
denotative meaning of the terms used. In a field like psychology, where the scientific or humanistic status of the subject is
itself at issue, the austerity or richness of a writer's style may
reflect how the writer construes the discipline in the first
place.

Most writers, of course, even if they only write within the
province of their fields, change their dress continuously. Can
you imagine (Dr.) Lewis Thomas, writing a medical report in
his role as president of the Memorial Sloan Kettering Cancer
Institute in New York, using prose like this?

> Viewed from the distance of the moon, the astonishing
> thing about the earth, catching the breath, is that it is alive.
> The photographs show the dry, pounded surface of the
> moon in the foreground, dead as an old bone. Aloft, float-
> ing free beneath the moist, gleaming membrane of bright
> blue sky, is the rising earth, the only exuberant thing in
> this part of the cosmos. If you could look long enough, you
> would see the swirling of the great drifts of white cloud,
> covering and uncovering the half-hidden masses of land.

—Lewis Thomas, *Lives of a Cell* (1974)

For that matter, can you imagine one of us dropping something like the following paragraph into this book?

> Although schemes of instructional ideology vary considerably, as do the research methods that inform them, they all strongly suggest that teachers' underlying beliefs about why, what, and how students should write are powerful determinants of their actual behaviors in the classroom—even in the midst of external pressures such as curricular mandates.

(The one of us who wrote that was wearing a jacket and tie that day.)

The Question of Jargon Every discipline over time creates its own vocabulary, its shop terms, its jargon. Often these serve a vital function. They provide names and labels for entities that otherwise would take too long to describe whenever they were mentioned. On the other hand, if you use them too freely (or incorrectly), they can sound pretentious and ugly. They can also distort the meaning of what you're trying to get across. Two safe principles for the use of jargon are, be *sparing* and be *precise*.

Don't use jargon when ordinary English words will do. Don't show off. Use it only when it's genuinely necessary in the context of your disciplinary writing and study. Try to use plain standard English as often as possible. English is still the first language of the most rarefied of specialists. Anything you can write in plain English has a higher chance of actually being understood than its jargonistic translation.

On the other hand, when you're working within your discipline and it is necessary and appropriate, feel free to use the specialized terminology—but *get it right*. Don't call *mass* "weight"—it's not. Don't call *punishment* "negative reinforcement." They're not the same. Don't use "phenomenology" when you mean "epistemology," or "ideology" when you mean "phenomenology." And if you don't know just what the term means, look it up or don't use it at all.

- Turning once more to your article, what do you notice about its prose style? How professional or casual is it? What does "professional" seem to mean in this case? How would you describe the persona of the author?

Does the prose change at all from section to section, or is it uniform throughout? Finally, write down any special terms you find and define them as precisely as you can.

TWO RHETORICAL DISSECTIONS

To give a better idea of the sort of anatomical research we've been discussing, we give here two examples. These are detailed analyses of a mathematical proof and a social psychology research article. (The originals are reprinted in full at the end of the chapter.) Our first example, the mathematical proof, shows how much you can ascertain about the construction of a text without even understanding the subject matter. We're not even raising the question here of the validity of the proof. We're simply describing as fully as possible *how the proof looks on paper*—so that, if we did have a contribution to make in this area, we would know how to present it for publication in this journal.

A Mathematical Proof

Title   The article is titled "Using Pythagorean Triangles to Approximate Angles." The title is obviously more functional than decorative; it labels the contents of the article without making any attempt to sell it.

Author and Audience   The article appears in *The American Mathematical Monthly*, published by the *Mathematical Association of America*. The author, W. S. Anglin, works in the Department of Mathematics and Statistics at McGill University (a Canadian "Ivy League" school), as can be seen from the credit under his name. His audience consists of other professional and academic mathematicians. Few will read this piece with anything less than a college degree in the field—most with a specialized advanced degree.

Purpose   The author states his purpose explicitly as a question at the end of the second paragraph:

The question we answer in this note is: what is the smallest Pythagorean triangle which approximates B degrees to within e?

Gross Anatomy The article falls into five major divisions: four paragraphs introducing the problem, three theorems, and a paragraph in conclusion. The first four paragraphs are largely occupied with definitions and other preliminaries. Though they have no special label, the placement and content of these paragraphs reflect their introductory nature.

The three central sections are distinctly marked. In each case, we see the word THEOREM, a number, and then a brief statement in italics.

THEOREM 1. $a^2 + b^2 = c^2$ *with a an even integer and a, b, c relatively prime integers . . .*

The second and third THEOREMS are followed by sections marked *Proof,* demonstrating how each theorem was arrived at.

The article concludes with one paragraph showing how the principle demonstrated can be used: "For example, suppose we want the smallest Pythagorean triangle approximating 20 degrees to within $\frac{1}{100}$. . . ." There is no heading labeling this as a "Conclusion" or "Discussion," but the nature of it is clear enough upon reading it.

You might sketch the skeleton of the article as follows:

Introductory paragraphs: definitions and purpose

THEOREM 1. *Statement in italics.*

THEOREM 2. *Statement in italics. Proof.*

THEOREM 3. *Statement in italics. Proof.*

Conclusion: application

Minor Organs The only extras the article contains are a brief thank-you note at the end of the body of the text, and a section marked REFERENCES.

Use of Outside Sources The writer used only one outside source for this work. Where we would expect to find the *Proof* section after THEOREM 1, we find instead this statement:

For a proof the reader may consult [**1,** pp. 138–139].

Someone has apparently already demonstrated the validity of THEOREM 1, and the author finds no reason to redo the work. The sentence itself is strikingly laconic. The author doesn't quote, paraphrase, or even summarize the previous work. The proof doesn't change or add anything; it merely validates one step in his reasoning.

Documentation   The flag for the original source within the text is the bracketed information. Note that the brackets do not contain the title of the source, the author's name, or the year of publication—simply a number, comma, "pp." and the numbers of the pages involved. This is a markedly different way of handling documentation from either New MLA or APA format.

In the REFERENCES section you find number 1 (not raised) and then the full source information. The sole reference is a book, and the schematic for its listing would look like this:

1. Author's Name and Second Author's Name, *Name of Book*, Nth ed., Name of Publisher, City of Publication, year of publication.

If you intended to write for this journal, you would need to study a few more articles first. From just this one, you still wouldn't know how to cite a journal article or unpublished thesis.

Graphics   The article uses no figures, drawings, diagrams, graphs, or other visual aids. If your prospective article for this journal included any of these, you'd have to search further for suitable examples to follow.

Coloration   Stylistically, this is mathematician's prose *par excellence*. Since the nature of the material is inherently complex, the writer has made his prose as clean, simple, and direct as possible. Here's the opening paragraph:

A Pythagorean triangle is a right triangle with integer sides. A well-known example is the triangle with sides 3, 4, and 5. Unfortunately, the angles of these triangles are not as "nice" as the sides: whether expressed in degrees or radians, they are always irrational.

There you have it: four simple declarative sentences (reading the colon as a period). None has more than two clauses or thirteen words. A children's story will not beat that for simplicity.

Professor Anglin is writing as a mathematician to mathematicians. The prose, simple as it is, is ruthlessly formal and austere. The one hint of color is the mildly whimsical description of the angles of a Pythagorean triangle as not "nice"—a caprice the author delicately frames with quotation marks.

Jargon Finally, the article is necessarily full of special terminology. In the world of mathematics even common English words take on special denotations. Notice how the author begins the third paragraph: "We begin by defining 'smaller.'" Outside of mathematics, you probably wouldn't need to do that! Needless to say, any misuse of the special terminology and symbolism would reduce such an article to gibberish.

To render the ideas here into common English prose, including all the mathematical notation in the proofs, would require volumes—and serve no purpose for this audience whatsoever. The translation of this sort of writing into immediately comprehensible English is the perilous and estimable labor of the humble textbook author, whose praises we shall put off to another time.

A Social Psychology Research Report

Title and Audience Our second piece is a standard research article in the social sciences. It's titled "Friendship and Freedom of Movement as Moderators of Sex Differences in Interpersonal Distancing," and appears in *The Journal of Social Psychology*. The title is well designed to show up in all the right computer searches; notice how many key words it contains. Other psychologists, moreover, will have no trouble guessing whether it's relevant to their own professional concerns, once they find it. In this case, the title and journal tell us a good deal about the nature of the audience: primarily researchers in the field of social psychology. Many will be scholars at colleges and universities; others will be practicing psychologists and social workers who like to keep abreast of new developments in the field.

Authors   There are three authors listed for the article: Paul A. Bell, Linda Mannik Kline, and William A. Barnard, all affiliated with the Department of Psychology at Colorado State University (again, a detail that tells us that the authors work and teach at a major academic institution). Notice that although three people are credited with authoring the article, their names are not alphabetized—or else Paul A. Bell would have followed William A. Barnard, who in this case appears last. It would appear then—and this is, in fact, the case in many academic disciplines—that Paul A. Bell is to be considered the "first author," a term that usually designates the leader of a research team or the person who did the most work on the project and/or the article. In some fields, such as medicine, there may be a substantial team of people who each played some sort of role in a research project (such as a lab technician who processed some blood products for analysis) but are not listed as authors. Such peripheral contributors are often thanked for their help in a footnote or, if the work is a book, in the Preface or Acknowledgments. Another clue to Paul A. Bell's leadership is a note which asks readers to write to Bell for reprints of the article.

Purpose   The purpose of the article is plainly stated in the last paragraph of the introduction: "The present study was designed to address these issues by examining . . ." This is a common place to find such a statement.

Skeleton and Major Organs   The names, placement, purpose, and typography of the subheadings is as follows:

[four introductory paragraphs with no subheading; review of previous research and problem definition]

Method
[what the experimenters did]

Subjects and Design [who they did it to]

Procedure [how they did it]

Results
[what numbers came up]

Discussion
[what the results mean for the question itself]

The overall pattern of the report is that of a narrative, presenting the experiment as a sort of story. "People have been wondering for a long time about X. So here's what we did. Here's what happened. And here's what we think it means." Much research reporting follows this pattern.

Minor Organs   In addition to the major sections, the article includes an abstract, a list of references, and several small notes. The abstract is informative rather than merely descriptive; it succinctly summarizes the article as a whole. The notes, at the bottom of the first page, include expressions of gratitude to helpers, addresses of two of the authors, and where to send for reprints of the article.

Outside Sources   With one exception, all outside sources show up in the first four paragraphs, and all serve the same purpose: to establish the nature and complexity of the problem at hand. The authors are working in a field with a long and confusing past. Dozens of studies exist on the topic, pointing in different and seemingly contradictory directions. The authors' brief review of the literature makes this clear.

At one point the authors start polling their studies— producing, in effect, thumbnail summaries *en masse:*

> Indeed, considerable research supports such a generalization (e.g., Brady & Walker, 1978; Hartnett, Bailey, & Gibson, 1970; Pellegrini & Empey, 1970).

Two sentences later they cease citing separate studies altogether and simply count votes:

> At least 27 personal space studies have found sex differences, 54 studies have found mixed results, and 29 studies have found no differences attributable to gender.

Beyond these thumbnail summaries, you find here no real paraphrases or direct quotations. They simply aren't necessary.

Documentation   Since this is APA format, the flag in the text marking each source is a parenthesis containing the author's last name and the year of publication. All coauthors are listed;

multiple studies in one parenthesis are separated by a semi-colon.

(e.g., Edwards, 1972; Heshka & Nelson, 1972)

If the author's name appears in the text itself, however, it is not repeated in the parenthetical reference:

As Hayduk (1983) pointed out, however . . .

The full bibliographic information for each outside source is presented in a section marked REFERENCES. The list is arranged alphabetically and includes books, articles, and unpublished papers. You would draw the schematics of these as follows:

Book
Name, Author's, & Name, Author's. (year). *Title of Book* (Nth ed.). City of Publication: Publisher.

Article
Name, Author's, & Name, Author's. (year). Title of Article. *Title of Journal,* Volume #, xxx–xxx.

Unpublished Paper
Name, Author's, & Name, Author's. (year, Month). Paper presented at . . . , City, State.

Graphics   The article does contain one graphic: Table 1 ("Table," mind you, not "Figure"). The label and title go above it, centered:

TABLE 1

Interpersonal Distance Means

Then follows the chart, with all rows and columns properly labeled, and a note beneath. Though the table is never explicitly mentioned anywhere in the text itself, its most important results are presented—in prose this time—in the **Results** section.

Coloration The opening sentences of the article establish the prose style it maintains throughout:

> As the volume of American research on personal space has grown increasingly large, inconsistencies with respect to determinants of personal space differences have also grown in complexity. Among the most perplexing inconsistencies is the influence of gender on interpersonal distancing. Probably the most often cited generality is that female-female dyads interact at closer distances than male-male dyads, with male-female dyads either between the other two or closer than the other two. . . .

Notice the formality and density of the prose. The persona is a *social scientist*—with the emphasis on *science*. Compare this with the prose of the mathematician, above. While the words and sentences there were short and simple, the diction and syntax here are markedly more latinate, abstruse, difficult.

Some of this is simply unnecessary. "As the *volume of American* research on personal space has grown *increasingly large* . . ." can only gain by cutting out the italicized words. "As the research on personal space has grown" says the same thing more simply and clearly. The difference is solely the degree of clutter—what a scientist might refer to as the noise-to-signal ratio.

More of an issue are terms such as "interpersonal distancing" and "female-female dyad." The former means how close people choose to stand to each other to talk. The technical term may *sound* a bit pretentious, but it certainly has an advantage over our paraphrase in terms of brevity. The article would be longer and clumsier without its use. It's harder to say if anything is gained by "female-female dyad" beyond merely *sounding* more scientific. (A "pair of women" you might find in any back yard; a "female-female dyad" is clearly a creature of the laboratory.)

If the opening sentences were translated for a general audience, they might come out like this:

> The more researchers have studied what makes people willing to stand closer together or farther apart to talk, the

more they've found inconsistent results. The effect of gender has been especially confusing. On the whole, pairs of women stand closer together to talk than do pairs of men. Mixed pairs have sometimes been found to stand closer together than either, though at other times they have fallen between men and women on this measure.

This is not, after all, an especially difficult idea, though the prose of the original makes it seem so. So what happened? Did the authors write an originally clear, plain-spoken English version and then go back and rewrite it into more abstruse, scientific prose? No, they did not. They wrote it in the style they did from the very beginning because they found all the other research in social psychology written this way. They were in Rome, doing as the Romans do.

Every writer sooner or later runs into this problem and has to decide what to do about it. Our own advice, again, is vulgarly pragmatic. Use the jargon when it helps. Otherwise, write the plainest, clearest English you can. You raise, thereby, your odds of being understood, even by the smartest of your colleagues.

Using Pythagorean Triangles to Approximate Angles

W. S. ANGLIN
Department of Mathematics and Statistics, McGill University, Montreal, PQ, Canada H3A 2K6

A Pythagorean triangle is a right triangle with integer sides. A well-known example is the triangle with sides 3, 4, and 5. Unfortunately, the angles of these triangles are not as "nice" as the sides: whether expressed in degrees or radians, they are always irrational.

If a Pythagorean triangle has an angle of A degrees and $|A - 20| < 1/100$, we shall say that the triangle "approximates 20 degrees to within one hundredth." Let B be any given angle in degrees with $0 < B < 90$. Let e be any real number such that $0 < e < 1$, $e < B$, and $e < 90 - B$. The question we answer in this note is: what is the smallest Pythagorean triangle which approximates B degrees to within e?

We begin by defining "smaller." If (a, b, c) and (a', b', c') are two Pythagorean triangles with sides $a < b < c$ and sides $a' < b' < c'$, then (a, b, c) is "smaller" than (a', b', c') just in case (i) $c < c'$ or (ii) $c = c'$ and $b < b'$. Roughly speaking, this means we order the triangles by hypotenuse. For example, the triangle $(3, 4, 5)$ is the smallest of all Pythagorean triangles since it has the smallest hypotenuse.

Pythagorean triangles whose sides are relatively prime are called "primitive." For the purpose of finding a *smallest* triangle approximating a given angle, we need only consider primitive triangles. We thus confine our attention to them. Since exactly one of the two smaller sides of a primitive Pythagorean triangle is even, the following well-known theorem gives a complete characterization of these triangles.

THEOREM 1. $a^2 + b^2 = c^2$ *with a an even integer and a, b, c relatively prime integers iff for some relatively prime positive integers u and v with v < u and u, v not both odd,*

$$a = 2uv, \qquad b = u^2 - v^2, \qquad and \quad c = u^2 + v^2.$$

For a proof the reader may consult [1, pp. 138–139].

Roughly speaking, we shall approximate a given angle B by means of approximating its tangent or cotangent. In this connection we need the following definitions.

$$X = \tan(B - e) + \sec(B - e)$$

$$Y = \tan(B + e) + \sec(B + e)$$

$$X' = \cot(B + e) + \csc(B + e)$$

$$Y' = \cot(B - e) + \csc(B - e).$$

We now have the "Approximation Theorem."

THEOREM 2. *Let u and v be positive integers. Then $X < u/v < Y$ iff $(2uv, u^2 - v^2, u^2 + v^2)$ approximates B to within e by means of the angle opposite $u^2 - v^2$ and $X' < u/v < Y'$ iff $(2uv, u^2 - v^2, u^2 + v^2)$ approximates B to within e by means of the angle opposite 2uv.*

Proof. Suppose $X < u/v < Y$. The given conditions on B and e imply that $1 < X$ and, hence, $v < u$ (since $X = (\sin(B - e) + 1)/\cos(B - e))$). Since $X < u/v < Y$, it follows that $-1/X < -v/u < -1/Y$. Adding these inequalities, we obtain $X - 1/X < (u^2 - v^2)/uv < Y - 1/Y$. Moreover, as a straightforward calculation will show, $X - 1/X = 2\tan(B - e)$ and $Y - 1/Y = 2\tan(B + e)$. Hence, we obtain $\tan(B - e) < (u^2 - v^2)/2uv < \tan(B + e)$. Hence, in $(2uv, u^2 - v^2, u^2 + v^2)$ the angle opposite $u^2 - v^2$ is between $B - e$ and $B + e$ degrees.

Suppose now that the right-hand side of the first equivalence holds. Then where $z = u/v$ we have $2\tan(B - e) < z - 1/z < 2\tan(B + e)$. Hence, $z^2 - (2\tan(B + e))z - 1 < 0$ and $0 < z^2 - (2\tan(B - e))z - 1$. The first of these inequalities implies that z is between the two roots of $z^2 - (2\tan(B + e))z - 1$. Thus $z < \tan(B + e) + \sqrt{\tan^2(B + e) + 1} = \tan(B + e) + \sec(B + e) = Y$. Similarly, from $0 < z^2 - (2\tan(B - e))z - 1$ it follows that $X < z$.

The proof for the second equivalence is similar.

Finally, we have the "Ordering Theorem."

THEOREM 3. *Let V be the smallest positive integer such that $[XV] + 1 < YV$ and let $U = [XV] + 1$. Then $(2UV, U^2 - V^2, U^2 + V^2)$ is the smallest Pythagorean triangle approximating B degrees to within e by means of the angle opposite the odd side.*

Moreover, the corresponding result holds for the "even side case" (with X', Y' replacing X, Y, respectively).

Proof. Since $X < U/V < Y$, the above triangle does approximate B degrees to within e by means of the angle opposite $U^2 - V^2$.

Let $T = (2u'v', u'^2 - v'^2, u'^2 + v'^2)$ be the smallest such triangle. Then $X < u'/v' < Y$ and, hence, $[Xv'] + 1 < Yv'$. Thus $V \leqslant v'$. If $U < u'$, then $U^2 + V^2 < u'^2 + v'^2$ against T's minimality. Hence, $u' \leqslant U$. Since $Xv' < u'$, it follows that $U = [XV] + 1 \leqslant [Xv'] + 1 \leqslant u'$. Thus $u' = U$. By T's minimality, $v' \leqslant V$ and, hence, $v' = V$. Thus the two triangles are the same.

The proof for the corresponding "even side result" is similar.

For example, suppose we want the smallest Pythagorean triangle approximating 20 degrees to within $1/100$. We compute $X = 1.42788278$, $Y = 1.42841330$, $X' = 5.66838919$ and $Y' = 5.67417730$. By straightforward testing (on a programmable calculator) we find that $V = 208$ is the smallest positive integer such that $[XV] + 1 < YV$ and $V' = 46$ is the smallest positive integer such that $[X'V'] + 1 < Y'V'$. Let $U = [XV] + 1 = 297$ and let $U' = [X'V'] + 1 = 261$. The smallest triangle to approximate 20 degrees to within $1/100$ by means of the angle opposite the odd side is $(2UV, U^2 - V^2, U^2 + V^2) = (123552, 44945, 131473)$ and the smallest triangle to approximate 20 degrees to within $1/100$ by means of the angle opposite the even side is $(2U'V', U'^2 - V'^2, U'^2 + V'^2) = (24012, 66005, 70237)$. The second is smaller.

I thank Professor J. Lambek for his kind help and encouragement.

REFERENCES

1. Ivan Niven and H. S. Zuckerman, An Introduction to the Theory of Numbers, 4th ed., John Wiley & Sons, New York, 1980.

Friendship and Freedom of Movement as Moderators of Sex Differences in Interpersonal Distancing

PAUL A. BELL
LINDA MANNIK KLINE
WILLIAM A. BARNARD
Department of Psychology
Colorado State University

ABSTRACT. American undergraduates (96 males, 96 females) interacted face-to-face with a same-sex or opposite-sex target person who was either a friend or a stranger. Half the subjects were free to move and approach the target person, stopping at the point where approaching "any closer would be uncomfortable." The other half were stationary and were approached by the target person, who was asked to stop at a similar uncomfortable point. As expected, friends maintained closer distances than strangers. Moreover, both sexes kept closer distances with males when subjects were free to move than when stationary, but freedom of movement made no difference when the target was female. Though not statistically reliable, our experiments showed that male-male dyads generally maintained greater distances than female-female dyads, with male-female dyads closest among friends. The results suggest that freedom of movement and friendship were important moderators of gender differences in interpersonal distancing.

AS THE VOLUME of American research on personal space has grown increasingly large, inconsistencies with respect to determinants of personal space differences have also grown in complexity. Among the most perplexing inconsistencies is the influence of gender on interpersonal distancing.

The authors express their sincere appreciation to Jerri Spear, Tony Hoag, and Richard Kirnan for their assistance in the collection of the data.
   Linda Kline is now at Murray State University and William Barnard is at the University of Northern Colorado.
   Requests for reprints should be sent to Paul Bell, Department of Psychology, Colorado State University, Ft. Collins, CO 80523.

Probably the most often cited generality is that female-female dyads interact at closer distances than male-male dyads, with male-female dyads either between the other two or closer than the other two (e.g., Fisher, Bell, & Baum, 1984). Indeed, considerable research supports such a generalization (e.g., Brady & Walker, 1978; Hartnett, Bailey, & Gibson, 1970; Pellegrini & Empey, 1970). As Hayduk (1983) pointed out, however, there are exceptions: At least 27 personal space studies have found sex differences, 54 studies have found mixed results, and 29 studies have found no differences attributable to gender.

Some of the inconsistency in gender differences may be mediated by another often cited generalization: Attraction or friendship is inversely related to interpersonal distance, except for male-male dyads. Again, numerous studies are consistent in this respect (e.g., Edwards, 1972; Heshka & Nelson, 1972), although there are also exceptions (e.g., Knowles, 1980 on one measure). Studies reporting distancing differences attributable to gender or attraction rarely use a fully crossed design (i.e., male vs. female subject by male vs. female target person by friend vs. stranger); hence, the independent or interaction effects of gender and friendship cannot be discerned.

Another potential mediator of inconsistencies in personal-space gender differences is freedom of movement. One function of the rules of personal space is protection: Maintaining a distance from strangers affords some degree of defense (e.g., Dosey & Meisels, 1969; Evans & Howard, 1973). Being in control of interpersonal distances, and perceiving that control, may be necessary for principles of personal-space regulation to be manifested in a given situation (e.g., Edney, Walker, & Jordan, 1976). Having the freedom to move toward or away from another may be crucial to that control. For example, Barnard and Bell (1982) found unreliable sex differences in distancing when subjects were unable to move toward or away from a (stranger) target person, but reliable differences (female-female closer than mixed-sex closer than male-male) when subjects were free to move toward or away from the target person. Such methodological considerations may mediate at least some gender difference inconsistencies in the literature.

The present study was designed to address these issues by examining the effects of sex of subject, sex of target, subject-target acquaintance (friend vs. stranger), and freedom of movement (subject moving vs. target moving) in a full factorial design. We hypothesized that friends would maintain closer distances than strangers, regardless of freedom of movement. Moreover, we expected that, for male-female dyads, closer distances would occur if the female was free to move than if she was stationary. Finally, we hypothesized that, among strangers, female-female dyads would maintain closer distances than male-female dyads, who would in turn maintain closer distances than male-male dyads, but that among friends, female-female dyads and male-female dyads would maintain equally close distances, with both sets maintaining closer distances than male-male dyads.

Method

Subjects and Design

Subjects were 96 male and 96 female students in introductory psychology classes, whose participation satisfied part of a course requirement. Twelve subjects were randomly assigned by gender to each cell of a $2 \times 2 \times 2 \times 2$ between-subjects factorial design, having as factors Sex of Subject, Sex of Other Person, Relationship to Other Person (friend, stranger), and Freedom of Movement (subject stationary, subject mobile). For those interacting with a stranger, one of four confederates participated. For those interacting with a friend, subjects were asked to bring a friend along for their experimental appointment.

Procedure

Subjects were recruited through a sign-up folder associated with the psychology subject pool. On the folder, no information was revealed about the experiment, except that on one fourth of the sign-up lines participants were asked to bring a male friend and on another fourth they were asked to bring a female friend. As subjects arrived for the experiment, the experimenter led the subject and the other person (confederate stranger or personal friend) to a room containing an interpersonal distance mat (Barnard & Bell, 1982). The mat measured 5 ft × 6 ft, 6 in. (153.6 cm × 199.68 cm) and contained wires across its width at 2-in. (2.54 cm) intervals. The wires tripped microswitches that illuminated a light-emitting diode (LED) panel in an adjoining room. The circuitry was such that, with one person standing at a reference point on the mat, another person walking on the mat would illuminate the LED corresponding to the tripped wire closest to the stationary person. The subject and other person (half males, half females) stood at opposite ends of the mat facing each other. In the subject-mobile condition, the other person was stationary and the subject was instructed to approach him or her and stop at a point such that "any closer would be uncomfortable." In the subject-stationary condition, the subject did not move but the other person slowly approached until the subject said "Stop!" at the point where "any closer would be uncomfortable." The experimenter recorded the distance between the two participants by noting the number of the LED illuminated on the panel. The subject was then taken to another room and asked to indicate the degree of acquaintance with the other participant on a 9-point scale ranging from *total stranger* (1) to *close friend* (9). The subject was thanked for participating and debriefed.

Results

The manipulation check on degree of acquaintance indicated highly reliable differences for this variable, with friends rated much higher ($M = 7.71$) than strangers ($M = 1.97$) on the stranger-friend scale, $F(1, 176) = 604.24$, $p < .0001$. Means for the distance measure are presented in Table 1. An analysis of variance on these distances indicated significant main effects for sex of other person (closer distances with female others), $F(1, 176) = 7.01$, $p < .01$, and for relationship (friends closer than strangers), $F(1, 176) = 28.17$, $p < .001$.

These main effects were qualified by two interactions. Sex of other person interacted with freedom of movement, $F(1, 176) = 4.83$, $p < .05$, with a Newman-Keuls analysis ($p < .05$) indicating that the mean for a male other who moved ($M = 27.26$ in., 69.24 cm) was larger than the mean for a female other who moved ($M = 18.30$ in., 46.48 cm), a male other who was stationary ($M = 20.88$ in., 53.04 cm), or a female other who was stationary ($M = 20.04$ in., 50.90 cm). The interaction between sex of subject, sex of other, and relationship (friend/stranger) also approached conventional standards of reliability, $F(1, 176) = 3.80$, $p < .053$. This interaction was appropriate for testing the hypotheses concerning relative distancing differences due to gender composition of dyads. The pattern of means was suggestive, though differences were not statistically reliable. Among strangers, female-female dyads ($M = 21.34$ in., 54.20 cm) did maintain closer distances than male-male dyads ($M = 28.50$ in., 72.39 cm, $p < .06$), but the

TABLE 1
Interpersonal Distance Means

	Male subjects				Female subjects			
	Male target		Female target		Male target		Female target	
Condition	Subject moved	Other moved	Subject moved	Other moved	Subject moved	Other moved	Subject moved	Other moved
Friends	20.84 (14.28)	20.34 (12.90)	14.66 (12.54)	12.66 (10.00)	14.00 (7.58)	17.50 (14.84)	17.84 (11.80)	15.84 (10.00)
Strangers	22.84 (15.26)	34.16 (13.28)	28.16 (15.74)	21.50 (15.54)	25.84 (5.94)	37.00 (14.80)	19.50 (7.44)	23.16 (16.48)

Note. Standard deviations are in parentheses. All distances are expressed in inches.

relationship of these conditions to mixed-sex dyads varied across the male subject-female other (M = 24.84 in., 63.09 cm) and female subject-male other (M = 31.42 in., 79.81 cm) circumstances, which is unusual given that all of these means are collapsed across the Freedom of Movement factor. Among friends, mixed-sex dyads were closer (M = 13.66 in., 34.70 cm, for male subjects; M = 15.76 in., 40.03 cm, for female subjects) than either male-male dyads (M = 20.60 in., 52.32 cm) or female-female dyads (M = 16.84 in., 42.77 cm), although it must be emphasized that none of these differences reached statistical significance.

Discussion

Consistent with one hypothesis, friends maintained closer distances than strangers, regardless of which member of the dyad was stationary and which was free to move. Also consistent with another hypothesis, females kept closer distances with males when the female was free to move. That relationship was true for males as well, however: Both sexes kept closer distances with males when subjects were free to move than when stationary, but freedom of movement made no difference when the target was female. Apparently, freedom of movement was a crucial variable in the expression of rules governing interpersonal distancing, presumably because it carried with it a degree of perceived control or perceived protection from an unwanted interaction. This Gender by Movement interaction was independent of degree of friendship: Even among friends, subjects kept more distance from male others when subjects were stationary.

With respect to gender differences in distancing with dyads, the results offer mixed evidence. Male-male dyads generally maintained greater distances than female-female dyads, with male-female dyads closest among friends. As a result of large within-cell variances, however, these relationships were not statistically reliable. Other individual difference variables may, accordingly, have a greater impact than gender on distancing preferences under the methodological constraints of the present study.

In sum, the confusion in the research literature concerning gender differences in interpersonal distancing may in part be mediated by differences in friendship and in freedom of movement. Moreover, it should be noted that the present study used face-to-face encounters in a standing mode, and that these relationships may also be dependent on angle of orientation and seated versus standing interactions (Kline & Bell, 1983, 1986).

REFERENCES

Barnard, W. A., & Bell, P. A. (1982). An unobtrusive apparatus for measuring interpersonal distances. *Journal of General Psychology, 107,* 85–90.

Brady, A., & Walker, M. (1978). Interpersonal distance as a function of situationally induced anxiety. *British Journal of Social and Clinical Psychology, 17,* 127–133.

Dosey, M., & Meisels, M. (1969). Personal space and self-protection. *Journal of Personality and Social Psychology, 11,* 93–97.

Edney, J. J., Walker, C. A., & Jordan, N. L. (1976). Is there reactance in personal space? *Journal of Social Psychology, 100,* 207–217.

Edwards, D. J. A. (1972). Approaching the unfamiliar: A study of human interaction distances. *Journal of Behavioral Sciences, 1,* 249–250.

Evans, G. W., & Howard, R. B. (1973). Personal space. *Psychological Bulletin, 80,* 334–344.

Fisher, J. D., Bell, P. A., & Baum, A. (1984). *Environmental psychology* (2nd ed.). New York: Holt, Rinehart and Winston.

Heshka, S., & Nelson, Y. (1972). Interpersonal speaking distance as a function of age, sex, and relationship. *Sociometry, 35,* 491–498.

Hartnett, J. J., Bailey, F, & Gibson, W. (1970). Personal space as influenced by sex and type of movement. *Journal of Psychology, 76,* 139–144.

Hayduk, L. A. (1983). Personal space: Where we now stand. *Psychological Bulletin, 94,* 293–335.

Kline, L. M., & Bell, P. A. (1983). Privacy preference and interpersonal distancing. *Psychological Reports, 53,* 1214.

Kline, L. M., & Bell, P. A. (1986, April). *Effects of gender, noise, music, and social interaction on interpersonal behaviors.* Paper presented at the meeting of the Rocky Mountain Psychological Association, Denver, CO.

Knowles, E. S. (1980). Convergent validity of personal space measures: Consistent results with low intercorrelations. *Journal of Nonverbal Behavior, 4,* 240–248.

Pellegrini, R. J., & Empey, J. (1970). Interpersonal spatial orientation in dyads. *Journal of Psychology, 76,* 67–70.

Received September 10, 1987

Index